# The Rediscovery of the Mind

Representation and Mind
Hilary Putnam and Ned Block, editors

# The Rediscovery of the Mind

John R. Searle

A Bradford Book

The MIT Press
Cambridge, Massachusetts
London, England

Third printing, 1992
© 1992 Massachusetts Institute of Technology

This book was set in Palatino by Chiron, Inc. and printed and bound in the United States of America.

Library of Congress Cataloging-in-Publication Data

Searle, John R.
    The rediscovery of the mind / John R. Searle.
        p.   cm. -- (Representation and mind)
    "A Bradford book."
    Includes bibliographical references and index.
    ISBN 0-262-19321-3
    1. Philosophy of mind.   2. Consciousness.   3. Intentionality
(Philosophy)   4. Mind-brain identity theory--Controversial
literature.   I. Title.   II. Series.
BD418.3.S43   1992
128'.2--dc20                                        92-12747
                                                          CIP

For Dagmar

# Contents

# Acknowledgments

I have benefited over a period of several years from discussions and conversations with friends, students, and colleagues about the issues considered in this book. I do not suppose I can thank all of them, but I want to offer special expressions of gratitude to the following: M. E. Aubert, John Batali, Catharine Carlin, Anthony Dardis, Hubert Dreyfus, Hana Filip, Jerry Fodor, Vinod Goel, Stevan Harnad, Jennifer Hudin, Paul Kube, Ernest Lepore, Elisabeth Lloyd, Kirk Ludwig, Thomas Nagel, Randal Parker, Joëlle Proust, Irvin Rock, Charles Siewart, Melissa Vaughn, and Kayley Vernallis.

These, however, are only a few of the many who helped me so much. I have presented these ideas in lectures that I have given not only in Berkeley but as a visiting professor at the universities of Frankfurt, Venice, Florence, Berlin, and Rutgers. Among my best and severest critics have been my students, and I am grateful for their relentless skepticism. Among my institutional benefactors, I want to thank the Committee on Research of the Academic Senate and the Office of the Chancellor of the University of California, Berkeley, and especially the Rockefeller Foundation Center at Bellagio, Italy.

Some of the material in this book has appeared elsewhere in a preliminary form. Specifically, portions of chapters 7 and 10 were developed from my article "Consciousness, Explanatory Inversion, and Cognitive Science" (*Behavioral and Brain Sciences*, 1990), and chapter 9 is based on my Presidential Address to the American Philosophical Association for 1990.

I am especially grateful to Ned Block, who read the entire manuscript in draft form and made many helpful comments. Most of all I thank my wife, Dagmar Searle, for her constant

help and advice. As always, she has been my greatest intellectual influence and my strongest source of encouragement and
inspiration. It is to her that this book is dedicated.

# Introduction

This book has several objectives, some of which do not admit of quick summary but will only emerge as the reader progresses. Its most easily statable objectives are these: I want to criticize and overcome the dominant traditions in the study of mind, both "materialist" and "dualist." Because I think consciousness is the central mental phenomenon, I want to begin a serious examination of consciousness on its own terms. I want to put the final nail in the coffin of the theory that the mind is a computer program. And I want to make some proposals for reforming our study of mental phenomena in a way that would justify the hope of rediscovering the mind.

Nearly two decades ago I began working on problems in the philosophy of mind. I needed an account of intentionality, both to provide a foundation for my theory of speech acts and to complete the theory. On my view, the philosophy of language is a branch of the philosophy of mind; therefore no theory of language is complete without an account of the relations between mind and language and of how meaning—the derived intentionality of linguistic elements—is grounded in the more biologically basic intrinsic intentionality of the mind/brain.

When I read the standard authors and tried to explain their views to my students, I was appalled to discover that with few exceptions these authors routinely denied what I thought were simple and obvious truths about the mind. It was then, and still is, quite common to deny, implicitly or explicitly, such claims as the following: We all have inner subjective qualitative states of consciousness, and we have intrinsically intentional mental states such as beliefs and desires, intentions and perceptions. Both consciousness and intentionality are biological processes caused by lower-level neuronal processes in the brain, and neither is reducible to something else. Furthermore, consciousness and intentionality are essentially connected in that we understand the notion of an unconscious intentional state only in terms of its accessibility to consciousness.

Then and now, all this and more was denied by the prevailing views. Mainstream orthodoxy consists of various versions of "materialism." Just as bad, the opponents of materialism usually embrace some doctrine of "property dualism," thus accepting the Cartesian apparatus that I had thought long discredited. What I argued for then (Searle 1984b) and repeat here is that one can accept the obvious facts of physics—that the world consists entirely of physical particles in fields of force—without denying that among the physical features of the world are biological phenomena such as inner qualitative states of consciousness and intrinsic intentionality.

About the same time as my interest in problems of the mind began, the new discipline of cognitive science was born. Cognitive science promised a break with the behaviorist tradition in psychology because it claimed to enter the black box of the mind and examine its inner workings. But unfortunately most mainstream cognitive scientists simply repeated the worst mistake of the behaviorists: They insisted on studying only objectively observable phenomena, thus ignoring the essential features of the mind. Therefore, when they opened up the big black box, they found only a lot of little black boxes inside.

So I got little help from either mainstream philosophy of mind or cognitive science in my investigations, and I went ahead to try to develop my own account of intentionality and its relation to language (Searle 1983). However, just developing a theory of intentionality left many major problems undiscussed, and worse yet, left what seemed to me the major prevailing mistakes unanswered. This book is an attempt to fill at least some of those gaps.

One of the hardest—and most important—tasks of philosophy is to make clear the distinction between those features of the world that are *intrinsic*, in the sense that they exist independent of any observer, and those features that are *observer relative*, in the sense that they only exist relative to some outside observer or user. For example, that an object has a certain mass is an intrinsic feature of the object. If we all died, it would still have that mass. But that the same object is a bathtub is not an intrinsic feature; it exists only relative to users and observers who assign the function of a bathtub to it. Having mass is intrinsic, but being a bathtub is observer relative, even though the object both has mass and is a bathtub. That is why there is a natural science that includes mass in its domain, but there is no natural science of bathtubs.

One of the themes that runs throughout this book is the attempt to get clear about which of the predicates in the philosophy of mind name features that are intrinsic and which observer relative. A dominant strain in the philosophy of mind and cognitive science has been to suppose that computation is an intrinsic feature of the world and that consciousness and intentionality are somehow eliminable, either in favor of something else or because they are observer relative, or reducible to something more basic, such as computation. In this book I argue that these suppositions are exactly backward: Consciousness and intentionality are intrinsic and ineliminable, and computation—except for the few cases in which the computation is actually being performed by a conscious mind—is observer relative.

Here is a brief map to help the reader find his or her way about the book. The first three chapters contain criticisms of the dominant views in the philosophy of mind. They are an attempt to overcome both dualism and materialism, with more attention devoted in these chapters to materialism. At one time I thought of calling the whole book *What's Wrong with the Philosophy of Mind*, but in the end that idea emerges as the theme of the first three chapters and is the title of the first. The next five chapters, 4 to 8, are a series of attempts to give a characterization of consciousness. Once we have gone beyond both materialism and dualism, how do we locate consciousness in relation to the rest of the world (chapter 4)? How do we account for its apparent irreducibility according to the standard patterns of scientific reduction (chapter 5)? Most important, what are the structural features of consciousness (chapter 6)? How do we account for the unconscious and its relation to consciousness (chapter 7)? And what are the relations between consciousness, intentionality, and the Background capacities that enable us to function as conscious beings in the world (chapter 8)? In the course of these discussions I try to overcome various Cartesian shibboleths such as property dualism, introspectionism, and incorrigibility, but the main effort in these chapters is not critical. I am trying to locate consciousness within our general conception of the world and the rest of our mental life. Chapter 9 extends my earlier (Searle 1980 a and b) criticisms of the dominant paradigm in cognitive science, and the final chapter makes some suggestions as to how we might study the mind without making so many obvious mistakes.

In this book I have more to say about the opinions of other writers than in any of my other books—maybe more than all of them put together. This makes me extremely nervous, because it is always possible that I might be misunderstanding them as badly as they misunderstand me. Chapter 2 gave me the most headaches in this regard, and I can only say that I tried as hard as I could to make a fair summary of a whole family of views that I find uncongenial. As for references: The books I read in my philosophical childhood—books by Wittgenstein, Austin, Strawson, Ryle, Hare, etc.—contain few or no references to other authors. I think unconsciously I have come to believe that philosophical quality varies inversely with the number of bibliographical references, and that no great work of philosophy ever contained a lot of footnotes. (Whatever its other faults, Ryle's *Concept of Mind* is a model in this regard: it has none.) In the present instance, however, there is no escaping bibliographical references, and I am likely to be faulted more for what I have left out than for what I have put in.

The title is an obvious homage to Bruno Snell's classic, *The Discovery of the Mind.* May we in rediscovering consciousness—the real thing, not the Cartesian ersatz nor the behaviorist doppelgänger—also rediscover the mind.

# Chapter 1

# What's Wrong with the Philosophy of Mind

---

*I. The Solution to the Mind-Body Problem and Why Many Prefer the Problem to the Solution*

The famous mind-body problem, the source of so much controversy over the past two millennia, has a simple solution. This solution has been available to any educated person since serious work began on the brain nearly a century ago, and, in a sense, we all know it to be true. Here it is: Mental phenomena are caused by neurophysiological processes in the brain and are themselves features of the brain. To distinguish this view from the many others in the field, I call it "biological naturalism." Mental events and processes are as much part of our biological natural history as digestion, mitosis, meiosis, or enzyme secretion.

Biological naturalism raises a thousand questions of its own. What exactly is the character of the neurophysiological processes and how exactly do the elements of the neuroanatomy—neurons, synapses, synaptic clefts, receptors, mitochondria, glial cells, transmitter fluids, etc.—produce mental phenomena? And what about the great variety of our mental life—pains, desires, tickles, thoughts, visual experiences, beliefs, tastes, smells, anxiety, fear, love, hate, depression, and elation? How does neurophysiology account for the range of our mental phenomena, both conscious and unconscious? Such questions form the subject matter of the neurosciences, and as I write this, there are literally thousands of people investigating these questions.[1] But not all the questions are neurobiological. Some are philosophical or psychological or part of cognitive science generally. Some of the philosophical questions are: What exactly is consciousness and how exactly do conscious mental phenomena relate to the unconscious? What are the special features of the "mental," features such as consciousness, intentionality, subjectivity, mental causation; and how exactly do they function? What are the causal relations between "mental" phenomena and "physical" phenomena? And can we characterize those causal relations in a way that avoids epiphenomenalism?

I will try to say something about some of these questions later, but at this point I want to note a remarkable fact. I said that the solution to the mind-body problem should be obvious to any educated person, but at present in philosophy and cognitive science many, perhaps most, of the experts claim to find it not at all obvious. In fact, they don't even think the solution I have proposed is true. If one surveys the field of the philosophy of mind over the past few decades, one finds it occupied by a small minority who insist on the reality and irreducibility of consciousness and intentionality and who tend to think of themselves as property dualists, and a much larger mainstream group who think of themselves as materialists of one type or another. The property dualists think that the mind-body problem is frightfully difficult, perhaps altogether insoluble.[2] The materialists agree that if intentionality and consciousness really do exist and are irreducible to physical phenomena, then there really would be a difficult mind-body problem, but they hope to "naturalize" intentionality and perhaps consciousness as well. By "naturalizing" mental phenomena, they mean reducing them to physical phenomena. They think that to grant the reality and irreducibility of consciousness and other mental phenomena commits one to some form of Cartesianism, and they do not see how such a view can be made consistent with our overall scientific world picture.

I believe that both sides are profoundly mistaken. They both accept a certain vocabulary and with it a set of assumptions. I intend to show that the vocabulary is obsolete and the assumptions are false. It is essential to show that both dualism and monism are false because it is generally supposed that these exhaust the field, leaving no other options. Most of my discussion will be directed at the various forms of materialism because it is the dominant view. Dualism in any form is today generally regarded as out of the question because it is assumed to be inconsistent with the scientific world view.

So the question I want to pose in this chapter and the next is: What is it about our intellectual history and environment that makes it difficult to see these rather simple points that I have made about the "mind-body problem"? What has made "materialism" appear to be the only rational approach to the philosophy of mind? This chapter and the next are about the current situation in the philosophy of mind, and this one might have had the title, "What Is Wrong with the Materialist Tradition in the Philosophy of Mind."

Seen from the perspective of the last fifty years, the philosophy of mind, as well as cognitive science and certain branches of psychology, present a very curious spectacle. The most striking feature is how much of mainstream philosophy of mind of the past fifty years seems obviously false. I believe there is no other area of contemporary analytic philosophy where so much is said that is so implausible. In the philosophy of language, for example, it is not at all common to deny the existence of sentences and speech acts; but in the philosophy of mind, obvious facts about the mental, such as that we all really do have subjective conscious mental states and that these are not eliminable in favor of anything else, are routinely denied by many, perhaps most, of the advanced thinkers in the subject.

How is it that so many philosophers and cognitive scientists can say so many things that, to me at least, seem obviously false? Extreme views in philosophy are almost never unintelligent; there are generally very deep and powerful reasons why they are held. I believe one of the unstated assumptions behind the current batch of views is that they represent the only scientifically acceptable alternatives to the antiscientism that went with traditional dualism, the belief in the immortality of the soul, spiritualism, and so on. Acceptance of the current views is motivated not so much by an independent conviction of their truth as by a terror of what are apparently the only alternatives. That is, the choice we are tacitly presented with is between a "scientific" approach, as represented by one or another of the current versions of "materialism," and an "antiscientific" approach, as represented by Cartesianism or some other traditional religious conception of the mind. Another odd fact, closely related to the first, is that most of the standard authors are deeply committed to the traditional vocabulary and categories. They really think there is some more or less clear meaning attaching to the archaic vocabulary of "dualism," "monism," "materialism," "physicalism," etc., and that the issues have to be posed and resolved in these terms. They use these words with neither embarrassment nor irony. One of the many aims I have in this book is to show that both these assumptions are mistaken. Properly understood, many of the currently fashionable views are inconsistent with what we know about the world both from our own experiences and from the special sciences. To state what we all know to be true, we are going to have to challenge the assumptions behind the traditional vocabulary.

Before identifying some of these incredible views, I want to make an observation about presentational style. Authors who are about to say something that sounds silly very seldom come right out and say it. Usually a set of rhetorical or stylistic devices is employed to avoid having to say it in words of one syllable. The most obvious of these devices is to beat around the bush with a lot of evasive prose. I think it is obvious in the writings of several authors, for example, that they think we really don't have mental states, such as beliefs, desires, fears, etc. But it is hard to find passages where they actually say this straight out. Often they want to keep the commonsense vocabulary, while denying that it actually stands for anything in the real world. Another rhetorical device for disguising the implausible is to give the commonsense view a name and then deny it by name and not by content. Thus, it is very hard even in the present era to come right out and say, "No human being has ever been conscious." Rather, the sophisticated philosopher gives the view that people are sometimes conscious a name, for example, "the Cartesian intuition," then he or she sets about challenging, questioning, denying something described as "the Cartesian intuition." Again, it is hard to come right out and say that no one in the history of the world ever drank because she was thirsty or ate because he was hungry; but it's easy to challenge something if you can label it in advance as "folk psychology." And just to give this maneuver a name, I will call it the "give-it-a-name" maneuver. Another maneuver, the most favored of all, I will call the "heroic-age-of-science" maneuver. When an author gets in deep trouble, he or she tries to make an analogy with his or her own claim and some great scientific discovery of the past. Does the view seem silly? Well, the great scientific geniuses of the past seemed silly to their ignorant, dogmatic, and prejudiced contemporaries. Galileo is the favorite historical analogy. Rhetorically speaking, the idea is to make you, the skeptical reader, feel that if you don't believe the view being advanced, you are playing Cardinal Bellarmine to the author's Galileo.[3] Other favorites are *phlogiston* and *vital spirits*, and again the idea is to bully the reader into supposing that if he or she doubts, for example, that computers are actually thinking, it can only be because the reader believes in something as unscientific as phlogiston or vital spirits.

## II. Six Unlikely Theories of Mind

I will not attempt to provide a complete catalogue of all the fashionable, implausible materialist views in contemporary philosophy and cognitive science, but will list only half a dozen to give the feel of the thing. What these views share is a hostility toward the existence and mental character of our ordinary mental life. In one way or another they all attempt to downgrade ordinary mental phenomena such as beliefs, desires, and intentions and to cast doubt on the existence of

such general features of the mental as consciousness and subjectivity.[4]

First, perhaps the most extreme version of these views is the
idea that mental states, as such, don't exist at all. This view is
held by those who call themselves "eliminative materialists."
The idea is that, contrary to a widely held belief, there really
aren't any such things as beliefs, desires, hopes, fears, etc.
Early versions of this view were put forth by Feyerabend
(1963) and Rorty (1965).

A second view, often used to support eliminative materialism, is the claim that folk psychology is—in all probability—
simply and entirely false. This view has been advanced by
P. M. Churchland (1981) and Stich (1983). Folk psychology
includes such claims as that people sometimes drink because
they are thirsty and eat because they are hungry; that they
have desires and beliefs, that some of these beliefs are true, or
at least false; that some beliefs are better supported than others; that people sometimes do something because they want to
do it; that they sometimes have pains; and that these are often
unpleasant. And so—more or less indefinitely—on. The connection between folk psychology and eliminative materialism
is this: Folk psychology is supposed to be an empirical theory
and the entities it "postulates"—pains, tickles, itches, and so
on—are supposed to be theoretical entities on all fours, ontologically speaking, with quarks and muons. If the theory goes,
the theoretical entities go with it: to demonstrate the falsehood
of folk psychology would be to remove any justification for
accepting the existence of the folk psychological entities. I sincerely hope I am not being unfair in characterizing these views
as implausible, but I have to confess that that is how they
strike me. Let me continue the list.

A third view of this same type holds that there is nothing
specifically *mental* about the so-called mental states. Mental
states consist entirely in their causal relations to each other and
to the inputs and outputs of the system of which they are a
part. These causal relations could be duplicated by any system
that had the right causal properties. Thus, a system made of

stones or beer cans, if it had the right causal relations, would have to have the same beliefs, desires, etc., as we do, because that is all there is to having beliefs and desires. The most influential version of this view is called "functionalism," and it is so widely held as to constitute a contemporary orthodoxy.

A fourth implausible view, and indeed the most famous and widely held of the current catalogue, is the view that a computer could have—indeed must have—thoughts, feelings, and understanding solely in virtue of implementing an appropriate computer program with the appropriate inputs and outputs. I have elsewhere baptized this view "strong artificial intelligence," but it has also been called "computer functionalism."

A fifth form of incredibility is to be found in the claim that we should not think of our mental vocabulary of "belief" and "desire," "fear" and "hope," etc., as actually standing for intrinsically mental phenomena, but rather as just a manner of speaking. It is just a useful vocabulary for explaining and predicting behavior, but not to be taken literally as referring to real, intrinsic, subjective, psychological phenomena. Adherents of this view think that the use of the commonsense vocabulary is a matter of taking an "intentional stance" toward a system.[5]

Sixth, another extreme view is that maybe consciousness as we normally think of it—as inner, private, subjective, qualitative phenomena of sentience or awareness—does not exist at all. This view is seldom advanced explicitly.[6] Very few people are willing to come right out and say that consciousness does not exist. But it has recently become common for authors to redefine the notion of consciousness so that it no longer refers to actual conscious states, that is, inner, subjective, qualitative, first-person mental states, but rather to publicly observable third-person phenomena. Such authors pretend to think that consciousness exists, but in fact they end up denying its existence.[7]

Sometimes mistakes in the philosophy of mind produce mistakes in the philosophy of language. One, to my mind, unbelievable thesis in the philosophy of language, which comes from the same stable as the examples we have just been considering, is the view that where meanings are concerned, there just aren't any facts of the matter in addition to patterns of verbal behavior. On this view, most famously held by Quine (1960), there just isn't any fact of the matter about whether when you or I say "rabbit" we mean rabbit, unde-tached part of a rabbit, or stage in the life history of a rabbit.[8]

Now what is one to do in the face of all this? It is not enough for me to say that it all seems implausible, rather I think a phi-losopher with patience enough and time should sit down and do a point by point, line by line refutation of the whole tradi-tion. I have tried to do that with one specific thesis in the tra-dition, the claim that computers have thoughts and feelings and understanding solely in virtue of instantiating a computer program (the "right" computer program with the "right" inputs and outputs) (Searle 1980a). This view, strong artificial intelligence, is an attractive target because it is reasonably clear, there is a simple and decisive refutation, and the refuta-tion can be extended to other versions of functionalism. I have also tried to refute Quine's thesis of indeterminacy (Searle 1987), which I believe also lends itself to a frontal assault. With some of the views, however, the situation is much messier. How, for example, would one go about refuting the view that consciousness does not exist? Should I pinch its adherents to remind them that they are conscious? Should I pinch myself and report the results in the *Journal of Philosophy*?

To conduct an argument in the traditional sense, it is essen-tial that there be some common ground. Unless the partici-pants agree on the premises, there is no point in trying to derive a conclusion. But if somebody denies the existence of consciousness from the very start, it is difficult to know what the common ground in the study of mind would be. On my view, if your theory results in the view that consciousness does not exist, you have simply produced a reductio ad absurdum of the theory, and similarly with many other views in contem-porary philosophy of mind.

Several years of debating these issues, both in public forums and in print, have convinced me that quite often the fundamental issues in the debate do not rise to the surface. If you debate people, for example, about strong artificial intelligence or the indeterminacy of translation, the sheer implausibility of such theories is disguised by the apparently technical character of the arguments bandied back and forth. Worse yet, it is hard to get the assumptions that lead to these theories out in the open. When, for example, somebody feels comfortable with the idea that a computer would suddenly and miraculously have mental states just in virtue of running a certain sort of program, the underlying assumptions that make this view seem possible are seldom stated explicitly. So, in this discussion I want to try an approach different from direct refutation. I am not going to present one more "refutation of functionalism"; rather, I want to begin the task of exposing and thereby undermining the foundations on which this whole tradition rests. If you are tempted to functionalism, I believe you do not need refutation, you need help.

The materialist tradition is massive, complex, ubiquitous, and yet elusive. Its various elements—its attitude toward consciousness, its conception of scientific verification, its metaphysics and theory of knowledge—are all mutually supporting, so that when one part is challenged, the defenders can easily fall back on another part whose certainty is taken for granted. Here I speak from personal experience. When you offer a refutation of strong AI or of the indeterminacy thesis or of functionalism, the defenders do not feel it necessary to try to meet your actual arguments, because they know in advance that you must be wrong. They know that the materialist tradition—which they often mistakenly call "science"—is on their side. And the tradition is not just part of academic philosophy. If you hear lectures in cognitive science or read popular articles on artificial intelligence, you will encounter the same tradition. It is too large to summarize in a paragraph or even a chapter, but I believe that if I continue to allow it to unfold itself, the reader will have no difficulty recognizing it.

Before beginning an assault on the foundations, I need to specify certain elements of the structure a little more precisely and to say something about its history.

### III. The Foundations of Modern Materialism

By "the tradition," I mean in large part the cluster of views and methodological presuppositions that centers around the following (often unstated) assumptions and theses:

1. Where the scientific study of the mind is concerned, consciousness and its special features are of rather minor importance. It is quite possible, indeed desirable, to give an account of language, cognition, and mental states in general without taking into account consciousness and subjectivity.[9]

2. Science is objective. It is objective not only in the sense that it strives to reach conclusions that are independent of personal biases and points of view, but more important, it concerns a reality that is objective. Science is objective because reality itself is objective.

3. Because reality is objective, the best method in the study of the mind is to adopt the objective or third-person point of view. The objectivity of science requires that the phenomena studied be completely objective, and in the case of cognitive science this means that it must study objectively observable *behavior*. As far as a mature cognitive science is concerned, the study of the mind and the study of intelligent behavior (including the causal foundations of behavior) are pretty much the same study.

4. From the third-person, objective point of view, the only answer to the epistemological question "How would we know about the mental phenomena of another system?" is: We know by observing its *behavior*. This is the only solution to the "other minds problem."

Epistemology plays a special role in cognitive science because an objective science of cognition must be able to distinguish such things as *cognition, intelligent behavior, information processing,* etc., from other natural phenomena. A basic question, perhaps the basic question, in the study of the mind is the epistemological question: How would we know whether or not some other "system" has such-and-such mental properties? And the only scientific answer is: By its behavior.

5. Intelligent behavior and causal relations to intelligent behavior are in some way the essence of the mental. Adherence to the view that there is an essential connection between mind and behavior range all the way from the extreme version of behaviorism that says there isn't anything to having mental states except having dispositions to behavior, to the functionalists attempt to define mental notions in terms of internal and external causal relations, to Wittgenstein's (1953, para. 580) puzzling claim, "An 'inner process' stands in need of outward criteria."[10]

6. Every fact in the universe is in principle knowable and understandable by human investigators. Because reality is physical, and because science concerns the investigation of physical reality, and because there are no limits on what we can know of physical reality, it follows that all of the facts in the universe are knowable and understandable by us.

7. The only things that exist are ultimately physical, *as the physical is traditionally conceived,* that is, as opposed to the mental. This means that in the traditional oppositions—dualism versus monism, mentalism versus materialism—the right-hand term names the correct view; the left-hand term names the false view.

Already it should be clear that these views hang together; because reality is *objective* (point 2), it must be ultimately *physical* (point 7). And the objectivist ontology of points 2 and 7 leads naturally to the objectivist methodology of points 3 and 4. But if the mind really exists and has an objective ontology, then it appears its ontology must be in some sense behavioral and causal (point 5). This, however, forces epistemology to the front of the stage (point 4), because it now becomes crucially important to be able to distinguish the behavior of those systems that lack mental states from those that really have mental states. From the fact that the reality is ultimately physical (point 7), and the fact that it is completely objective (point 2), it is natural to assume that everything in reality is knowable by us (point 6). Finally, one thing is obvious: There is no place— or at least very little place—for consciousness in this overall picture (point 1).

In the course of this book, I hope to show that each of these points is, at best, false, and that the total picture they present is not only profoundly unscientific, it is incoherent.

## IV. Historical Origins of the Foundations

Historically, how did we get into this situation? How did we get into a situation where people can say things that are inconsistent with obvious facts of their experiences?

What one wants to know is: What is it about the history of contemporary discussion in the philosophy of mind, psychology, cognitive science, and artificial intelligence that makes such views conceivable, that makes them seem perfectly respectable or acceptable? At any given time in intellectual history we are, all of us, working within certain traditions that make certain questions seem the right ones to ask and certain answers seem the only possible answers. In contemporary philosophy of mind, the historical tradition is blinding us to the obvious facts of our experiences, giving us a methodology and a vocabulary that make obviously false hypotheses seem acceptable. The tradition has risen from its early crude behaviorist beginnings more than a half century ago through "type-type" and "token-token" identity theories to the present sophisticated computational models of cognition. Now what is it about the tradition that makes it so powerful in such a counterintuitive way? I wish I understood these matters well enough to give a full historical analysis, but I fear I have only a few guesses and suggestions to make about the nature of the symptoms. It seems to me that there are at least four factors at work.

First, we have a terror of falling into Cartesian dualism. The bankruptcy of the Cartesian tradition, and the absurdity of supposing that there are two kinds of substances or properties in the world, "mental" and "physical," is so threatening to us and has such a sordid history that we are reluctant to concede anything that might smack of Cartesianism. We are reluctant to concede any of the commonsense facts that sound "Cartesian," because it seems that if we accept the facts, we will have to accept the whole of Cartesian metaphysics. Any sort of mentalism that recognizes the obvious facts of our existence is regarded as automatically suspect. At the most extreme, some philosophers are reluctant to admit the existence of consciousness because they fail to see that the *mental* state of consciousness is just an ordinary biological, that is, *physical*, feature of the brain. Perhaps even more exasperatingly, they are aided in this error by those philosophers who cheerfully acknowledge the existence of consciousness and in so doing suppose they must be asserting the existence of something nonphysical.

The view that consciousness, mental states, etc., exist, in the most naive and obvious sense, and play a real causal role in our behavior has nothing special to do with Cartesian dualism. After all, one does not have to read the *Meditations* to be conscious that one is conscious or that one's desires, as mental phenomena, conscious or unconscious, are real causal phenomena. But when one reminds philosophers of these "Cartesian intuitions," one is immediately accused of Cartesianism. I have, personally speaking, been accused of holding some crazy doctrine of "property dualism" and "privileged access," or believing in "introspection" or "neovitalism" or even "mysticism," even though I have never, implicitly or explicitly, endorsed any of these views. Why? Partly, no doubt, it is just intellectual carelessness (or perhaps even worse) on the part of the commentators, but there is also something deeper involved. They find it difficult to see that one could accept the obvious facts about mental states without accepting the Cartesian apparatus that traditionally went along with the acknowledgment of these facts. They think the only real choices available are between some form of materialism and some form of dualism. One of my many aims in writing this book is to show that this conception is mistaken, that one can give a coherent account of the facts about the mind without endorsing any of the discredited Cartesian apparatus.

Second, along with the Cartesian tradition we have inherited a vocabulary, and with the vocabulary a certain set of categories, within which we are historically conditioned to think about these problems. The vocabulary is not innocent, because implicit in the vocabulary are a surprising number of theoretical claims that are almost certainly false. The vocabulary includes a series of apparent oppositions: "physical" versus "mental," "body" versus "mind," "materialism" versus "mentalism," "matter" versus "spirit." Implicit in these oppositions is the thesis that the same phenomenon under the same aspects cannot literally satisfy both terms. Sometimes the semantics and even the morphology seems to make this opposition explicit, as in the apparent opposition between "materialism" and "immaterialism." Thus we are supposed to believe that if something is mental, it cannot be physical; that if it is a matter of spirit, it cannot be a matter of matter; if it is immaterial, it cannot be material. But these views seem to me obviously false, given everything we know about neurobiology. The brain causes certain "mental" phenomena, such as conscious mental states, and these conscious states are simply higher-level features of the brain. Consciousness is a higher-level or emergent property of the brain in the utterly harmless sense of "higher-level" or "emergent" in which solidity is a higher-level emergent property of $H_2O$ molecules when they are in a lattice structure (ice), and liquidity is similarly a higher-level emergent property of $H_2O$ molecules when they are, roughly speaking, rolling around on each other (water). Consciousness is a mental, and therefore physical, property of the brain in the sense in which liquidity is a property of systems of molecules. If there is one thesis that I would like to get across in this discussion, it is simply this: The fact that a feature is mental does not imply that it is not physical; the fact that a feature is physical does not imply that it is not mental. Revising Descartes for the moment, we might say not only "I think, therefore I am" and "I am a thinking being," but also *I am a thinking being, therefore I am a physical being.*

But notice how the vocabulary makes it difficult, if not impossible, to say what I mean using the traditional terminology. When I say that consciousness is a higher-level physical feature of the brain, the temptation is to hear that as meaning physical-as-opposed-to-mental, as meaning that consciousness should be described *only* in objective behavioral or neurophysiological terms. But what I really mean is consciousness *qua* consciousness, *qua* mental, *qua* subjective, *qua* qualitative is *physical*, and physical *because* mental. All of which shows, I believe, the inadequacy of the traditional vocabulary.

Along with the apparent oppositions are names that apparently exhaust the possible positions one can occupy: there is monism versus dualism, materialism and physicalism versus mentalism and idealism. The eagerness to stick with the traditional categories produces some odd terminology, such as "property dualism," "anomalous monism," "token identity," etc. My own views do not fit any of the traditional labels, but to many philosophers the idea that one might hold a view that does not fit these categories seems incomprehensible.[11] Perhaps worst of all, there are several nouns and verbs that look as if they had a clear meaning and actually stood for well-defined objects and activities—"mind," "self," and "introspection" are obvious examples. The contemporary cognitive science vocabulary is no better. We tend to assume uncritically that expressions like "cognition," "intelligence," and "information processing" have clear definitions and actually stand for some natural kinds. I believe such assumptions are mistaken. This point is worth emphasizing: "intelligence," "intelligent behavior," "cognition," and "information processing," for example, are not precisely defined notions. Even more amazingly, a lot of very technical sounding notions are poorly defined—notions such as "computer," "computation," "program," and "symbol," for example. It does not much matter for most purposes in computer science that these notions are ill defined (just as it is not important to furniture manufacturers that they do not have a philosophically precise definition of "chair" and "table" either); but when cognitive scientists say such things as that brains are computers, minds are programs, etc., then the definition of these notions becomes crucial.

Third, there is a persistent objectifying tendency in contemporary philosophy, science, and intellectual life generally. We have the conviction that if something is real, it must be equally accessible to all competent observers. Since the seventeenth century, educated people in the West have come to accept an absolutely basic metaphysical presupposition: *Reality is objective.* This assumption has proved useful to us in many ways, but it is obviously false, as a moment's reflection on one's own subjective states reveals. And this assumption has led, perhaps inevitably, to the view that the only "scientific" way to study the mind is as a set of objective phenomena. Once we adopt the assumption that anything that is objective must be equally accessible to any observer, the questions are automatically shifted away from the subjectivity of mental states toward the objectivity of the external behavior. And this has the consequence that instead of asking the questions, "What is it to have a belief?," "What is it to have a desire?," "What is it like to be in certain sorts of conscious states?", we ask the third-person question, "Under what conditions would we from outside *attribute* beliefs, desires, etc., to some *other* system?" This seems perfectly natural to us, because, of course, most of the questions we need to answer about mental phenomena concern other people and not just ourselves.

But the third-person character of the epistemology should not blind us to the fact that the actual ontology of mental states is a first-person ontology. The way that the third-person point of view is applied in practice makes it difficult for us to see the difference between something really having a mind, such as a human being, and something behaving *as if* it had a mind, such as a computer. And once you have lost the distinction between a system's really having mental states and merely acting as if it had mental states, then you lose sight of an essential feature of the mental, namely that its ontology is essentially a first-person ontology. Beliefs, desires, etc., are always *somebody's* beliefs and desires, and they are always potentially conscious, even in cases where they are actually unconscious.

I present an argument for this last point in chapter 7. Now I am trying to diagnose a historically conditioned pattern of investigation that makes the third-person point of view seem the only scientifically acceptable standpoint from which to examine the mind. It would take an intellectual historian to answer such questions as when did the under-what-conditions-would-we-attribute-mental-states question come to seem the right question to ask? But the intellectual effects of its persistence seem clear. Just as Kant's commonsense distinction between the appearances of things and things in themselves eventually led to the extremes of absolute idealism, so the persistence of the commonsense question "Under what conditions would we attribute mental states?" has led us into behaviorism, functionalism, strong AI, eliminative materialism, the intentional stance, and no doubt other confusions known only to experts.

Fourth, because of our conception of the history of the growth of knowledge we have come to suffer from what Austin called the *"ivresse des grands profondeurs."* It does not seem enough somehow to state humble and obvious truths about the mind—we want something deeper. We want a theoretical discovery. And of course our model of a great theoretical discovery comes from the history of the physical sciences. We dream of some great "breakthrough" in the study of the mind, we look forward to a "mature" cognitive science. So the fact that the views in question are implausible and counterintuitive does not count against them. On the contrary, it can even seem a great merit of contemporary functionalism and artificial intelligence that they run dead counter to our intuitions. For is this not the very feature that makes the physical sciences so dazzling? Our ordinary intuitions about space and time or, for that matter, about the solidity of the table in front of us, have been shown to be mere illusions replaced by a much deeper knowledge of the inner workings of the universe. Could not a great breakthrough in the study of the mind similarly show that our most firmly held beliefs about our mental states are equally illusory? Can we not reasonably expect great discoveries that will overthrow our commonsense assumptions? And, who knows, might not some of those great discoveries be made by some of us?

## V. Undermining the Foundations

One way to state some of the salient features of the argument that I will be presenting is to state them in opposition to the seven principles I mentioned earlier. To do this, I need first to make explicit the distinctions between *ontology*, *epistemology*, and *causation*. There is a distinction between answers to the questions, What is it? (ontology), How do we find out about it? (epistemology), and What does it do? (causation). For example, in the case of the heart, the ontology is that it is a large piece of muscle tissue in the chest cavity; the epistemology is that we find out about it by using stethescopes, EKGs, and in a pinch we can open up the chest and have a look; and the causation is that the heart pumps blood through the body. With these distinctions in mind, we can go to work.

*1. Consciousness does matter.* I will argue that there is no way to study the phenomena of the mind without implicitly or explicitly studying consciousness. The basic reason for this is that we really have no notion of the mental apart from our notion of consciousness. Of course, at any given point in a person's life, most of the mental phenomena in that person's existence are not present to consciousness. In the formal mode, most of the mental predicates that apply to me at any given instant will have conditions of application independent of my conscious states at that moment. However, though most of our mental life at any given point is unconscious, I will argue that we have no conception of an unconscious mental state except in terms derived from conscious mental states. If I am right about this, then all of the recent talk about mental states that are in principle inaccessible to consciousness is really incoherent (more about this in chapter 7).

*2. Not all of reality is objective; some of it is subjective.* There is a persistent confusion between the claim that we should try as much as possible to eliminate personal subjective prejudices from the search for truth and the claim that the real world contains no elements that are irreducibly subjective. And this confusion in turn is based on a confusion between the epistemological sense of the subjective/objective distinction, and the ontological sense. Epistemically, the distinction marks different degrees of independence of claims from the vagaries of special values, personal prejudices, points of view, and emotions. Ontologically, the distinction marks different categories of empirical reality (more about these distinctions in chapter 4). Epistemically, the ideal of objectivity states a worthwhile, even if unattainable goal. But ontologically, the claim that all of reality is objective is, neurobiologically speaking, simply false. In general mental states have an irreducibly subjective ontology, as we will have occasion to see in some detail later.

If I am right in thinking that consciousness and subjectivity are essential to the mind, then the conception of the mental employed by the tradition is misconceived from the beginning, for it is essentially an objective, third-person conception. The tradition tries to study the mind as if it consisted of neutral phenomena, independent of consciousness and subjectivity. But such an approach leaves out the crucial features that distinguish mental from nonmental phenomena. And this more than any other reason accounts for the implausibility of the views I mentioned at the beginning. If you try to treat beliefs, for example, as phenomena that have no essential connection with consciousness, then you are likely to wind up with the idea that they can be defined solely in terms of external behavior (behaviorism), or in terms of cause and effect relations (functionalism), or that they do not really exist at all (eliminative materialism), or that talk of beliefs and desires is just to be construed as a certain manner of speaking (the intentional stance). The ultimate absurdity is to try to treat consciousness itself independently of consciousness, that is, to treat it solely from a third-person point of view, and that leads to the view that consciousness as such, as "inner," "private" phenomenal events, does not really exist.

Sometimes the tension between the methodology and the absurdity of the results becomes visible. In recent literature, there is a dispute about something called "qualia" and the problem is supposed to be, "Can functionalism account for qualia?" What the issue reveals is that the mind consists of qualia, so to speak, right down to the ground. Functionalism can't account for qualia because it was designed around a different subject matter, namely attributions of intentionality based on third-person evidence, whereas actual mental phenomena have to do not with attributions but with the existence of conscious and unconscious mental states, both of which are first-person, subjective phenomena.

*3. Because it is a mistake to suppose that the ontology of the mental is objective, it is a mistake to suppose that the methodology of a science of the mind must concern itself only with objectively observable behavior.* Because mental phenomena are essentially connected with consciousness, and because consciousness is essentially subjective, it follows that the ontology of the mental is essentially a first-person ontology. Mental states are always somebody's mental states. There is always a "first person," an "I," that has these mental states. The consequence of this for the present discussion is that the first-person point of view is primary. In the actual practice of investigation, we will of course study other people, simply because most of our research is not on ourselves. But it is important to emphasize that what we are trying to get at when we study other people is precisely the first-person point of view. When we study *him* or *her*, what we are studying is the *me* that is him or her. And this is not an epistemic point.

In light of the distinctions between ontology, epistemology, and causation, if one had to summarize the crisis of the tradition in one paragraph, it would be this:

The subjectivist ontology of the mental seems intolerable. It seems intolerable metaphysically that there should be irreducibly subjective, "private" entities in the world, and intolerable epistemologically that there should be an asymmetry between the way that each person knows of his or her inner mental phenomena and the way that others from outside know of them. This crisis produces a flight from subjectivity and the direction of the flight is to rewrite the *ontology* in terms of the *epistemology* and the *causation*. We first get rid of subjectivity by redefining the ontology in terms of the third-person, epistemic basis, behavior. We say, "Mental states just are dispositions to behavior" (behaviorism), and when the absurdity of that becomes unbearable we fall back on causation. We say, "Mental states are defined by their causal relations" (functionalism), or "Mental states are computational states" (strong AI).

The tradition assumes, falsely in my view, that in the study of the mind one is forced to choose between "introspection" and "behavior." There are several mistakes involved in this, among them:

4. *It is a mistake to suppose that we know of the existence of mental phenomena in others only by observing their behavior.* I believe that the traditional "solution" to the "problem of other minds," though it has been with us for centuries, will not survive even a moment's serious reflection. I will have more to say about these issues later (in chapter 3), but at present just this: If you think for a moment about how we know that dogs and cats are conscious, and that computers and cars are not conscious (and by the way, there is no doubt that you and I know both of these things), you will see that the basis of our certainty is not

"behavior," but rather a certain causal conception of how the world works. One can see that dogs and cats are in certain important respects relevantly similar to us. Those are eyes, this is skin, these are ears, etc. The "behavior" only makes sense as the expression or manifestation of an underlying mental reality, because we can see the causal basis of the mental and thereby see the behavior as a manifestation of the mental. The principle on which we "solve" the problem of other minds, I shall argue, is not: same-behavior-ergo-same-mental-phenomena. That is the old mistake enshrined in the Turing test. If this principle were correct, we would all have to conclude that radios are conscious because they exhibit intelligent verbal behavior. But we do not draw any such conclusion, because we have a "theory" about how radios work. The principle on which we "solve the other minds problem" is: same-causes-same-effects, and relevantly-similar-causes-relevantly-similar-effects. Where knowledge of other minds is concerned, behavior *by itself* is of no interest to us; it is rather *the combination of behavior with the knowledge of the causal underpinnings of the behavior* that form the basis of our knowledge.

But even the foregoing seems to me to concede too much to the tradition, because it suggests that our basic stance toward dogs, cats, radios, and other people is epistemic; it suggests that in our everyday dealings with the world we are busy "solving the other minds problem" and that dogs and cats are passing the test and radios and cars failing. But that suggestion is wrong. Except in odd cases, we do not solve the other minds problem, because it does not arise. Our Background capacities for dealing with the world enable us to cope with people in one way and cars in another, but we do not in addition generate a hypothesis to the effect that this person is conscious and that car is not conscious, except in unusual cases. I will have more to say about this later (in chapters 3 and 8).

In the sciences, epistemic questions do of course arise, but epistemic questions are no more essential to understanding the nature of the mind than they are to understanding the nature of the phenomena studied in any other discipline. Why should they be? There are interesting epistemic questions about knowledge of the past in history, or knowledge of unobserved entities in physics. But the question *"How* is the existence of the phenomena to be verified?" should not be confused with the question *"What* is the nature of the phenomena whose existence is verified?" The crucial question is not "Under what conditions would we *attribute* mental states to other people?" but rather, "What is it that people *actually have* when they have mental states?" "What are mental phenomena?" as distinct from "How do we find out about them and how do they function causally in the life of the organism?"

I do not want this point to be misunderstood: I am not saying that it is easy to find out about mental states, and that we don't have to worry about epistemic questions. That's not the point at all. I think that it is immensely difficult to study mental phenomena, and the only guide for methodology is the universal one—use any tool or weapon that comes to hand, and stick with any tool or weapon that works. The point I am making here is different: The epistemology of studying the mental no more determines its ontology than does the epistemology of any other discipline determine its ontology. On the contrary, in the study of the mind as elsewhere, the whole point of the epistemology is to get at the preexisting ontology.

5. *Behavior or causal relations to behavior are not essential to the existence of mental phenomena.* I believe that the relation of mental states to behavior is purely contingent. It is easy to see this when we consider how it is possible to have the mental states without the behavior, and the behavior without the mental states (I will give some examples in chapter 3). Causally we know that brain processes are sufficient for any mental state and that the connection between those brain processes and the motor nervous system is a contingent neurophysiological connection like any other.

6. *It is inconsistent with what we in fact know about the universe and our place in it to suppose that everything is knowable by us.*

Our brains are the products of certain evolutionary processes, and as such they are simply the most developed in a whole series of evolutionary paths that include the brains of dogs, baboons, dolphins, etc. Now, no one supposes that, for example, dogs can be brought to understand quantum mechanics; the dog's brain is simply not developed to that extent. And it is easy to imagine a being that is further developed along the same evolutionary progression than we are, that stands to us roughly as we stand to dogs. Just as we think that dogs cannot understand quantum mechanics, so this imaginary evolutionary product would conclude that though humans can understand quantum mechanics, there is a great deal that the human brain cannot grasp.[12] It's a good idea to ask ourselves, who do we think we are? And at least part of the answer is that we are biological beasts selected for coping with hunter-gatherer environments, and as far as we know, we have had no significant change in our gene pool for several thousand years. Fortunately (or unfortunately), nature is profligate, and just as every male produces enough sperm to repopulate the earth, so we have a lot more neurons than we need for a hunter-gatherer existence. I believe that the phenomenon of surplus neurons—as distinct from, say, opposed thumbs—is the key to understanding how we got out of hunter-gatherering and produced philosophy, science, technology, neuroses, advertising, etc. But we should never forget who we are; and for such as us, it is a mistake to assume that everything that exists is comprehensible to our brains. Of course, methodologically we have to act as if we could understand everything, because there is no way of knowing what we can't: to know the limits of knowledge, we would have to know both sides of the limit. So potential omniscience is acceptable as a heuristic device, but it would be self-deception to suppose it a fact.

Furthermore, we know that many beings on our earth have neurophysiological structures that are different enough from ours so that it may be literally unknowable to us what the experiences of those beings are really like. I will discuss an example of this in chapter 3.

7. *The Cartesian conception of the physical, the conception of physical reality as res* extensa, *is simply not adequate to describe the facts that correspond to statements about physical reality.* When we come to the proposition that reality is physical, we come to what is perhaps the crux of the whole discussion. When we think of the "physical," we think perhaps of things like molecules and atoms and subatomic particles. And we think that they are physical, in a sense that is opposed to the mental, and that things like sensations of pain are mental. And if we are brought up in our culture, we also think these two categories must exhaust everything that exists. But the poverty of these categories becomes apparent as soon as you start to think about the different kinds of things the world contains, that is, as soon as you start to think about the facts that correspond to various sorts of empirical statements. So if you think about balance-of-payments problems, ungrammatical sentences, reasons for being suspicious of modal logic, my ability to ski, the state government of California, and points scored in football games, you are less inclined to think that everything must be categorized as either mental or physical. Of the list I gave, which are mental and which are physical?

There are at least three things wrong with our traditional conception that reality is physical. First, as I have noted, the terminology is designed around a false opposition between the "physical" and the "mental," and as I have already claimed, that is a mistake. Second, if we think of the physical in Cartesian terms as *res extensa*, then it is obsolete even as a matter of physics to suppose that physical reality is physical on this definition. Since relativity theory, we have come to think of, for example, electrons as points of mass/energy. So on the Cartesian definition of "physical," electrons would not count as physical. Third, and most important for our present discussion, it is a very deep mistake to suppose that the crucial question for ontology is, "What sorts of things exist in the world?" as opposed to, "What must be the case in the world in order that our empirical statements be true?"

Noam Chomsky once said (in conversation) that as soon as we come to understand anything, we call it "physical." On this view, trivially, anything is either physical or unintelligible. If we think of the make-up of the world, then of course everything in the world is made of particles, and particles are among our paradigms of the physical. And if we are going to call anything that is made up of physical particles physical; then, trivially, everything in the world is physical. But to say that is not to deny that the world contains points scored in football games, interest rates, governments, and pains. All of these have their own way of existing—athletic, economic, political, mental, etc.

The conclusion is this: Once you see the incoherence of dualism, you can also see that monism and materialism are just as mistaken. Dualists asked, "How many kinds of things and properties are there?" and counted up to two. Monists, confronting the same question, only got as far as one. But the real mistake was to start counting at all. Monism and materialism are defined in terms of dualism and mentalism, and because the definitions of dualism and mentalism are incoherent, monism and materialism inherit that incoherence. It is customary to think of dualism as coming in two flavors, substance dualism and property dualism; but to these I want to add a third, which I will call "conceptual dualism." This view consists in taking the dualistic concepts very seriously, that is, it consists in the view that in some important sense "physical" implies "nonmental" and "mental" implies "nonphysical." Both traditional dualism and materialism presuppose conceptual dualism, so defined. I introduce this definition to make it clear why it seems to me best to think of materialism as really a form of dualism. It is that form of dualism that begins by accepting the Cartesian categories. I believe that if you take those categories seriously—the categories of mental and physical, mind and body—as a consistent dualist, you will eventually be forced to materialism. Materialism is thus in a sense the finest flower of dualism, and to a discussion of its difficulties and recent history I now turn.

# Chapter 2

# The Recent History of Materialism:
# The Same Mistake Over and Over

---

*I. The Mystery of Materialism*

What exactly is the doctrine known as "materialism" supposed
to amount to? One might think that it would consist in the
view that the microstructure of the world is entirely made up
of material particles. The difficulty, however, is that this view
is consistent with just about any philosophy of mind, except
possibly the Cartesian view that in addition to physical particles there are "immaterial" souls or mental substances, spiritual entities that survive the destruction of our bodies and live
on immortally. But nowadays, as far as I can tell, no one
believes in the existence of immortal spiritual substances
except on religious grounds. To my knowledge, there are no
purely philosophical or scientific motivations for accepting the
existence of immortal mental substances. So leaving aside
opposition to religiously motivated belief in immortal souls,
the question remains: What exactly is materialism in the philosophy of mind supposed to amount to? To what views is it
supposed to be opposed?

If one reads the early works of our contemporaries who
describe themselves as materialists—J. J. C. Smart (1965), U. T.
Place (1956), and D. Armstrong (1968), for example—it seems
clear that when they assert the identity of the mental with the
physical, they are claiming something more than simply the
denial of Cartesian substance dualism. It seems to me they
wish to deny the existence of any irreducible mental
phenomena in the world. They want to deny that there are any
irreducible phenomenological properties, such as consciousness, or *qualia*. Now why are they so anxious to deny the

existence of irreducible intrinsic mental phenomena? Why don't they just concede that these properties are ordinary higher-level biological properties of neurophysiological systems such as human brains?

I think the answer to that is extremely complex, but at least part of the answer has to do with the fact that they accept the traditional Cartesian categories, and along with the categories the attendant vocabulary with its implications. I think from this point of view to grant the existence and irreducibility of mental phenomena would be equivalent to granting some kind of Cartesianism. In their terms, it might be a "property dualism" rather than a "substance dualism," but from their point of view, property dualism would be just as inconsistent with materialism as substance dualism. By now it will be obvious that I am opposed to the assumptions behind their view. What I want to insist on, ceaselessly, is that one can accept the obvious facts of physics—for example, that the world is made up entirely of physical particles in fields of force—without at the same time denying the obvious facts about our own experiences—for example, that we are all conscious and that our conscious states have quite specific *irreducible* phenomenological properties. The mistake is to suppose that these two theses are inconsistent, and that mistake derives from accepting the presuppositions behind the traditional vocabulary. My view is emphatically not a form of dualism. I reject both property and substance dualism; but precisely for the reasons that I reject dualism, I reject materialism and monism as well. The deep mistake is to suppose that one must choose between these views.

It is the failure to see the consistency of naive mentalism with naive physicalism that leads to those very puzzling discussions in the early history of this subject in which the authors try to find a "topic-neutral" vocabulary or to avoid something they call "nomological danglers" (Smart 1965). Notice that nobody feels that, say, digestion has to be described in a "topic-neutral" vocabulary. Nobody feels the urge to say, "There is something going on in me which is like what goes on when I digest pizza." Though they do feel the urge to say, "There is something going on in me which is like what goes on when I see an orange." The urge is to try to find a description of the phenomena that doesn't use the mentalistic vocabulary. But what is the point of doing that? The facts remain the same. The fact is that the mental phenomena have mentalistic properties, just as what goes on in my stomach has digestive properties. We don't get rid of those properties simply by finding an alternative vocabulary. Materialist philosophers wish to deny the existence of mental properties without denying the reality of *some* phenomena that underly the use of our mentalistic vocabulary. So they have to find an alternative vocabulary to describe the phenomena.[1] But on my account, this is all a waste of time. One should just grant the mental (hence, physical) phenomena to start with, in the same way that one grants the digestive phenomena in the stomach.

In this chapter I want to examine, rather briefly, the history of materialism over the past half century. I believe that this history exhibits a rather puzzling but very revealing pattern of argument and counterargument that has gone on in the philosophy of mind since the positivism of the 1930s. This pattern is not always visible on the surface. Nor is it even visible on the surface that the same issues are being talked about. But I believe that, contrary to surface appearances, there really has been only one major topic of discussion in the philosophy of mind for the past fifty years or so, and that is the mind-body problem. Often philosophers purport to talk about something else—such as the analysis of belief or the nature of consciousness—but it almost invariably emerges that they are not really interested in the special features of belief or consciousness. They are not interested in how believing differs from supposing and hypothesizing, but rather they want to test their convictions about the mind-body problem against the *example* of belief. Similarly with consciousness: There is surprisingly little discussion of consciousness as such; rather, materialists see consciousness as a special "problem" for a materialist theory of mind. That is, they want to find a way to "handle" consciousness, given their materialism.[2]

The pattern that these discussions almost invariably seem to take is the following. A philosopher advances a materialist theory of the mind. He does this from the deep assumption that some version of the materialist theory of the mind must be the correct one—after all, do we not know from the discoveries of science that there is really nothing in the universe but physical particles and fields of forces acting on physical particles? And surely it must be possible to give an account of human beings in a way that is consistent and coherent with our account of nature generally. And surely, does it not follow from that that our account of human beings must be thoroughgoing materialism? So the philosopher sets out to give a materialist account of the mind. He then encounters difficulties. It always seems that he is leaving something out. The general pattern of discussion is that criticisms of the materialist theory usually take a more or less technical form, but in fact, underlying the technical objections is a much deeper objection, and the deeper objection can be put quite simply: The theory in question has left out the mind; it has left out some essential feature of the mind, such as consciousness or "qualia" or semantic content. One sees this pattern over and over. A materialist thesis is advanced. But the thesis encounters difficulties; the difficulties take different forms, but they are always manifestations of an underlying deeper difficulty, namely, the thesis in question denies obvious facts that we all know about our own minds. And this leads to ever more frenzied efforts to stick with the materialist thesis and try to defeat the arguments put forward by those who insist on preserving the facts. After some years of desperate maneuvers to account for the difficulties, some new development is put forward that allegedly solves the difficulties, but then we find that it encounters new difficulties, only the new difficulties are not so new—they are really the same old difficulties.

If we were to think of the philosophy of mind over the past fifty years as a single individual, we would say of that person that he is a compulsive neurotic, and his neurosis takes the form of repeating the same pattern of behavior over and over. In my experience, the neurosis cannot be cured by a frontal assault. It is not enough just to point out the logical mistakes that are being made. Direct refutation simply leads to a repetition of the pattern of neurotic behavior. What we have to do is go behind the symptoms and find the unconscious assumptions that led to the behavior in the first place. I am now convinced, after several years of discussing these issues, that with very few exceptions all of the parties to the disputes in the current issues in the philosophy of mind are captives of a certain set of verbal categories. They are the prisoners of a certain terminology, a terminology that goes back at least to Descartes if not before, and in order to overcome the compulsive behavior, we will have to examine the unconscious origins of the disputes. We will have to try to uncover what it is that everyone is taking for granted to get the dispute going and keep it going.

I would not wish my use of a therapeutic analogy to be taken to imply a general endorsement of psychoanalytic modes of explanation in intellectual matters. So let's vary the therapeutic metaphor as follows: I want to suggest that my present enterprise is a bit like that of an anthropologist undertaking to describe the exotic behavior of a distant tribe. The tribe has a set of behavior patterns and a metaphysic that we must try to uncover and understand. It is easy to make fun of the antics of the tribe of philosophers of mind, and I must confess that I have not always been able to resist the temptation to do so. But at the beginning, at least, I must insist that the tribe is us— we are the possessors of the metaphysical assumptions that make the behavior of the tribe possible. So before I actually present an analysis and a criticism of the behavior of the tribe, I want to present an idea that we should all find acceptable, because the idea is really part of our contemporary scientific culture. And yet, I will later on argue that the idea is incoherent; it is simply another symptom of the same neurotic pattern.

Here is the idea. We think the following question must make sense: How is it possible for unintelligent bits of matter to produce intelligence? How is it possible for the unintelligent bits of matter in our brains to produce the intelligent behavior that we all engage in? Now that seems to us like a perfectly intelligible question. Indeed, it seems like a very valuable research project, and in fact it is a research project that is widely pursued[3] and incidentally, very well funded.

Because we find the question intelligible, we find the following answer plausible: Unintelligent bits of matter can produce intelligence because of their *organization*. The unintelligent bits of matter are *organized* in certain dynamic ways, and it is the dynamic organization that is constitutive of the intelligence. Indeed, we can actually artificially reproduce the form of dynamic organization that makes intelligence possible. The underlying structure of that organization is called "a computer," the project of programming the computer is called "artificial intelligence"; and when operating, the computer produces intelligence because it is implementing the right computer program with the right inputs and outputs.

Now doesn't that story sound at least plausible to you? I must confess that it can be made to sound very plausible to me, and indeed I think if it doesn't sound even remotely plausible to you, you are probably not a fully socialized member of our contemporary intellectual culture. Later on I will show that both the question and the answer are incoherent. When we pose the question and give that answer in these terms, we really haven't the faintest idea of what we are talking about. But I present this example here because I want it to seem natural, indeed promising, as a research project.

I said a few paragraphs back that the history of philosophical materialism in the twentieth century exhibits a curious pattern, a pattern in which there is a recurring tension between the materialist's urge to give an account of mental phenomena that makes no reference to anything intrinsically or irreducibly mental, on the one hand, and the general intellectual requirement that every investigator faces of not saying anything that is obviously false, on the other. To let this pattern show itself, I want now to give a very brief sketch, as neutrally and objectively as I can, of the pattern of theses and responses that materialists have exemplified. The aim of what follows is to provide evidence for the claims made in chapter 1 by giving actual illustrations of the tendencies that I identified.

## II. Behaviorism

In the beginning was behaviorism. Behaviorism came in two varieties: "methodological behaviorism" and "logical behaviorism." Methodological behaviorism is a research strategy in psychology to the effect that a science of psychology should consist in discovering the correlations between stimulus inputs and behavioral outputs (Watson 1925). A rigorous empirical science, according to this view, makes no reference to any mysterious introspective or mentalistic items.

Logical behaviorism goes even a step further and insists that there are no such items to refer to, except insofar as they exist in the form of behavior. According to logical behaviorism, it is a matter of definition, a matter of logical analysis, that mental terms can be defined in terms of behavior, that sentences about the mind can be translated without any residue into sentences about behavior (Hempel 1949; Ryle 1949). According to the logical behaviorist, many of the sentences in the translation will be hypothetical in form, because the mental phenomena in question consist not of actual occurring patterns of behavior, but rather of dispositions to behavior. Thus, according to a standard behaviorist account, to say that John believes that it is going to rain is simply to say that John will be disposed to close the windows, put the garden tools away, and carry an umbrella if he goes out. In the material mode of speech, behaviorism claims that the mind is just behavior and dispositions to behavior. In the formal mode of speech, it consists in the view that sentences about mental phenomena can be translated into sentences about actual and possible behavior.

Objections to behaviorism can be divided into two kinds: commonsense objections and more or less technical objections. An obvious commonsense objection is that the behaviorist seems to leave out the mental phenomena in question. There is nothing left for the subjective experience of thinking or feeling in the behaviorist account; there are just patterns of objectively observable behavior.

Several more or less technical objections have been made to logical behaviorism. First, the behaviorists never succeeded in making the notion of a "disposition" fully clear. No one ever succeeded in giving a satisfactory account of what sorts of antecedents there would have to be in the hypothetical statements to produce an adequate dispositional analysis of mental terms in behavioral terms (Hampshire 1950; Geach 1957). Second, there seemed to be a problem about a certain form of circularity in the analysis: to give an analysis of belief in terms of behavior, it seems that one has to make reference to desire; to give an analysis of desire, it seems that one has to make reference to belief (Chisholm 1957). Thus, to consider our earlier example, we are trying to analyze the hypothesis that John believes that it is going to rain in terms of the hypothesis that if the windows are open, John will close them, and other similar hypotheses. We want to analyze the categorical statement that John believes that it is going to rain in terms of certain hypothetical statements about what John will do under what conditions. However, John's belief that it is going to rain will be manifested in the behavior of closing the windows only if we assume such additional hypotheses as that John doesn't want the rainwater to come in through the windows and John believes that open windows admit rainwater. If there is nothing he likes better than rain streaming in through the windows, he will not be disposed to close them. Without some such hypothesis about John's desires (and his other beliefs), it looks as if we cannot begin to analyze any sentence about his original beliefs. Similar remarks can be made about the analysis of desires; such analyses seem to require reference to beliefs.

A third technical objection to behaviorism was that it left out the causal relations between mental states and behavior (Lewis 1966). By identifying, for example, the pain with the disposition to pain behavior, behaviorism leaves out the fact that pains *cause* behavior. Similarly, if we try to *analyze* beliefs and desires in terms of behavior, we are no longer able to say that beliefs and desires *cause* behavior.

Though perhaps most of the discussions in the philosophical literature concern the "technical" objections, in fact it is the commonsense objections that are the most embarrassing. The absurdity of behaviorism lies in the fact that it denies the existence of any inner mental states in addition to external behavior (Ogden and Richards 1926). And this, we know, runs dead counter to our ordinary experiences of what it is like to be a human being. For this reason, behaviorists were sarcastically accused of "feigning anesthesia"[4] and were the target of a number of bad jokes (e.g., First behaviorist to second behaviorist just after making love, "It was great for you, how was it for me?"). This commonsense objection to behaviorism was sometimes put in the form of arguments appealing to our intuitions. One of these is the superactor/superspartan objection (Putnam 1963). One can easily imagine an actor of superior abilities who could give a perfect imitation of the behavior of someone in pain even though the actor in question had no pain, and one can also imagine a superspartan who was able to endure pain without giving any sign of being in pain.

## III. Type Identity Theories

Logical behaviorism was supposed to be an analytic truth. It asserted a definitional connection between mental and behavioral concepts. In the recent history of materialist philosophies of mind it was replaced by the "identity theory," which claimed that as a matter of contingent, synthetic, empirical fact, mental states were identical with states of the brain and of the central nervous system (Place 1956; Smart 1965). According to the identity theorists, there was no logical absurdity in supposing that there might be separate mental phenomena, independent of material reality; it just turned out as a matter of fact that our mental states, such as pains, were identical with states of our nervous system. In this case, pains were claimed to be identical with stimulations of C-fibers.[5] Descartes *might* have been right in thinking that there were separate mental phenomena; it just turned out *as a matter of fact* that he was wrong. Mental phenomena were nothing but states of the brain and central nervous system. The identity between the mind and the brain was supposed to be an empirical identity, just as the identity between lightning and electrical discharges (Smart 1965), or between water and $H_2O$ molecules (Feigl 1958; Shaffer 1961), were supposed to be empirical and contingent identities. It just turned out as a matter of scientific discovery that lightning bolts were nothing but streams of electrons, and that water in all its various forms was nothing but collections of $H_2O$ molecules.

As with behaviorism, we can divide the difficulties of the identity theory into the "technical" objections and the commonsense objections. In this case, the commonsense objection takes the form of a dilemma. Suppose that the identity theory is, as its supporters claim, an empirical truth. If so, then there must be logically independent features of the phenomena in question that enable it to be identified on the left-hand side of the identity statement in a different way from the way it is identified on the right-hand side of the identity statement (Stevenson 1960). If, for example, pains are identical with neurophysiological events, then there must be two sets of features, pain features and neurophysiological features, and these two sets of features enable us to nail down both sides of the synthetic identity statement. Thus, for example, suppose we have a statement of the form:

Pain event $x$ is identical with neurophysiological event $y$.

We understand such a statement because we understand that one and the same event has been identified in virtue of two different sorts of properties, pain properties and neurophysiological properties. But if so, then we seem to be confronted with a dilemma: either the pain features are subjective, mental, intro-spective features, or they are not. Well if they are, then we have not really gotten rid of the mind. We are still left with a form of dualism, albeit property dualism rather than substance dualism. We are still left with sets of mental properties, even though we have gotten rid of mental substances. If on the other hand we try to treat "pain" as not naming a subjective mental feature of certain neurophysiological events, then its meaning is left totally mysterious and unexplained. As with behaviorism, we have left out the mind. For we now have no way to specify these subjective mental features of our experi-ences.

I hope it is clear that this is just a repetition of the common-sense objection to behaviorism. In this case we have put it in the form of a dilemma: either materialism of the identity variety leaves out the mind or it does not; if it does, it is false; if it does not, it is not materialism.

The Australian identity theorists thought they had an answer to this objection. The answer was to try to describe the so-called mental features in a "topic-neutral" vocabulary. The idea was to get a description of the mental features that did not mention the fact that they were mental (Smart 1965). This can surely be done: One can mention pains without mentioning the fact that they are pains, just as one can mention airplanes without mentioning the fact that they are airplanes. That is, one can mention an airplane by saying, "a certain piece of property belonging to United Airlines," and one can refer to a yellow-orange afterimage by saying, "a certain event going on in me that is like the event that goes on in me when I see an orange." But the fact that one can mention a phenomenon without specifying its essential characteristics doesn't mean that it doesn't exist and doesn't have those essential charac-teristics. It still is a pain or an afterimage, or an airplane, even if our descriptions fail to mention these facts.

Another more "technical" objection to the identity theory was this: it seems unlikely that for every type of mental state there will be one and only one type of neurophysiological state with which it is identical. Even if my belief that Denver is the capital of Colorado is identical with a certain state of my brain, it seems too much to expect that everyone who believes that Denver is the capital of Colorado must have an identical neurophysiological configuration in his or her brain (Block and Fodor 1972; Putnam 1967). And across species, even if it is true that in all humans pains are identical with human neurophysiological events, we don't want to exclude the possibility that in some other species there might be pains that were identical with some other type of neurophysiological configuration. It seems, in short, too much to expect that every *type* of mental state is identical with some *type* of neurophysiological state. And indeed, it seems a kind of "neuronal chauvinism" (Block 1978) to suppose that only entities with neurons like our own can have mental states.

A third "technical" objection to the identity theory derives from Leibniz's law. If two events are identical only if they have all of their properties in common, then it seems that mental states cannot be identical with physical states, because mental states have certain properties that physical states do not have (Smart 1965; Shaffer 1961). For example, my pain is in my toe, but my corresponding neurophysiological state goes all the way from the toe to the thalamus and beyond. So where is the pain, really? The identity theorists did not have much difficulty with this objection. They pointed out that the unit of analysis is really the *experience* of having pain, and that experience (together with the experience of the entire body image) presumably takes place in the central nervous system (Smart 1965). On this point it seems to me that materialists are absolutely right.

A more radical technical objection to the identity theory was posed by Saul Kripke (1971), with the following modal argument: If it were really true that pain is identical with C-fiber stimulation, then it would have to be a necessary truth, in the same way that the identity statement "Heat is identical with the motion of molecules" is a necessary truth. This is because in both cases the expressions on either side of the identity statement are "rigid designators." By this he means that each expression identifies the object it refers to in terms of its essential properties. This feeling of pain that I now have is *essentially* a feeling of pain because anything identical with this feeling would have to be a pain, and this brain state is *essentially* a brain state because anything identical with it would have to be a brain state. So it appears that the identity theorist who claims that pains are certain types of brain states, and that this particular pain is identical with this particular brain state, would be forced to hold both that it is a necessary truth that in general pains are brain states, and that it is a necessary truth that this particular pain is a brain state. But neither of these seems right. It does not seem right to say either that pains in general are necessarily brain states, or that my present pain is necessarily a brain state; because it seems easy to imagine that some sort of being could have brain states like these without having pains and pains like these without being in these sorts of brain states. It is even possible to conceive a situation in which I had this very pain without having this very brain state, and in which I had this very brain state without having a pain.

Debate about the force of this modal argument went on for some years and still continues (Lycan 1971, 1987; Sher 1977). From the point of view of our present interests, I want to call attention to the fact that it is essentially the commonsense objection in a sophisticated guise. The commonsense objection to any identity theory is that you can't identify anything mental with anything nonmental, without leaving out the mental. Kripke's modal argument is that the identification of mental states with physical states would have to be necessary, and yet it cannot be necessary, because the mental could not be necessarily physical. As Kripke says, quoting Butler, "Everything is what it is and not another thing."[6]

In any case, the idea that any type of mental state is identical with some type of neurophysiological state seemed really much too strong. But it seemed that the underlying philosophical motivation of materialism could be preserved with a much weaker thesis, the thesis that for every token instance of a mental state, there will be some token neurophysiological event with which that token instance is identical. Such views were called "token-token identity theories" and they soon replaced type-type identity theories. Some authors indeed felt that a token-token identity theory could evade the force of Kripke's modal arguments.[7]

## IV. Token-Token Identity Theories

The token identity theorists inherited the commonsense objection to type identity theories, the objection that they still seemed to be left with some form of property dualism; but they had some additional difficulties of their own.

One was this. If two people who are in the same mental state are in different neurophysiological states, then what it is about those different neurophysiological states that makes them the same mental state? If you and I both believe that Denver is the capital of Colorado, then what is it that we have in common that makes our different neurophysiological squiggles the same belief? Notice that the token identity theorists cannot give the commonsense answer to this question; they cannot say that what makes two neurophysiological events the same type of mental event is that it has the same type of mental features, because it was precisely the elimination or reduction of these mental features that materialism sought to achieve. They must find some nonmentalistic answer to the question, "What is it about two different neurophysiological states that makes them into tokens of the same type of mental state?" Given the entire tradition within which they were working, the only plausible answer was one in the behaviorist style. Their answer was that a neurophysiological state was a particular mental state in virtue of its function, and this naturally leads to the next view.

## V. Black Box Functionalism

What makes two neurophysiological states into tokens of the the same type of mental state is that they perform the same function in the overall life of the organism. The notion of a function is somewhat vague, but the token identity theorists fleshed it out as follows. Two different brain-state tokens would be tokens of the same type of mental state iff the two brain states had the same causal relations to the input stimulus that the organism receives, to its various other "mental" states, and to its output behavior (Lewis 1972; Grice 1975). Thus, for example, my belief that it is about to rain will be a state in me which is caused by my perception of the gathering of clouds and the increasing thunder; and together with my desire that the rain not come in the windows, it will in turn cause me to close them. Notice that by identifying mental states in terms of their causal relations—not only to input stimuli and output behavior, but also to other mental states—the token identity theorists immediately avoided two objections to behaviorism. One was that behaviorism had neglected the causal relations of mental states, and the second was that there was a circularity in behaviorism, in that beliefs had to be analyzed in terms of desires, desires in terms of beliefs. The token identity theorist of the functionalist stripe can cheerfully accept this circularity by arguing that the entire system of concepts can be cashed out in terms of the system of causal relations.

Functionalism had a beautiful technical device with which to make this system of relations completely clear without invoking any "mysterious mental entities." This device is called a Ramsey sentence,[8] and it works as follows: Suppose that John has the belief that $p$, and that this is caused by his perception that $p$; and, together with his desire that $q$, the belief that $p$ causes his action $a$. Because we are defining beliefs in terms of their causal relations, we can eliminate the explicit use of the word "belief" in the previous sentence, and simply say that there is a *something* that stands in such-and-such causal relations. Formally speaking, the way we eliminate the explicit mention of belief is simply by putting a variable, "$x$," in place of any expression referring to John's belief that $p$; and we preface the whole sentence with an existential quantifier (Lewis 1972). The whole story about John's belief that $p$ can then be told as follows:

$(\exists x)$ (John has $x$ & $x$ is caused by the perception that $p$
& $x$ together with a desire that $q$ causes action $a$)

Further Ramsey sentences are supposed to get rid of the occurrence of such remaining psychological terms as "desire" and "perception." Once the Ramsey sentences are spelled out in this fashion, it turns out that functionalism has the crucial advantage of showing that there is nothing especially mental about mental states. Talk of mental states is just talk of a neutral set of causal relations; and the apparent "chauvinism" of type-type identity theories—that is, the chauvinism of supposing that only systems with brains like ours can have mental states—is now avoided by this much more "liberal" view.[9] Any system whatever, no matter what it was made of, could have mental states provided only that it had the right causal relations between its inputs, its inner functioning, and its outputs. Functionalism of this variety says nothing about how the belief works to have the causal relations that it does. It just treats the mind as a kind of a black box in which these various causal relations occur, and for that reason it was sometimes labeled "black box functionalism."

Objections to black box functionalism revealed the same mixture of the commonsensical and the technical that we have seen before. The commonsense objection was that the functionalist seems to leave out the qualitative subjective feel of at least some of our mental states. There are certain quite specific qualitative experiences involved in seeing a red object or having a pain in the back, and just describing these experiences in terms of their causal relations leaves out these special *qualia*. A proof of this was offered as follows: Suppose that one section of the population had their color spectra reversed in such a way that, for example, the experience they call "seeing red" a normal person would call "seeing green"; and what they call "seeing green" a normal person would call "seeing red" (Block and Fodor 1972). Now we might suppose that this "spectrum inversion" is entirely undetectable by any of the usual color blindness tests, since the abnormal group makes exactly the same color discriminations in response to exactly the same stimuli as the rest of the population. When asked to put the red pencils in one pile and the green pencils in another they do exactly what the rest of us would do; it *looks different* to them on the inside, but there is no way to detect this difference from the outside.

Now if this possibility is even intelligible to us—and it surely is—then black box functionalism must be wrong in supposing that neutrally specified causal relations are sufficient to account for mental phenomena; for such specifications leave out a crucial feature of many mental phenomena, namely, their qualitative feel.

A related objection was that a huge population, say the entire population of China, might behave so as to imitate the functional organization of a human brain to the extent of having the right input-output relations and the right pattern of inner cause-and-effect relations. But all the same, the system would still not feel anything as a system. The entire population of China would not feel a pain just by imitating the functional organization appropriate to pain (Block 1978).

Another more technical-sounding objection to black box functionalism was to the "black box" part: Functionalism so defined failed to state in material terms what it is about the different physical states that gives different material phenomena the same causal relations. How does it come about that these quite different physical structures are causally equivalent?

## VI. Strong Artificial Intelligence

At this point there occurred one of the most exciting developments in the entire two-thousand-year history of materialism. The developing science of artificial intelligence provided an answer to this question: different material structures can be mentally equivalent if they are different hardware implementations of the same computer program. Indeed, given this answer, we can see that the mind just is a computer program and the brain is just one of the indefinite range of different computer hardwares (or "wetwares") that can have a mind. The mind is to the brain as the program is to the hardware (Johnson-Laird 1988). Artificial intelligence and functionalism coalesced, and one of the most stunning aspects of this union was that it turned out that one can be a thoroughgoing materialist about the mind and still believe, with Descartes, that the brain does not really matter to the mind. Because the mind is a computer program, and because a program can be implemented on any hardware whatever (provided only that the hardware is powerful and stable enough to carry out the steps in the program), the specifically mental aspects of the mind can be specified, studied, and understood without knowing how the brain works. Even if you are a materialist, you do not have to study the brain to study the mind.

This idea gave birth to the new discipline of "cognitive science." I will have more to say about it later (in chapters 7, 9, and 10); at this point I am just tracing the recent history of materialism. Both the discipline of artificial intelligence and the philosophical theory of functionalism converged on the idea that the mind was just a computer program. I have baptized this view "strong artificial intelligence" (Searle 1980a), and it was also called "computer functionalism" (Dennett 1978).

Objections to strong AI seem to me to exhibit the same mixture of commonsense objections and more or less technical objections that we found in the other cases. The technical difficulties and objections to artificial intelligence in either its strong or weak version are numerous and complex. I will not attempt to summarize them. In general, they all have to do with certain difficulties in programming computers in a way that would enable them to satisfy the Turing test. Within the AI camp itself, there were always difficulties such as the "frame problem" and the inability to get adequate accounts of "nonmonotonic reasoning" that would mirror actual human behavior. From outside the AI camp, there were objections such as those of Hubert Dreyfus (1972) to the effect that the way the human mind works is quite different from the way a computer works.

The commonsense objection to strong AI was simply that the computational model of the mind left out the crucial things about the mind such as consciousness and intentionality. I believe the best-known argument against strong AI was my Chinese room argument (Searle 1980a) that showed that a system could instantiate a program so as to give a perfect simulation of some human cognitive capacity, such as the capacity to understand Chinese, even though that system had no understanding of Chinese whatever. Simply imagine that someone who understands no Chinese is locked in a room with a lot of Chinese symbols and a computer program for answering questions in Chinese. The input to the system consists in Chinese symbols in the form of questions; the output of the system consists in Chinese symbols in answer to the questions. We might suppose that the program is so good that the answers to the questions are indistinguishable from those of a native Chinese speaker. But all the same, neither the person inside nor any other part of the system literally understands Chinese; and because the programmed computer has nothing that this system does not have, the programmed computer, qua computer, does not understand Chinese either. Because the program is purely formal or syntactical and because minds have mental or semantic contents, any attempt to produce a mind purely with computer programs leaves out the essential features of the mind.

In addition to behaviorism, type identity theories, token identity theories, functionalism, and strong AI, there were other theories in the philosophy of mind within the general materialist tradition. One of these, which dates back to the early 1960s in the work of Paul Feyerabend (1963) and Richard Rorty (1965), has recently been revived in different forms by such authors as P. M. Churchland (1981) and S. Stich (1983). It is the view that mental states don't exist at all. This view is called "eliminative materialism" and I now turn to it.

## VII. Eliminative Materialism

In its most sophisticated version, eliminative materialism argued as follows: our commonsense beliefs about the mind constitute a kind of primitive theory, a "folk psychology." But as with any theory, the entities postulated by the theory can only be justified to the extent that the theory is true. Just as the failure of the phlogiston theory of combustion removed any justification for believing in the existence of phlogiston, so the failure of folk psychology removes the rationale for folk psychological entities. Thus, if it turns out that folk psychology is false, then we would be unjustified in believing in the existence of beliefs, desires, hopes, fears, etc. According to the eliminative materialists, it seems very likely that folk psychology will turn out to be false. It seems likely that a "mature cognitive science" will show that most of our commonsense beliefs about mental states are completely unjustified. This result would have the consequence that the entities that we have always supposed to exist, our ordinary mental entities, do not really exist. And therefore, we have at long last a theory of mind that simply eliminates the mind. Hence, the expression "eliminative materialism."

A related argument used in favor of "eliminative materialism" seems to me so breathtakingly bad that I fear I must be misunderstanding it. As near as I can tell, here is how it goes:

> Imagine that we had a perfect science of neurobiology. Imagine that we had a theory that really explained how the brain worked. Such a theory would cover the same domain as folk psychology, but would be much more powerful. Furthermore, it seems very unlikely that our ordinary folk psychological concepts, such as belief and desire, hope, fear, depression, elation, pain, etc., would exactly match or even remotely match the taxonomy provided by our imagined perfect science of neurobiology. In all probability there would be no place in this neurobiology for expressions like "belief," "fear," "hope" and "desire," and no smooth reduction of these supposed phenomena would be possible.

That is the premise. Here is the conclusion:

> Therefore, the entities purportedly named by the expressions of folk psychology, beliefs, hopes, fears, desires, etc., do not really exist.

To see how bad this argument really is, just imagine a parallel argument from physics:

> Consider our existing science of theoretical physics. Here we have a theory that explains how physical reality works, and is vastly superior to our commonsense theories by all the usual criteria. Physical theory covers the same domain as our commonsense theories of golf clubs, tennis rackets, Chevrolet station wagons, and split-level ranch houses. Furthermore, our ordinary folk physical concepts such as "golf club," "tennis racket," "Chevrolet station wagon," and "split-level ranch house" do not exactly, or even remotely, match the taxonomy of theoretical physics. There simply is no use in theoretical physics for any of these expressions and no smooth type reductions of these phenomena is possible. The way that an ideal physics— indeed the way that our actual physics—taxonomizes reality is really quite different from the way our ordinary folk physics taxonomizes reality.

> Therefore, split-level ranch houses, tennis rackets, golf clubs, Chevrolet station wagons, etc., do not really exist.

I have not seen this mistake discussed in the literature. Perhaps it is so egregious that it has simply been ignored. It rests on the obviously false premise that for any empirical theory and corresponding taxonomy, unless there is a type-type reduction of the entities taxonomized to the entities of better theories of basic science, the entities do not exist. If you have any doubts that this premise is false, just try it out on anything you see around you—or on yourself![10]

With eliminative materialism, once again, we find the same pattern of technical and commonsense objections that we noted earlier. The technical objections have to do with the fact that folk psychology, if it is a theory, is nonetheless not a research project. It isn't itself a rival field of scientific research, and indeed, the eliminative materialists who attack folk psychology, according to their critics, are often unfair. According to its defenders, folk psychology isn't such a bad theory after all; many of its central tenets are quite likely to turn out to be true. The commonsense objection to eliminative materialism is just that it seems to be crazy. It seems crazy to say that I never felt thirst or desire, that I never had a pain, or that I never actually had a belief, or that my beliefs and desires don't play any role in my behavior. Unlike the earlier materialist theories, eliminative materialism doesn't so much leave out the mind, it denies the existence of anything to leave out in the first place. When confronted with the challenge that eliminative materialism seems too insane to merit serious consideration, its defenders almost invariably invoke the heroic-age-of-science maneuver (P. S. Churchland 1987). That is, they claim that giving up the belief that we have beliefs is analogous to giving up the belief in a flat earth or sunsets, for example.

It is worth pointing out in this entire discussion that a certain paradoxical asymmetry has come up in the history of materialism. Earlier type-type identity theories argued that we could get rid of mysterious, Cartesian mental states because such states were *nothing but* physical states (nothing "over and above" physical states); and they argued this on the assumption that types of mental states could be shown to be identical with types of physical states, that we would get a match between the deliverances of neurobiology and our ordinary notions such as pain and belief. Now in the case of eliminative materialism, it is precisely the alleged failure of any such match that is regarded as the vindication of the elimination of these mental states in favor of a thoroughgoing neurobiology. Earlier materialists argued that there aren't any such things as separate mental phenomena, because mental phenomena *are* *identical* with brain states. More recent materialists argue that there aren't any such things as separate mental phenomena because they *are not identical* with brain states. I find this pattern very revealing, and what it reveals is an urge to get rid of mental phenomena at any cost.

## VIII. Naturalizing Content

After half a century of this recurring pattern in debates about materialism, one might suppose that the materialists and the dualists would think there is something wrong with the terms of the debate. But so far the induction seems not to have occurred to either side. As I write this, the same pattern is being repeated in current attempts to "naturalize" intentional content.

Strategically the idea is to carve off the problem of consciousness from the problem of intentionality. Perhaps, one admits, consciousness is irreducibly mental and thus not subject to scientific treatment, but maybe consciousness does not matter much anyway and we can get along without it. We need only to naturalize intentionality, where "to naturalize intentionality" means to explain it completely in terms of—to reduce it to—nonmental, physical phenomena. Functionalism was one such attempt at naturalizing intentional content, and it has been rejuvenated by being joined to externalist causal theories of reference. The idea behind such views is that semantic content, that is, meanings, cannot be entirely in our heads because what is in our heads is insufficient to determine how language relates to reality. In addition to what is in our heads, "narrow content," we need a set of actual physical causal relations to objects in the world, we need "wide content." These views were originally developed around problems in the philosophy of language (Putnam 1975b), but it is easy to see how they extend to mental contents generally. If the meaning of the sentence "Water is wet" cannot be explained in terms of what is inside the heads of speakers of English, then the belief that water is wet is not a matter solely of what is in their heads either. Ideally one would like an account of intentional content stated solely in terms of causal relations between people, on the one hand, and objects and states of affairs in the world, on the other.

A rival to the externalist causal attempt to naturalize content, and I believe an even less plausible account, is that intentional contents can be individuated by their Darwinian, biological, teleological function. For example, my desires will have a content referring to water or food iff they function to help me obtain water or food (Millikan 1984).

So far no attempt at naturalizing content has produced an explanation (analysis, reduction) of intentional content that is even remotely plausible. Consider the simplest sort of belief. For example, I believe that Flaubert was a better novelist than Balzac. Now, what would an analysis of that content, stated in terms of brute physical causation or Darwinian natural selection, without using any mental terms, look like? It should be no surprise to anyone that these attempts do not even get off the ground.

Once again such naturalized conceptions of content are subject to both technical and commonsense objections. The most famous of the technical problems is probably the disjunction problem (Fodor 1987). If a certain concept is caused by a certain sort of object, then how do we account for cases of mistaken identity? If "horse" is caused by horses or by cows that are mistakenly identified as horses, then do we have to say that the analysis of "horse" is disjunctive, that it means either horse or certain sorts of cows?

As I write this, naturalistic (externalist, causal) accounts of content are all the rage. They will all fail for reasons that I hope by now are obvious. They will leave out the subjectivity of mental content. By way of technical objections there will be counterexamples, such as the disjunction cases, and the counterexamples will be met with gimmicks—nomological relations, and counterfactuals, or so I would predict—but the most you could hope from the gimmicks, even if they were successful in blocking the counterexamples, would be a parallelism between the output of the gimmick and intuitions about mental content. You still would not get at the essence of mental content.

I do not know if anyone has yet made the obvious common-sense objection to the project of naturalizing intentional content, but I hope it is clear from the entire discussion what it will be. In case no one has done it yet, here goes: Any attempt to reduce intentionality to something nonmental will always fail because it leaves out intentionality. Suppose for example that you had a perfect causal externalist account of the belief that water is wet. This account is given by stating a set of causal relations in which a system stands to water and to wetness and these relations are entirely specified without any mental component. The problem is obvious: a system could have all of these relations and still not believe that water is wet. This is just an extension of the Chinese room argument, but the moral it points to is general: You cannot reduce intentional content (or pains or "qualia") to something else, because if you could they would be something else, and they are not something else. The opposite of my view is stated very succinctly by Fodor: "If aboutness is real, it must really be something else" (1987, p. 97). On the contrary, aboutness (i.e., intentionality) is real, and it is not something else.

A symptom that something is radically wrong with the project is that the intentional notions are inherently normative. They set standards of truth, rationality, consistency, etc., and there is no way that these standards can be intrinsic to a system consisting entirely of brute, blind, nonintentional causal relations. There is no normative component to billiard ball causation. Darwinian biological attempts at naturalizing content try to avoid this problem by appealing to what they suppose is the inherently teleological, normative character of biological evolution. But this is a very deep mistake. There is nothing normative or teleological about Darwinian evolution. Indeed, Darwin's major contribution was precisely to remove purpose and teleology from evolution, and substitute for it purely natural forms of selection. Darwin's account shows that the apparent teleology of biological processes is an illusion.

It is a simple extension of this insight to point out that notions such as "purpose" are never intrinsic to biological organisms, (unless of course those organisms themselves have conscious intentional states and processes). And even notions like "biological function" are always made relative to an observer who assigns a normative value to the causal processes. There is no *factual* difference about the heart that corresponds to the difference between saying

    1.  The heart causes the pumping of blood.

and saying,

    2.  The function of the heart is to pump blood.

But 2 assigns a normative status to the sheer brute causal facts about the heart, and it does this because of our interest in the relation of this fact to a whole lot of other facts, such as our interest in survival. In short, the Darwinian mechanisms and even biological functions themselves are entirely devoid of purpose or teleology. All of the teleological features are entirely in the mind of the observer.[11]

## IX. The Moral So Far

My aim so far in this chapter has been to illustrate a recurring pattern in the history of materialism. This pattern is made graphic in table 2.1. I have been concerned not so much to defend or refute materialism as to examine its vicissitudes in the face of certain commonsense facts about the mind, such as the fact that most of us are, for most of our lives, conscious. What we find in the history of materialism is a recurring tension between the urge to give an account of reality that leaves out any reference to the special features of the mental, such as consciousness and subjectivity, and at the same time account for our "intuitions" about the mind. It is, of course, impossible to do these two things. So there are a series of attempts, almost neurotic in character, to cover over the fact that some crucial element about mental states is being left out. And when it is pointed out that some obvious truth is being denied by the materialist philosophy, the upholders of this view almost invariably resort to certain rhetorical strategies

**Table 2.1**
The general pattern exhibited by recent materialism.

| Theory | Common-sense objections | Technical objections |
| --- | --- | --- |
| Logical behaviorism | Leaves out the mind: superspartan/super-actor objections | 1. Circular; needs desires to explain beliefs, and conversely 2. Can't do the conditionals 3. Leaves out causation |
| Type identity theory | Leaves out the mind: or else it leads to property dualism | 1. Neural chauvinism 2. Leibniz's law 3. Can't account for mental properties 4. Modal arguments |
| Token identity theory | Leaves out the mind: absent qualia | Can't identify the mental features of mental content |
| Black box functionalism | Leaves out the mind: absent qualia and spectrum inversion | Relation of structure and function is unexplained |
| Strong AI (Turing machine functionalism) | Leaves out the mind: Chinese room | Human cognition is nonrepresentational and therefore noncomputational |
| Eliminative materialism (rejection of folk psychology) | Denies the existence of the mind: unfair to folk psychology | Defense of folk psychology |
| Naturalizing intentionality | Leaves out intentionality | Disjunction problem |

designed to show that materialism must be right, and that the philosopher who objects to materialism must be endorsing some version of dualism, mysticism, mysteriousness, or general antiscientific bias. But the unconscious motivation for all of this, the motivation that never somehow manages to surface, is the assumption that materialism is necessarily inconsistent with the reality and causal efficacy of consciousness, subjectivity, etc. That is, the basic assumption behind materialism is essentially the Cartesian assumption that materialism implies antimentalism and mentalism implies antimaterialism.

There is something immensely depressing about this whole history because it all seems so pointless and unnecessary. It is all based on the false assumption that the view of reality as entirely physical is inconsistent with the view that world really contains subjective ("qualitative," "private," "touchy-feely," "immaterial," "nonphysical") conscious states such as thoughts and feelings.

The weird feature about this entire discussion is that materialism inherits the worst assumption of dualism. In denying the dualist's claim that there are two kinds of substances in the world or in denying the property dualist's claim that there are two kinds of properties in the world, materialism inadvertently accepts the categories and the vocabulary of dualism. It accepts the terms in which Descartes set the debate. It accepts, in short, the idea that the vocabulary of the mental and the physical, of material and immaterial, of mind and body, is perfectly adequate as it stands. It accepts the idea that if we think consciousness exists we are accepting dualism. What I believe—as is obvious from this entire discussion—is that the vocabulary, and the accompanying categories, are the source of our deepest philosophical difficulties. As long as we use words like "materialism," we are almost invariably forced to suppose that they imply something inconsistent with naive mentalism. I have been urging that in this case, one can have one's cake and eat it too. One can be a "thoroughgoing materialist" and not in any way deny the existence of (subjective, internal, intrinsic, often conscious) mental phenomena. However, since my use of these terms runs dead counter to over three hundred years of philosophical tradition, it would probably be better to abandon this vocabulary altogether.

If one had to describe the deepest motivation for materialism, one might say that it is simply a terror of consciousness. But should this be so? Why should materialists have a fear of consciousness? Why don't materialists cheerfully embrace consciousness as just another material property among others? Some, in fact, such as Armstrong and Dennett, claim to do so. But they do this by so redefining "consciousness" as to deny the central feature of consciousness, namely, its subjective quality. The deepest reason for the fear of consciousness is that consciousness has the essentially terrifying feature of subjectivity. Materialists are reluctant to accept that feature because they believe that to accept the existence of subjective consciousness would be inconsistent with their conception of what the world must be like. Many think that, given the discoveries of the physical sciences, a conception of reality that denies the existence of subjectivity is the only one that it is possible to have. Again, as with "consciousness," one way to cope is to redefine "subjectivity" so that it no longer means subjectivity but means something objective (for an example, see Lycan 1990a).

I believe all of this amounts to a very large mistake, and in chapters 4, 5, and 6, I will examine in some detail the character and the ontological status of consciousness.

## X. The Idols of the Tribe

I said earlier in this chapter that I would explain why a certain natural-sounding question was really incoherent. The question is: How do unintelligent bits of matter produce intelligence? We should first note the form of the question. Why are we not asking the more traditional question: How do unconscious bits of matter produce consciousness? That question seems to me perfectly coherent. It is a question about how the brain works to cause conscious mental states even though the individual neurons (or synapses or receptors) in the brain are not themselves conscious. But in the present era, we are reluctant to ask the question in that form because we lack "objective" criteria of consciousness. Consciousness has an ineliminable subjective ontology, so we think it more scientific to rephrase the question as one about intelligence, because we think that for intelligence we have objective, impersonal criteria. But now we immediately encounter a difficulty. If by "intelligence" we mean anything that satisfies the objective third-person criteria of intelligence, then the question contains a false presupposition. Because if intelligence is defined behavioristically, then it is simply not the case that neurons are not intelligent. Neurons, like just about everything else in the world, behave in certain regular, predictable patterns. Furthermore, considered in a certain way, neurons do extremely sophisticated "information processing." They take in a rich set of signals from other neurons at their dendritic synapses; they process this information at their somae and send out information through their axonal synapses to other neurons. If intelligence is to be defined behavioralistically, then neurons are pretty intelligent by anybody's standards. In short, if our criteria of intelligence are entirely objective and third-person— and the whole point of posing the question in this way was to get something that satisfied those conditions—then the question contains a presupposition that on its own terms is false. The question falsely presupposes that the bits do not meet the criteria of intelligence.

The answer to the question, not surprisingly, inherits the same ambiguity. There are two different sets of criteria for applying the expression "intelligent behavior." One of these sets consists of third-person or "objective" criteria that are not necessarily of any psychological interest whatever. But the other set of criteria are essentially mental and involve the first-person point of view. "Intelligent behavior" on the second set of criteria involves thinking, and thinking is essentially a mental process. Now, if we adopt the third-person criteria for intelligent behavior, then of course computers—not to mention pocket calculators, cars, steam shovels, thermostats, and indeed just about everything in the world—engages in intelligent behavior. If we are consistent in adopting the Turing test or some other "objective" criterion for intelligent behavior, then the answer to such questions as "Can unintelligent bits of matter produce intelligent behavior?" and even, "How exactly do they do it?" are ludicrously obvious. Any thermostat, pocket calculator, or waterfall produces "intelligent behavior," and we know in each case how it works. Certain artifacts are designed to behave as if they were intelligent, and since everything follows laws of nature, then everything will have some description under which it behaves as if it were intelligent. But this sense of "intelligent behavior" is of no psychological relevance at all.

In short, we tend to hear both the question and the answer as oscillating between two different poles: (a) How do unconscious bits of matter produce consciousness? (a perfectly good question to which the answer is: In virtue of specific—though largely unknown—neurobiological features of the brain); and (b) How do "unintelligent" (by first- or third-person criteria?) bits of matter produce "intelligent" ( by first- or third-person criteria?) behavior? But to the extent that we make the criteria of intelligence third-person criteria, the question contains a false presupposition, and this is concealed from us because we tend to hear the question on interpretation (a).

# Appendix

## Is There a Problem about Folk Psychology?

The aim of chapter 2 was not so much to present my own views but to describe the contemporary history of a philosophical tradition. I want now to state some of my own views on so-called folk psychology (FP), because I do not believe they have been represented in the literature so far. The standard discussions, both pro and con (Churchland 1981, Stich 1983, Horgan and Woodward 1985, and Fodor 1986) have been within the tradition.

I will state the argument stepwise as a series of theses and answers.

*Thesis*: FP is an empirical thesis like any other, and as such it is subject to empirical confirmation and disconfirmation.

*Answer*: The actual capacities that people have for coping with themselves and others are for the most part not in propositional form. They are, in my sense, Background capacities. For example, how we respond to facial expressions, what we find natural in behavior, and even how we understand utterances are in large part matters of know-how, not theories. You distort these capacities if you think of them as theories. See chapter 8 for more about this.

*Thesis*: All the same, you could state theoretical correlates or principles underlying these capacities. This would constitute a folk psychology and will in all likelihood be false, since in general folk theories are false.

*Answer*: You can, with some distortion, state a theoretical analogue to a practical skill. But it would be miraculous if these were in general false. Where it really matters, where something is at stake, folk theories have to be in general true or we would not have survived. Folk physics can be wrong about peripheral issues, such as the movement of the celestial spheres and the origin of the earth, because it doesn't much matter. But when it comes to which way your body moves if you jump off a cliff or what happens if a huge rock falls on you, folk theories had better be right or we would not have survived.

*Thesis*:  It now becomes a specific matter for cognitive science (CS) to decide which theses of FP are true and which of its ontological commitments are warranted. For example, FP postulates beliefs and desires to account for behavior, but if it turns out that the CS account of behavior is inconsistent with this, then beliefs and desires do not exist.

*Answer*:  Just about everything is wrong with this claim. First, we do not *postulate* beliefs and desires to account for anything. We simply experience conscious beliefs and desires. Think about real-life examples. It is a hot day and you are driving a pickup truck in the desert outside of Phoenix. No air conditioning. You can't remember when you were so thirsty, and you want a cold beer so bad you could scream. Now where is the "postulation" of a desire? Conscious desires are experienced. They are no more postulated than conscious pains.

Second, beliefs and desires sometimes cause actions, but there is no essential connection. Most beliefs and desires never issue in actions. For example, I believe that the sun is 94 million miles away, and I would like to be a billionaire. Which of my actions do this belief and this desire explain? That if I want to buy a ticket to the sun I will be sure to get a 94-million-mile ticket? That the next time somebody gives me a billion, I won't refuse?

*Thesis*:  All the same, postulated or not, there is unlikely to be a smooth reduction of the entities of FP to the more basic science of neurobiology, so it seems that elimination is the only alternative.

*Answer*: I have already said what a bad argument this is. Most types of real entities, from split-level ranch houses to cocktail parties, from interest rates to football games, do not undergo a smooth reduction to the entities of some fundamental theory. Why should they? I guess I have a "theory" of cocktail parties—at least as much as I have a theory of "folk psychology"—and cocktail parties certainly consist of molecule movements; but my theory of cocktail parties is nowhere near as good a theory as my theory of molecular physics, and there is no type reduction of cocktail parties to the taxonomy of physics. But all the same, cocktail parties really do exist. The question of the reducibility of such entities is irrelevant to the question of their existence.

Why would anyone make such an egregious mistake? That is, why would anyone suppose that the "smooth reduction" of beliefs and desires to neurobiology is even relevant to the existence of beliefs and desires? The answer is that they are drawing a false analogy with the history of certain parts of physics. Churchland thinks that "belief" and "desire" have the same status in the theory of folk psychology that "phlogiston" and "caloric fluid" had in physics. But the analogy breaks down in all sorts of ways: Beliefs and desires, unlike phlogiston and caloric fluid, were not postulated as part of some special theory, they are actually experienced as part of our mental life. Their existence is no more theory-relative than is the existence of ranch houses, cocktail parties, football games, interest rates, or tables and chairs. One can always describe one's commonsense beliefs about such things as a "theory," but the existence of the phenomena is prior to the theory. Again, always think about actual cases. My theory of cocktail parties would include such things as that big cocktail parties are likely to be noisier than small ones, and my theory of ranch houses would include the claim that they tend to spread out more than most other types of houses. Such "theories" are no doubt hopelessly inadequate, and the entities do not undergo smooth reduction to physics, where I have a much better theories for describing the same phenomena. But what has all that got to do with the existence of split-level ranch houses? Nothing. Similarly the inadequacy of commonsense psychology and the failure of commonsense taxonomy to match the taxonomy of brain science ( this is what is meant by the failure of "smooth reduction") have nothing to do with the existence of beliefs and desires. In a word, beliefs and split-level ranch houses are totally unlike phlogiston because their ontology is not dependent on the truth of a special theory, and their irreducibility to a more fundamental science is irrelevant to their existence.

*Thesis*:   Yes, but what you are saying begs the question. You are just saying that beliefs and desires, like cocktail parties and split-level ranch houses, are not theoretical entities—their evidentiary base is not derived from some theory. But isn't that precisely one of the points at issue?

*Answer*:   I think is is obvious that beliefs and desires are experienced as such, and they are certainly not "postulated" to explain behavior, because they are not postulated at all. However even "theoretical entities" do not in general get their legitimacy from reducibility. Consider economics. Interest rates, effective demand, marginal propensity to consume—are all referred to in mathematical economics. But none of the types of entities in question undergoes a smooth reduction to physics or neurobiology, for example. Again, why should they?

Reducibility is a weird requirement for ontology anyway, because classically one way to show that an entity did *not* really exist has been to reduce it to something else. Thus sunsets are reducible to planetary movements in the solar system, which showed that, as traditionally conceived, sunsets do not exist. The appearance of the sun setting is caused by something else, that is, the rotation of the earth relative to the sun.

*Thesis*:   Still, it is possible to list a lot of folk psychological claims and see that many of them are doubtful.

*Answer*:   If you look at the actual lists given, there is something fishy going on. If I were going to list some propositions of FP, I would list such things as:

1.  In general, beliefs can be either true or false.
2.  Sometimes people get hungry, and when they are hungry they often want to eat something.
3.  Pains are often unpleasant. For this reason people often try to avoid them.

It is hard to imagine what kind of empirical evidence could refute these propositions. The reason is that on a natural construal they are not empirical hypotheses, or not *just* empirical hypotheses. They are more like constitutive principles of the phenomena in question. Proposition 1, for example, is more like the "hypothesis" that a touchdown in American football counts six points. If you are told that a scientific study has shown that touchdowns actually count only 5.999999999 points, you know that somebody is seriously confused. It is part of the current definition of a touchdown that it counts six points. We can change the definition but not discover a different fact. Similarly, it is part of the definition of "belief" that beliefs are candidates for truth or falsity. We could not "discover" that beliefs are not susceptible to being true or false.

If you look at lists of candidates that have been given for "laws" of FP, they tend to be either obviously false on their face or they are constitutive principles. For example, Churchland (1981) lists the principle that, "barring confusion, distraction, etc." anyone who believes $p$ and if $p$ then $q$ , believes $q$ (p. 209 in Lycan 1990b). As a candidate for a commonsense belief, this is literally incredible. If it were true, then proving theorems would be no more difficult than examining one's beliefs (without "confusion, distraction, etc."). It is very easy to refute FP if you say it consists of such false principles to start with.

A candidate for a constitutive principle is Churchland's example that anyone who fears $p$ wants it to be the case that not $p$. How would you look for empirical evidence that this is false? It is part of the definition of "fear." So the deeper mistake is not just to suppose that FP is a theory, but that all the propositions of the theory are empirical hypotheses.

Since they are constitutive, not empirical, the only way to show them false would be to show that they have no range of application. For example, the "constitutive principles" of witchcraft don't apply to anything because there aren't any witches. But you could not show that conscious desires and pains do not exist in the way that you can show that witches do not exist, because these are conscious experiences, and you cannot make the usual appearance reality distinction for conscious experiences (more about this in chapter 3).

Lots of commonsense psychological beliefs have been shown to be false, and no doubt more will be. Consider a spectacular example: Common sense tells us that our pains are located in physical space within our bodies, that for example, a pain in the foot is literally inside the area of the foot. But we now know that is false. The brain forms a body image, and pains, like all bodily sensations, are parts of the body image. The pain-in-the-foot is literally in the physical space of the brain.

So common sense was wildly wrong about some aspects of the location of pains in physical space. But even such an extreme falsehood does not show—and could not show—that pains do not exist. What is actually likely to happen, indeed is happening, is that common sense will be supplemented with additional scientific knowledge. For example, we now recognize distinctions between long- and short-term memory, and between those and iconic memories, and these distinctions are the result of neurobiological investigations.

# Chapter 3

# Breaking the Hold: Silicon Brains, Conscious Robots, and Other Minds

The view of the world as completely objective has a very powerful hold on us, though it is inconsistent with the most obvious facts of our experiences. As the picture is false, we ought to be able to break the hold. I don't know any simple way to do that. One of the many aims of this book, however, is to begin the task. In this chapter I want to describe some thought experiments that will challenge the accuracy of the picture. Initially the aim of the thought experiments is to challenge the conception of the mental as having some important internal connection to behavior.

To begin undermining the foundations of this whole way of thinking, I want to consider some of the relationships between consciousness, behavior, and the brain. Most of the discussion will concern conscious mental phenomena; but leaving out the unconscious at this point is not such a great limitation, because, as I will argue in detail in chapter 7, we have no notion of an unconscious mental state except in terms derived from conscious states. To begin the argument, I will employ a thought experiment that I have used elsewhere (Searle 1982). This *Gedankenexperiment* is something of an old chestnut in philosophy, and I do not know who was the first to use it. I have been using it in lectures for years, and I assume that anybody who thinks about these topics is bound to have something like these ideas occur to him or her eventually.

## I. Silicon Brains

Here is how it goes. Imagine that your brain starts to deteriorate in such a way that you are slowly going blind.

Imagine that the desperate doctors, anxious to alleviate your condition, try any method to restore your vision. As a last resort, they try plugging silicon chips into your visual cortex. Imagine that to your amazement and theirs, it turns out that the silicon chips restore your vision to its normal state. Now, imagine further that your brain, depressingly, continues to deteriorate and the doctors continue to implant more silicon chips. You can see where the thought experiment is going already: in the end, we imagine that your brain is entirely replaced by silicon chips; that as you shake your head, you can hear the chips rattling around inside your skull. In such a situation there would be various possibilities. One logical possibility, not to be excluded on any a priori grounds alone, is surely this: you continue to have all of the sorts of thoughts, experiences, memories, etc., that you had previously; the sequence of your mental life remains unaffected. In this case, we are imagining that the silicon chips have the power not only to duplicate your input-output functions, but also to duplicate the mental phenomena, conscious and otherwise, that are normally responsible for your input-output functions.

I hasten to add that I don't for a moment think that such a thing is even remotely empirically possible. I think it is empirically absurd to suppose that we could duplicate the causal powers of neurons entirely in silicon. But that is an empirical claim on my part. It is not something that we could establish a priori. So the thought experiment remains valid as a statement of logical or conceptual possibility.

But now let us imagine some variations on the thought experiment. A second possibility, also not to be excluded on any a priori grounds, is this: as the silicon is progressively implanted into your dwindling brain, you find that the area of your conscious experience is shrinking, but that this shows no effect on your external behavior. You find, to your total amazement, that you are indeed losing control of your external behavior. You find, for example, that when the doctors test your vision, you hear them say, "We are holding up a red object in front of you; please tell us what you see." You want to cry out, "I can't see anything. I'm going totally blind." But you hear your voice saying in a way that is completely out of your control, "I see a red object in front of me." If we carry this thought experiment out to the limit, we get a much more depressing result than last time. We imagine that your conscious experience slowly shrinks to nothing, while your externally observable behavior remains the same.

It is important in these thought experiments that you should always think of it from the first-person point of view. Ask yourself, "What would it be like for me?" and you will see that it is perfectly conceivable for you to imagine that your external behavior remains the same, but that your internal conscious thought processes gradually shrink to zero. From the outside, it seems to observers that you are just fine, but from the inside you are gradually dying. In this case, we are imagining a situation where you are eventually mentally dead, where you have no conscious mental life whatever, but your externally observable behavior remains the same.

It is also important in this thought experiment to remember our stipulation that you are becoming unconscious but that your behavior remains unaffected. To those who are puzzled how such a thing is possible, let us simply remind them: As far as we know, the basis of consciousness is in certain specific regions of the brain, such as, perhaps, the reticular formation. And we may suppose in this case that these regions are gradually deteriorating to the point where there is no consciousness in the system. But we further suppose that the silicon chips are able to duplicate the input-output functions of the whole central nervous system, even though there is no consciousness left in the remnants of the system.

Now consider a third variation. In this case, we imagine that the progressive implantation of the silicon chips produces no change in your mental life, but you are progressively more and more unable to put your thoughts, feelings, and intentions into action. In this case, we imagine that your thoughts, feelings, experiences, memories, etc., remain intact, but your observable external behavior slowly reduces to total paralysis. Eventually you suffer from total paralysis, even though your mental life is unchanged. So in this case, you might hear the doctors saying,

The silicon chips are able to maintain heartbeat, respiration, and other vital processes, but the patient is obviously brain dead. We might as well unplug the system, because the patient has no mental life at all.

Now in this case, you would know that they are totally mistaken. That is, you want to shout out,

No, I'm still conscious! I perceive everything going on around me. It's just that I can't make any physical movement. I've become totally paralyzed.

The point of these three variations on the thought experiment is to illustrate the *causal* relationships between brain processes, mental processes, and externally observable behavior. In the first case, we imagined that the silicon chips had causal powers equivalent to the powers of the brain, and thus we imagined that they caused both the mental states and the behavior that brain processes normally cause. In the normal case, such mental states mediate the relationship between input stimuli and output behavior.

In the second case, we imagined that the mediating relationship between the mind and the behavior patterns was broken. In this case, the silicon chips did not duplicate the causal powers of the brain to produce conscious mental states, they only duplicated certain input-output functions of the brain. The underlying conscious mental life was left out.

In the third case, we imagined a situation where the agent had the same mental life as before, but in this case, the mental phenomena had no behavioral expression. Actually, to imagine this case we need not even have imagined the silicon chips. It would have been very easy to imagine a person with the motor nerves cut in such a way that he or she was totally paralyzed, while consciousness and other mental phenomena remained unaffected. Something like these cases exists in clinical reality. Patients who suffer from the Guillain-Barré syndrome are completely paralyzed, but also fully conscious.

What is the philosophical significance of these three thought experiments? It seems to me there is a number of lessons to be learned. The most important is that they illustrate something about the relationship between mind and behavior. What exactly is the importance of behavior for the concept of mind? *Ontologically speaking, behavior, functional role, and causal relations are irrelevant to the existence of conscious mental phenomena.* Epistemically, we do learn about other people's conscious mental states *in part* from their behavior. *Causally,* consciousness serves to mediate the causal relations between input stimuli and output behavior; and from an *evolutionary* point of view, the conscious mind functions causally to control behavior. But *ontologically* speaking, the phenomena in question can exist completely and have all of their essential properties independent of any behavioral output.

Most of the philosophers I have been criticizing would accept the following two propositions:

1. Brains cause conscious mental phenomena.
2. There is some sort of conceptual or logical connection between conscious mental phenomena and external behavior.

But what the thought experiments illustrate is that these two cannot be held consistently with a third:

3. The capacity of the brain to cause consciousness is conceptually distinct from its capacity to cause motor behavior. A system could have consciousness without behavior and behavior without consciousness.

But given the truth of 1 and 3, we have to give up 2. So the first point to be derived from our thought experiments is what we might call "the principle of the independence of consciousness and behavior." In case number two, we imagined the circumstance in which the behavior was unaffected, but the mental states disappeared, so behavior is not a sufficient condition for mental phenomena. In case number three, we imagined the circumstance in which mental phenomena were present, but the behavior disappeared, so behavior is not a necessary condition for the presence of the mental either.

Two other points are illustrated by the thought experiments. First, the ontology of the mental is essentially a first-person ontology. That is just a fancy way of saying that every mental state has to be *somebody's* mental state. Mental states only exist as subjective, first-person phenomena. And the other point related to this is that, epistemically speaking, the first-person point of view is quite different from the third-person point of view. It is easy enough to imagine cases, such as those illustrated by our thought experiments, where from a third-person point of view, somebody might not be able to tell whether I had any mental states at all. He might even think I was unconscious, and it might still be the case that I was completely conscious. From the first-person point of view, there is no question that I am conscious, even if it turned out that third-person tests were not available.

## II. Conscious Robots

I want to introduce a second thought experiment to buttress the conclusions provided by the first. The aim of this one, as with the first, is to use our intuitions to try to drive a wedge between mental states and behavior. Imagine that we are designing robots to work on a production line. Imagine that our robots are really too crude and tend to make a mess of the more refined elements of their task. But imagine that we know enough about the electrochemical features of human consciousness to know how to produce robots that have a rather low level of consciousness, and so we can design and manufacture conscious robots. Imagine further that these conscious robots are able to make discriminations that unconscious robots could not make, and so they do a better job on the production line. Is there anything incoherent in the above? I have to say that according to my "intuitions," it is perfectly coherent. Of course, it is science fiction, but then, many of the most important thought experiments in philosophy and science are precisely science fiction.

But now imagine an unfortunate further feature of our conscious robots: Suppose that they are absolutely miserable.

Again, we can suppose that our neurophysiology is sufficient for us to establish that they are extremely unhappy. Now imagine we give our robotics research group the following task: Design a robot that will have the capacity to make the same discriminations as the conscious robots, but which will be totally unconscious. We can then allow the unhappy robots to retire to a more hedonically satisfying old age. This seems to me a well-defined research project; and we may suppose that, operationally speaking, our scientists try to design a robot with a "hardware" that they know will not cause or sustain consciousness, but that will have the same input-output functions as the robot that has a "hardware" that does cause and sustain consciousness. We might suppose then that they succeed, that they build a robot that is totally unconscious, but that has behavioral powers and abilities that are absolutely identical with those of the conscious robot.

The point of this experiment, as with the earlier ones, is to show that as far as the ontology of consciousness is concerned, behavior is simply irrelevant. We could have *identical behavior* in two different systems, one of which is conscious and the other totally unconscious.

### III. Empiricism and the "Other Minds Problem"

Many empirically minded philosophers will be distressed by these two thought experiments, especially the first. It will seem to them that I am alleging the existence of empirical facts about the mental states of a system that are not ascertainable by any empirical means. Their conception of the empirical means for ascertaining the existence of mental facts rests entirely on the presupposition of behavioral evidence. They believe that the only evidence we have for attributing mental states to other systems is the behavior of those systems.

In this section I want to continue the discussion of the other minds problem that was begun in chapter 1. Part of my aim will be to show that there is nothing incoherent or objectionable in the epistemic implications of the two thought experiments I just described, but my primary aim will be to give an account of the "empirical" basis we have for supposing that other people and higher animals have conscious mental phenomena more or less like our own.

It is worth emphasizing at the beginning of the discussion that in the history of empirical philosophy and of the philosophy of mind, there is a systematic ambiguity in the use of the word "empirical," an ambiguity between an ontological sense and an epistemic sense. When people speak of empirical facts, they sometimes mean actual, contingent facts in the world as opposed to, say, facts of mathematics or facts of logic. But sometimes when people speak of empirical facts, they mean facts that are testable by third-person means, that is, by "empirical facts" and "empirical methods," they mean facts and methods that are accessible to all competent observers. Now this systematic ambiguity in the use of the word "empirical" suggests something that is certainly false: that all empirical facts, in the ontological sense of being facts in the world, are equally accessible epistemically to all competent observers. We know independently that this is false. There are lots of empirical facts that are not equally accessible to all observers. The previous sections gave us some thought experiments designed to show this, but we actually have empirical data that suggest exactly the same result.

Consider the following example.[1] We can with some difficulty imagine what it would be like to be a bird flying. I say "with some difficulty" because, of course, the temptation is always to imagine what it would be like *for us* if we were flying, and not, strictly speaking, what it is like for *a bird* to be flying. But now some recent research tells us that there are some birds that navigate by detecting the earth's magnetic field. Let us suppose that just as the bird has a conscious experience of flapping its wings or feeling the wind pressing against its head and body, so it also has a conscious experience of a feeling of magnetism surging through its body. Now, what is it like to feel a surge of magnetism? In this case, I do not have the faintest idea what it feels like for a bird, or for that matter, for a human to feel a surge of magnetism from the earth's magnetic field. It is, I take it, an empirical fact whether or not birds that navigate by detecting the magnetic field actually have a conscious experience of the detection of the magnetic field. But the exact qualitative character of this empirical fact is not accessible to standard forms of empirical tests. And indeed, why should it be? Why should we assume that all the facts in the world are equally accessible to standard, objective, third-person tests? If you think about it, the assumption is obviously false.

I said that this result is not as depressing as it might seem. And the reason is simple. Although in some cases we do not have equal access to certain empirical facts because of their intrinsic subjectivity, in general we have indirect methods of getting at the same empirical facts. Consider the following example. I am completely convinced that my dog, as well as other higher animals, has conscious mental states, such as visual experiences, feelings of pain, and sensations of thirst and hunger, and of cold and heat. Now why am I so convinced of that? The standard answer is because of the dog's behavior, because by observing his behavior I infer that he has mental states like my own. I think this answer is mistaken. It isn't just because the dog behaves in a way that is appropriate to having conscious mental states, but also because I can see that the causal basis of the behavior in the dog's physiology is relevantly like my own. It isn't just that the dog has a structure like my own and that he has behavior that is interpretable in ways analogous to the way that I interpret my own. But rather, it is in the combination of these two facts that I can see that the behavior is appropriate and that it has the appropriate *causation* in the underlying physiology. I can see, for example, that these are the dog's ears; this is his skin; these are his eyes; that if you pinch his skin, you get behavior appropriate to pinching skin; if you shout in his ear, you get behavior appropriate to shouting in ears.

It is important to emphasize that I don't need to have a fancy or sophisticated anatomical and physiological theory of dog structure, but simple, so to speak, "folk" anatomy and physiology—the ability to recognize the structure of skin, eyes, teeth, hair, nose, etc., and the ability to suppose that the causal role that these play in his experiences is relevantly like the causal role that such features play in one's own experiences. Indeed, even describing certain structures as "eyes" or "ears" already implies that we are attributing to them functions and causal powers similar to our own eyes and ears. In short, though I don't have direct access to the dog's consciousness, nonetheless it seems to me a well-attested empirical fact that dogs are conscious, and it is attested by evidence that is quite compelling. I do not have anything like this degree of confidence when it comes to animals much lower on the phylogenetic scale. I have no idea whether fleas, grasshoppers, crabs, or snails are conscious. It seems to me that I can reasonably leave such questions to neurophysiologists. But what sort of evidence would the neurophysiologist look for? Here, it seems to me, is another thought experiment that we might well imagine.

Suppose that we had an account of the neurophysiological basis of consciousness in human beings. Suppose that we had quite precise, neurophysiologically isolable causes of consciousness in human beings, such that the presence of the relevant neurophysiological phenomena was both necessary and sufficient for consciousness. If you had it, you were conscious; if you lost it, you became unconscious. Now imagine that some animals have this phenomenon, call it "$x$" for short, and others lack it. Suppose that $x$ was found to occur in all those animals, such as ourselves, monkeys, dogs, etc., of which we feel quite confident that they are conscious on the basis of their gross physiology, and that $x$ was totally absent from animals, such as amoebae, to which we do not feel inclined to ascribe any consciousness. Suppose further that the removal of $x$ from any human being's neurophysiology immediately produced unconsciousness, and its reintroduction produced consciousness. In such a case, it seems to me we might reasonably assume that the presence of $x$ played a crucial causal role in the production of consciousness, and this discovery would enable us to settle doubtful cases of animals either having or lacking conscious states. If snakes had $x$, and mites lacked it, then we might reasonably infer that mites were operating on simple tropisms and snakes had consciousness in the same sense that we, dogs, and baboons do.

I don't for a moment suppose that the neurophysiology of consciousness will be as simple as this. It seems to me much more likely that we will find a great variety of forms of neurophysiologies of consciousness, and that in any real experimental situation we would seek independent evidence for the existence of mechanical-like tropisms to account for apparently goal-directed behavior in organisms that lacked consciousness. The point of the example is simply to show that we can have indirect means of an objective, third-person, empirical kind for getting at empirical phenomena that are intrinsically subjective and therefore inaccessible to direct third-person tests.

It shouldn't be thought, however, that there is something second rate or imperfect about the third-person empirical methods for discovering these first-person subjective empirical facts. The methods rest on a rough-and-ready principle that we use elsewhere in science and in daily life: *same causes-same effects*, and *similar causes-similar effects*. We can readily see in the case of other human beings that the causal bases of their experiences are virtually identical with the causal bases of our experiences. This is why in real life there is no "problem of other minds." Animals provide a good test case for this principle because, of course, they are not physiologically identical with us, but they are in certain important respects similar. They have eyes, ears, nose, mouth, etc. For this reason we do not really doubt that they have the experiences that go with these various sorts of apparatus. So far, all these considerations are prescientific. But let us suppose that we could identify for the human cases exact causes of consciousness, and then could discover precisely the same causes in other animals. If so, it seems to me we would have established quite conclusively that other species have exactly the same sort of consciousness that we have, because we can presume that the same causes produce the same effects. This would not be just a wild speculation, because we would have very good reason to suppose that those causes would produce the same effects in other species.

In actual practice, neurophysiology textbooks routinely report, for example, how the cat's perception of color is similar to and different from the human's *and even other animals.* What breathtaking irresponsibility! How could the authors pretend to have solved the other cat's mind problem so easily? The answer is that the problem is solved for cats' vision once we know exactly how the cat's visual apparatus is similar to and different from our own and other species'.[2]

Once we understand the causal basis of the ascription of mental states to other animals, then several traditional skeptical problems about "other minds" have an easy solution. Consider the famous problem of spectrum inversion that I mentioned in chapter 2. It is often said that, for all we know, one section of the population might have a red/green inversion such that though they make the same behavioral discriminations as the rest of us, the actual experiences they have when they see green, and which they call "seeing green," are experiences that we would, if we had them, call "seeing red," and vice versa. But now consider: Suppose we actually found that a section of the population actually did have the red and green receptors reversed in such a way, and so connected with the rest of their visual apparatus, that we had overwhelming neurophysiological evidence that though their molar discriminations were the same as ours, they actually had different experiences underlying them. This would not be a problem in philosophical skepticism, but a well-defined neurophysiological hypothesis. But then if there is no such section of the population, if all of the non-color-blind people have the same red/green perceptual pathways, we have solid empirical evidence that things look to other people the way they look to us. A cloud of philosophical skepticism condenses into a drop of neuroscience.

Notice that this solution to "the other minds problem," one that we use in science and in daily life, gives us sufficient but not necessary conditions for the correct ascription of mental phenomena to other beings. We would, as I suggested earlier in this chapter, need a much richer neurobiological theory of consciousness than anything we can now imagine to suppose that we could isolate necessary conditions of consciousness. I am quite confident that the table in front of me, the computer I use daily, the fountain pen I write with, and the tape-recorder I dictate into are quite unconscious, but, of course, I cannot *prove* that they are unconscious and neither can anyone else.

## IV. Summary

In this chapter I have so far had two objectives: First, I have tried to argue that as far as the ontology of the mind is concerned, behavior is simply irrelevant. Of course in real life our behavior is crucial to our very existence, but when we are examining the existence of our mental states as mental states, the correlated behavior is neither necessary nor sufficient for their existence. Second, I have tried to begin to break the hold of three hundred years of epistemological discussions of "the other minds problem," according to which behavior is the sole basis on which we know of the existence of other minds. This seems to me obviously false. It is only because of the *connection* between behavior and the causal structure of other organisms that behavior is at all relevant to the discovery of mental states in others.

A final point is equally important: except when doing philosophy, there really is no "problem" about other minds, because we do not hold a "hypothesis," "belief," or "supposition" that other people are conscious, and that chairs, tables, computers, and cars are not conscious. Rather, we have certain Background ways of behaving, certain Background capacities, and these are constitutive of our relations to the consciousness of other people. It is typical of philosophy that skeptical problems often arise when elements of the Background are treated as if they were hypotheses that have to be justified. I don't hold a "hypothesis" that my dog or my department chairman is conscious, and consequently the question doesn't arise except in philosophical debate.

*V. Intrinsic, As-If, and Derived Intentionality*

Before proceeding further, I need to introduce some simple distinctions that have been implicit in what I have said so far, but will need to be made explicit for what follows. To introduce these distinctions, let us consider the similarities and differences among the various sorts of truth-conditions of sentences that we use to ascribe intentional mental phenomena. Consider the similarities and differences among the following:

1.  I am now thirsty, really thirsty, because I haven't had anything to drink all day.
2.  My lawn is thirsty, really thirsty, because it has not been watered in a week.
3.  In French, "j'ai grand soif" means "I am very thirsty."

The first of these sentences is used literally to ascribe a real, intentional mental state to oneself. If I utter that sentence, making a true statement, then there is in me a conscious feeling of thirst that makes that statement true. That feeling has intentionality because it involves a desire to drink. But the second sentence is quite different. Sentence 2 is used only metaphorically, or figuratively, to ascribe thirst to my lawn. My lawn, lacking water, is in a situation in which I would be thirsty, so I figuratively describe it *as if* it were thirsty. I can, by analogy, quite harmlessly say that the lawn is thirsty even though I do not suppose for a moment that it is literally thirsty. The third sentence is like the first in that it literally ascribes intentionality, but it is like the second and unlike the first in that the intentionality described is not intrinsic to the system.

The first sort of ascription ascribes *intrinsic* intentionality. If such a statement is true, there must really be an *intentional state in the object of the ascription*. The second sentence does not ascribe any intentionality at all, intrinsic or otherwise; it is merely used to speak figuratively or metaphorically. Therefore, I will say that the "intentionality" in the ascription is merely *as-if*, and not intrinsic. To avoid confusion, it is important to emphasize that *as-if* intentionality is not a kind of intentionality, rather a system that has *as-if* intentionality is as-if-it-had-intentionality. In the third case I literally ascribe intentionality to the French sentence, that is, the French sentence literally means what I say it does. But the intentionality in the French sentence is not intrinsic to that particular sentence construed just as a syntactical object. That very sequence might have meant something very different or nothing at all. *Speakers* of French can use it to express *their* intentionality. Linguistic meaning is a real form of intentionality, but it is not intrinsic intentionality. It is derived from the intrinsic intentionality of the users of the language.

We can summarize these points as follows: intrinsic intentionality is a phenomenon that humans and certain other animals have as part of their biological nature. It is not a matter of how they are used or how they think of themselves or how they choose to describe themselves. It is just a plain fact about such beasts that, for example, sometimes they get *thirsty* or *hungry*, they *see* things, *fear* things, etc. All of the italicized expressions in the previous sentence are used to refer to intrinsic intentional states. It is very convenient to use the jargon of intentionality for talking about systems that do not have it, but that behave as if they did. I say about my thermostat that it *perceives* changes in the temperature; I say of my carburetor that it *knows* when to enrich the mixture; and I say of my computer that its *memory* is bigger than the *memory* of the computer I had last year. All of these attributions are perfectly harmless and no doubt they will eventually produce new literal meanings as the metaphors become dead. But it is important to emphasize that these attributions are psychologically irrelevant, because they do not imply the presence of any mental phenomena. The intentionality described in all of these cases is purely *as-if*.

Cases of the third sort are rendered interesting by the fact that that we often do literally endow nonmental phenomena with intentional properties. There is nothing metaphorical or *as-if* about saying that certain sentences *mean* certain things or certain maps are correct *representations of* the state of California or that certain pictures are *pictures of* Winston Churchill. These forms of intentionality are real, but they are derived from the intentionality of human agents.

I have been using the terminology of "intrinsic" for over a decade (see Searle 1980b), but it is subject to certain persistent misunderstandings. In common speech "intrinsic" is often opposed to "relational." Thus the moon intrinsically has a mass, but is not intrinsically a satellite. It is only a satellite relative to the earth. In this sense of intrinsic, people who believe in intentional states with "wide content," that is content essentially involving relations to objects outside the mind, would be forced to deny that such intentional states are intrinsic, because they are relational. I don't believe in the existence of wide content (see Searle 1983, ch. 7), so the problem does not arise for me. The distinctions I am making now are independent of the dispute about wide and narrow content. So I am just stipulating that by "intrinsic intentionality" I mean the real thing as opposed to the mere appearance of the thing (*as-if*), and as opposed to derived forms of intentionality such sentences, pictures, etc. You do not have to accept my objections to wide content to accept the distinctions I am trying to make.

Another—amazing to me—misunderstanding is to suppose that by calling cases of the real thing "intrinsic" I am implying that they are somehow mysterious, ineffable, and beyond the reach of philosophical explanation or scientific study. But this is nonsense. I have right now many intrinsic intentional states, for example, an urge to go to the bathroom, a strong desire for a cold beer, and a visual experience of a lot of boats on the lake. All of these are *intrinsic* intentional states, in my sense, which just means they are the real thing and not just something more or less like the real thing (*as-if*), or something that is the result of somebody else's uses of or attitudes toward the thing (*derived*).[3]

I have seen efforts to deny these distinctions, but it is very hard to take the denials seriously. If you think that there are no principled differences, you might consider the following from the journal *Pharmacology*.

> Once the food is past the chrico-pharyngus sphincter, its movement is almost entirely involuntary except for the final expulsion of feces during defecation. *The gastrointestinal tract is a highly intelligent organ that senses* not only the presence of food in the lumen but also its chemical composition, quantity, viscosity and adjusts the rate of propulsion and mixing by producing appropriate patterns of contractions. *Due to its highly developed decision making ability* the gut wall comprised of the smooth muscle layers, the neuronal structures and paracrine-endocrine cells *is often called the gut brain.* (Sarna and Otterson 1988, my italics).[4]

This is clearly a case of *as-if* intentionality in the "gut brain." Does anyone think there is no principled difference between the gut brain and the brain brain? I have heard it said that both sorts of cases are the same; that it is all a matter of taking an "intentional stance" toward a system. But just try in real life to suppose that the "perception" and the "decision making" of the gut brain are no different from that of the real brain.

This example reveals, among other things, that any attempt to deny the distinction between intrinsic and *as-if* intentionality faces a general reductio ad absurdum. If you deny the distinction, it turns out that everything in the universe has intentionality. Everything in the universe follows laws of nature, and for that reason everything behaves with a certain degree of regularity, and for that reason everything behaves *as if* it were following a rule, trying to carry out a certain project, acting in accordance with certain desires, etc. For example, suppose I drop a stone. The stone *tries* to reach the center of the earth, because it *wants* to reach the center of the earth, and in so doing it *follows the rule* $S = 1/2 \, gt.^2$ The price of denying the distinction between intrinsic and *as-if* intentionality, in short, is absurdity, because it makes everything in the universe mental.

No doubt there are marginal cases. About grasshoppers or fleas for example, we may not be quite sure what to say. And no doubt, even in some human cases we might be puzzled as to whether we should take the ascription of intentionality literally or metaphorically. But marginal cases do not alter the distinction between the sort of facts corresponding to ascriptions of intrinsic intentionality and those corresponding to *as-if* metaphorical ascriptions of intentionality. There is nothing harmful, misleading, or philosophically mistaken about *as-if* metaphorical ascriptions. The only mistake is to take them literally.

I hope the distinctions I have been making are painfully obvious. However, I have to report, from the battlefronts as it were, that the neglect of these simple distinctions underlies some of the biggest mistakes in contemporary intellectual life. A common pattern of mistake is to suppose that because we can make *as-if* ascriptions of intentionality to systems that have no intrinsic intentionality, that somehow or other we have discovered the nature of intentionality.[5]

# Chapter 4

# Consciousness and Its Place in Nature

---

## I. Consciousness and the "Scientific" World View

As with most words, it is not possible to give a definition of "consciousness" in terms of necessary and sufficient conditions, nor is it possible to define it in the Aristotelian fashion by way of genus and differentia. However, though we cannot give a noncircular verbal definition, it is still essential for me to say what I mean by this notion, because it is often confused with several others. For example, for reasons of both etymology and usage, "consciousness" is often confused with "conscience," "self-consciousness," and "cognition."

What I mean by "consciousness" can best be illustrated by examples. When I wake up from a dreamless sleep, I enter a state of consciousness, a state that continues as long as I am awake. When I go to sleep or am put under a general anesthetic or die, my conscious states cease. If during sleep I have dreams, I become conscious, though dream forms of consciousness in general are of a much lower level of intensity and vividness than ordinary waking consciousness. Consciousness can vary in degree even during our waking hours, as for example when we move from being wide awake and alert to sleepy or drowsy, or simply bored and inattentive. Some people introduce chemical substances into their brains for the purpose of producing altered states of consciousness, but even without chemical assistance, it is possible in ordinary life to distinguish different degrees and forms of consciousness. Consciousness is an on/off switch: a system is either conscious or not. But once conscious, the system is a rheostat: there are different degrees of consciousness.

A near synonym for "consciousness," in my sense, is "awareness," but I do not think they are exactly equivalent in meaning because "awareness" is more closely connected to cognition, to knowledge, than is the general notion of consciousness. Furthermore, it seems possible that one might allow for cases in which one is aware of something unconsciously (cf. Weiskrantz et al. 1974). It is also worth emphasizing that there is nothing so far in my account of consciousness that implies *self*-consciousness. I will later (in chapter 6) discuss the connection between consciousness and self-consciousness.

Some philosophers (e.g., Block, "Two Concepts of Consciousness,") claim that there is a sense of this word that implies no sentience whatever, a sense in which a total zombie could be "conscious." I know of no such sense, but in any case that is not the sense in which I am using the word.

Conscious states always have a content. One can never just be conscious, rather when one is conscious, there must be an answer to the question, "What is one conscious of?" But the "of" of "conscious of" is not always the "of" of intentionality. If I am conscious of a knock on the door, my conscious state is intentional, because it makes reference to something beyond itself, the knock on the door. If I am conscious of a pain, the pain is not intentional, because it does not represent anything beyond itself.[1]

The main aim of this chapter is to locate consciousness within our overall "scientific" conception of the world. The reason for emphasizing consciousness in an account of the mind is that it is the central mental notion. In one way or another, all other mental notions—such as intentionality, subjectivity, mental causation, intelligence, etc.—can only be fully understood as *mental* by way of their relations to consciousness (more about this in chapter 7). Because at any given point in our waking lives only a tiny fraction of our mental states is conscious, it may seem paradoxical to think of consciousness as the central mental notion, but I intend in the course of this book to try to resolve the appearance of paradox. Once we have located the place of consciousness in our overall world view, we can see that the materialist theories of the mind we discussed in chapter 2 are just as profoundly antiscientific as the dualism they thought they were attacking.

We will find that when we try to state the facts, the pressure on the traditional categories and terminology becomes almost unbearable and they begin to crack under the strain. What I say will sound almost self-contradictory: On the one hand I will claim that consciousness is just an ordinary biological feature of the world, but I will also try to show why we find it almost literally inconceivable that it should be so.

Our contemporary world view began to develop in the seventeenth century, and its development is continuing right through the late twentieth century. Historically, one of the keys to this development was the exclusion of consciousness from the subject matter of science by Descartes, Galileo, and others in the seventeenth century. On the Cartesian view, the natural sciences proper excluded "mind," *res cogitans*, and concerned themselves only with "matter," *res extensa*. The separation between mind and matter was a useful heuristic tool in the seventeenth century, a tool that facilitated a great deal of the progress that took place in the sciences. However, the separation is philosophically confused, and by the twentieth century it had become a massive obstacle to a scientific understanding of the place of consciousness within the natural world. One of the main aims of this book is to try to remove that obstacle, to bring consciousness back into the subject matter of science as a biological phenomenon like any other. To do that, we need to answer the dualistic objections of contemporary Cartesians.

It goes without saying that our "scientific" world view is extremely complex and includes all of our generally accepted theories about what sort of place the universe is and how it works. It includes, that is, theories ranging from quantum mechanics and relativity theory to the plate techtonic theory of geology and the DNA theory of hereditary transmission. At present, for example, it includes a belief in black holes, the germ theory of disease, and the heliocentric account of the solar system. Some features of this world view are very tentative, others well established. At least two features of it are so fundamental and so well established as to be no longer optional for reasonably well-educated citizens of the present era; indeed they are in large part constitutive of the modern world view. These are the atomic theory of matter and the evolutionary theory of biology. Of course, like any other theory, they might be refuted by further investigation; but at present the evidence is so overwhelming that they are not simply up for grabs. To situate consciousness within our understanding of the world, we have to situate it with respect to these two theories.

According to the atomic theory of matter, the universe consists entirely of extremely small physical phenomena that we find it convenient, though not entirely accurate, to call "particles." All the big and middle-sized entities in the world, such as planets, galaxies, cars, and overcoats, are made up of smaller entities that are in turn made up of yet smaller entities until finally we reach the level of molecules, themselves composed of atoms, themselves composed of subatomic particles. Examples of particles are electrons, hydrogen atoms, and water molecules. As these examples illustrate, bigger particles are made up of smaller particles; and there is still much uncertainty and dispute about the identification of the ultimately smallest particles. We are somewhat embarrassed to use the word "particle" for at least two reasons. First, it seems more accurate to describe the more basic of these entities as points of mass/energy rather than as extended spatial entities. And second, more radically, according to quantum mechanics, as long as they are not being measured or interfered with in some way, "particles," such as electrons, behave more like waves than like particles. However, for convenience I will stick with the word "particle."

Particles, as our earlier examples illustrated, are organized into larger *systems*. It would be tricky to try to define the notion of a system, but the simple intuitive idea is that systems are collections of particles where the spatio-temporal boundaries of the system are set by causal relations. Thus, a raindrop is a system, but so is a glacier. Babies, elephants, and mountain ranges are also examples of systems. It should be obvious from these examples that systems can contain subsystems.

Essential to the explanatory apparatus of atomic theory is not only the idea that big systems are made up of little systems, but that many features of the big ones can be *causally explained* by the behavior of the little ones. This conception of explanation gives us the possibility, indeed the requirement, that many sorts of macrophenomena be explicable in terms of microphenomena. And this in turn has the consequence that there will be different levels of explanation of the same phenomenon, depending on whether we are going left to right from macro to macro, or micro to micro, or bottom up from micro to macro. We can illustrate these levels with a simple example. Suppose I wish to explain why this pot of water is boiling. One explanation, a left-right macro-macro explanation, would be that I put the pot on the stove and turned on the heat under it. I call this explanation "left-right" because it cites an earlier event to explain a later event,[2] and I call it "macro-macro" because both explanans and explanandum are at the macrolevel. Another explanation—bottom-up micro-macro—would be that the water is boiling because the kinetic energy transmitted by the oxidization of hydrocarbons to the $H_2O$ molecules has caused them to move so rapidly that the internal pressure of the molecule movements equals the external air pressure, which pressure in turn is explained by the movement of the molecules of which the external air is composed. I call this explanation "bottom-up micro-macro" because it explains the features and behavior of surface or macrophenomena in terms of lower-level microphenomena. I do not mean to imply that these are the only possible levels of explanation. There are also left-right micro-micro explanations, and further subdivisions can be made within each micro or macro level.

This, then, is one of the chief lessons of atomic theory: many features of big things are explained by the behavior of little things. We regard the germ theory of disease or the DNA theory of genetic transmission as such major breakthroughs precisely because they fit this model. If someone had an explanation of diseases in terms of the movement of the planets we would never accept it as complete explanation, even if it worked for diagnoses and cures, until we understood how the macro causes and effects at the level of planets and symptoms were grounded in bottom-up micro-macro causal structures.

To these elementary notions of atomic theory let us now add the principles of evolutionary biology. Over long periods of time, certain *types* of living systems evolve in certain very special ways. On our little earth, the types of systems in question invariably contain carbon-based molecules, and they make extensive use of hydrogen, nitrogen, and oxygen. The ways in which they evolve are complicated, but the basic procedure is that token instances of the types cause similar tokens to come into existence. Thus, after the original tokens are destroyed, the type or pattern that they exemplify continues in other tokens and continues to be replicated as subsequent generations of tokens produce yet other tokens. Variations in the surface features, phenotypes, of the tokens give those tokens greater or lesser chances of survival, relative to the specific environments in which they find themselves. Those tokens that have a greater probability of survival relative to their environment will therefore have a greater probability of producing further tokens like themselves, tokens with the same genotype. And thus does the type evolve.

Part of the intellectual appeal of the theory of evolution, as supplemented by Mendelian and DNA genetics, is that it fits in with the explanatory model we have derived from atomic theory. Specifically, the grounding of genetic mechanisms in molecular biology allows for different levels of explanation of biological phenomena corresponding to the different levels of explanation we have for physical phenomena. In evolutionary biology, there are characteristically two levels of explanation, a "functional" level where we explain the survival of species in terms of "inclusive fitness," which depends on the phenotypical traits possessed by members of the species, and a "causal" level where we explain the causal mechanisms by which the traits in question actually relate the organism to the environment. We can illustrate this with a simple example. Why do green plants turn their leaves toward the sun? The functional explanation:[3] This trait has survival value. By increasing the plant's capacity to perform photosynthesis, it increases the plant's capacity to survive and reproduce. The plant does not turn toward the sun to survive; rather, the plant tends to survive because it is predisposed to turn toward the sun anyway. The causal explanation: The plant's biochemical structure as determined by its genetic makeup causes it to secrete the growth hormone auxin, and the varying concentrations of auxin in turn cause the leaves to turn in the direction of the light source.

If you put these two levels of explanation together, you get the following result: Because the phenotype, as produced by the interaction of the genotype with the environment, has survival value relative to the environment, the genotype survives and reproduces. Such, in very brief form, are the mechanisms of natural selection.

The products of the evolutionary process, organisms, are made of subsystems called "cells," and some of these organisms develop subsystems of nerve cells, which we think of as "nervous systems." Furthermore, and this is the crucial point, some extremely complex nervous systems are capable of causing and sustaining conscious states and processes. Specifically, certain big collections of nerve cells, that is, brains, cause and sustain conscious states and processes. We do not know the detail of how brains cause consciousness, but we know for a fact that this occurs in human brains, and we have overwhelming evidence that it also occurs in the brains of many species of animals (Griffin 1981). We do not know at present how far down the evolutionary scale consciousness extends.

Basic to our world view is the idea that human beings and other higher animals are part of the biological order like any other organisms. Humans are continuous with the rest of nature. But if so, the biologically specific characteristics of these animals—such as their possession of a rich system of consciousness, as well as their greater intelligence, their capacity for language, their capacity for extremely fine perceptual discriminations, their capacity for rational thought, etc.—are biological phenomena like any other biological phenomena. Furthermore, these features are all phenotypes. They are as much the result of biological evolution as any other phenotype. *Consciousness, in short, is a biological feature of human and certain animal brains. It is caused by neurobiological processes and is as much a part of the natural biological order as any other biological features such as photosynthesis, digestion, or mitosis.* This principle is the first stage in understanding the place of consciousness within our world view.[4] The thesis of this chapter so far has been that once you see that atomic and evolutionary theories are central to the contemporary scientific world view, then consciousness falls into place naturally as an evolved phenotypical trait of certain types of organisms with highly developed nervous systems. I am not in this chapter concerned to defend this world view. Indeed, many thinkers whose opinions I respect, most notably Wittgenstein, regard it as in varying degrees repulsive, degrading, and disgusting. It seems to them to allow no place—or at most a subsidiary place—for religion, art, mysticism, and "spiritual" values generally. But, like it or not, it is the world view we have. Given what we know about the details of the world — about such things as the position of elements in the periodic table, the number of chromosomes in the cells of different species, and the nature of the chemical bond—this world view is not an option. It is not simply up for grabs along with a lot of competing world views. Our problem is not that somehow we have failed to come up with a convincing proof of the existence of God or that the hypothesis of an afterlife remains in serious doubt, it is rather that in our deepest reflections we cannot take such opinions seriously. When we encounter people who claim to believe such things, we may envy them the comfort and security they claim to derive from these beliefs, but at bottom we remain convinced that either they have not heard the news or they are in the grip of faith. We remain convinced that somehow they must separate their minds into separate compartments to believe such things. When I lectured on the mind-body problem in India and was assured by several members of my audience that my views must be mistaken, because they personally had existed in their earlier lives as frogs or elephants, etc., I did not think, "Here is evidence for an alternative world view," or even "Who knows, perhaps they are right." And my insensitivity was much more than mere cultural provincialism: Given what I know about how the world works, I could not regard their views as serious candidates for truth.

And once you accept our world view the only obstacle to granting consciousness its status as a biological feature of organisms is the outmoded dualistic/materialistic assumption that the "mental" character of consciousness makes it impossible for it to be a "physical" property.

I have only discussed the relation of consciousness to carbon-based living systems of the sort we have on our earth, but of course, we cannot exclude the possibility that consciousness may have evolved on other planets in other solar systems in other parts of the universe. Given the sheer size of the universe, it would be statistically amazing if we were the only bearers of consciousness in it. Furthermore, we do not want to exclude the possibility that consciousness might have been evolved in systems that are not carbon-based, but use some other sort of chemistry altogether. For all we know at present, there might be no theoretical obstacle to developing consciousness in systems made up of other elements. We are at present very far from having an adequate theory of the neurophysiology of consciousness; but until we do, we have to keep an open mind about its possible chemical bases. My own hunch would be that the neurobiology of consciousness is likely to prove at least as restricted as, say, the biochemistry of digestion. There are different varieties of digestion, but not anything can be digested by anything. And similarly, it seems to me we are likely to find that though there may be biochemically different varieties of consciousness, not anything goes.

Furthermore, because consciousness is entirely caused by the behavior of lower-level biological phenomena, it would in principle be possible to produce it artificially by duplicating the causal powers of the brain in a laboratory situation. We know that many biological phenomena have been created artificially. We can synthesize certain organic compounds, and even artificially create certain biological processes such as photosynthesis. If we can artificially create photosynthesis, why not consciousness as well? For photosynthesis, the artificial form of the phenomenon was created by actually duplicating the chemical processes in the laboratory. Similarly, if one were going to create consciousness artificially, the natural way to go about it would be to try to duplicate the actual neurobiological basis that consciousness has in organisms like ourselves. Because at present we do not know exactly what that neurobiological basis is, the prospects for such "artificial intelligence" are very remote. Furthermore, as I suggested earlier, it might be possible to produce consciousness using some altogether different sort of chemistry from the one that our brains in fact use. However, one thing we know before we even begin the investigation is that *any system capable of causing consciousness must be capable of duplicating the causal powers of the brain.* If, for example, it is done with silicon chips instead of neurons, it must be because the chemistry of the silicon chips is capable of duplicating the specific causal powers of neurons to cause consciousness. It is a trivial logical consequence of the fact that brains cause consciousness that any other system capable of causing consciousness, but using completely different mechanisms, would have to have at least the equivalent power of brains to do it. (Compare: airplanes don't have to have feathers to fly, but they do have to share with birds the causal capacity to overcome the force of gravity in the earth's atmosphere.)

To summarize: Our world picture, though extremely complicated in detail, provides a rather simple account of the mode of existence of consciousness. According to the atomic theory, the world is made up of particles. These particles are organized into systems. Some of these systems are living, and these types of living systems have evolved over long periods of time. Among these, some have evolved brains that are capable of causing and sustaining consciousness. Consciousness is, thus, a biological feature of certain organisms in exactly the same sense of "biological" in which photosynthesis, mitosis, digestion, and reproduction are biological features of organisms.

I have tried to describe the position of consciousness in our overall world view in very simple terms, because I want it to seem absolutely obvious. Anyone who has had even a modicum of "scientific" education after about 1920 should find nothing at all contentious or controversial in what I have just said. It is worth emphasizing also that all of this has been said without any of the traditional Cartesian categories. There has been no question of dualism, monism, materialism, or anything of the sort. Furthermore, there has been no question of "naturalizing consciousness"; it already is completely natural. Consciousness, to repeat, is a natural biological phenomenon. The exclusion of consciousness from the natural world was a useful heuristic device in the seventeenth century, because it enabled scientists to concentrate on phenomena that were measurable, objective, and meaningless, that is, free of intentionality. But the exclusion was based on a falsehood. It was based on the false belief that consciousness is not part of the natural world. That single falsehood, more than anything else, more even than the sheer difficulty of studying consciousness with our available scientific tools, has prevented us from arriving at an understanding of consciousness.

## II. Subjectivity

Conscious mental states and processes have a special feature not possessed by other natural phenomena, namely, subjectivity. It is this feature of consciousness that makes its study so recalcitrant to the conventional methods of biological and psychological research, and most puzzling to philosophical analysis. There are several different senses of "subjectivity," none of them entirely clear, and I need to say at least a little bit to clarify the sense in which I am claiming that consciousness is subjective.

We often speak of judgments as being "subjective" when we mean that their truth or falsity cannot be settled "objectively" because the truth or falsity is not a simple matter of fact, but depends on certain attitudes, feelings, and points of view of the makers and the hearers of the judgment. An example of such a judgment might be, "Van Gogh is a better artist than Matisse." In this sense of "subjectivity," we contrast such subjective judgments with completely objective judgments, such as the judgment, "Matisse lived in Nice during the year 1917." For such objective judgments, we can ascertain what sorts of facts in the world make them true or false independent of anybody's attitudes or feelings about them.

Now this sense in which we speak of "objective" and "subjective" judgments is not the sense of "subjective" in which I am speaking of consciousness as subjective. In the sense in which I am here using the term, "subjective" refers to an ontological category, not to an epistemic mode. Consider, for example, the statement, "I now have a pain in my lower back." That statement is completely objective in the sense that it is made true by the existence of an actual fact and is not dependent on any stance, attitudes, or opinions of observers. However, the phenomenon itself, the actual pain itself, has a subjective mode of existence, and it is in that sense which I am saying that consciousness is subjective.

What more can we say about this subjective mode of existence? Well, first it is essential to see that in consequence of its subjectivity, the pain is not equally accessible to any observer. Its existence, we might say, is a first-person existence. For it to be a pain, it must be *somebody's* pain; and this in a much stronger sense than the sense in which a leg must be somebody's leg, for example. Leg transplants are possible; in that sense, pain transplants are not. And what is true of pains is true of conscious states generally. Every conscious state is always *someone's* conscious state. And just as I have a special relation to my conscious states, which is not like my relation to other people's conscious states, so they in turn have a relation to their conscious states, which is not like my relation to their conscious states.[5] Subjectivity has the further consequence that all of my conscious forms of intentionality that give me information about the world independent of myself are always from a special point of view. The world itself has no point of view, but my access to the world through my conscious states is always perspectival, always from my point of view.

It would be difficult to exaggerate the disastrous effects that the failure to come to terms with the subjectivity of consciousness has had on the philosophical and psychological work of the past half century. In ways that are not at all obvious on the surface, much of the bankruptcy of most work in the philosophy of mind and a great deal of the sterility of academic psychology over the past fifty years, over the whole of my intellectual lifetime, have come from a persistent failure to recognize and come to terms with the fact that the ontology of the mental is an irreducibly first-person ontology. There are very deep reasons, many of them embedded in our unconscious history, why we find it difficult if not impossible to accept the idea that the real world, the world described by physics and chemistry and biology, contains an ineliminably subjective element. How could such a thing be? How can we possibly get a coherent world picture if the world contains these mysterious conscious entities? Yet we all know that we are for most of our lives conscious, and that other people around us are conscious. And unless we are blinded by bad philosophy or some forms of academic psychology, we really don't have any doubts that dogs, cats, monkeys, and small children are conscious, and that their consciousness is just as subjective as our own.

So let us try to describe in a little more detail the world picture that contains subjectivity as a rock-bottom element, and then try to describe some of the difficulties we have in coming to terms with this world picture. If we think of the world as consisting of particles, and those particles as organized into systems, and some of those systems as biological systems, and some of those biological systems as conscious, and consciousness as essentially subjective—then what is it that we are being asked to imagine when we imagine the subjectivity of consciousness? After all, all those other things we imagined — particles, systems, organisms, etc.—were completely objective. In consequence, they are equally accessible to all competent observers. So what are we being asked to imagine if we are now to throw into this metaphysical pot something that is irreducibly subjective?

Actually, what we are being asked to "imagine" is simply the world that we know to exist. I know, for example, that I am now conscious, and that this conscious state that I am in has the subjectivity I have been referring to, and I know that a very large number of other organisms like myself are similarly conscious and have similar subjective states. Then why does it seem that I am asking us to imagine something that is difficult or in some way counterintuitive, when all I am doing is reminding us of facts that are right in front of our face all along? Part—but only part—of the answer has to do with the fact that quite naively I invoked the word "observer" in the previous paragraph. When we are asked to form a world *view* or a world *picture*, we form these on the model of vision. We tend literally to form an image of reality as consisting of very small bits of matter, "the particles," and then we imagine these organized into systems, again with gross visible features. But when we visualize the world with this inner eye, we can't see consciousness. Indeed, it is the very subjectivity of consciousness that makes it invisible in the crucial way. *If we try to draw a picture of someone else's consciousness, we just end up drawing the other person* (perhaps with a balloon growing out of his or her head). *If we try to draw our own consciousness, we end up drawing whatever it is that we are conscious of.* If consciousness is the rock-bottom epistemic basis for getting at reality, we cannot get at the reality of consciousness in that way. (Alternative formulation: We cannot get at the reality of consciousness in the way that, using consciousness, we can get at the reality of other phenomena.)

It is important to go over this rather slowly and not just zip past it in the usual fashion, so let me go through it step by step in low gear. If I try to observe the consciousness of another, what I observe is not his subjectivity but simply his conscious behavior, his structure, and the causal relations between structure and behavior. Furthermore, I observe the causal relations between both structure and behavior, on the one hand, and the environment that impinges on him and on which he in turn impinges, on the other. So there is no way I can observe someone else's consciousness as such; rather what I observe is him and his behavior and the relations between him, the behavior, the structure, and the environment. Well, what about my own inner goings-on? Can I not observe those? The very fact of subjectivity, which we were trying to observe, makes such an observation impossible. Why? Because where conscious subjectivity is concerned, there is no distinction between the observation and the thing observed, between the perception and the object perceived. The model of vision works on the presupposition that there is a distinction between the thing seen and the seeing of it. But for "introspection" there is simply no way to make this separation. Any introspection I have of my own conscious state is itself that conscious state. This is not to say that my conscious mental phenomena don't come in many different levels and varieties—we will have occasion to examine some of these in detail later—it is simply to say that the standard model of observation simply doesn't work for conscious subjectivity. It doesn't work for other people's consciousness, and it doesn't work for one's own. For that reason, the idea that there might be a special method of investigating consciousness, namely "introspection," which is supposed to be a kind of inner observation, was doomed to failure from the start, and it is not surprising that introspective psychology proved bankrupt.

We find it difficult to come to terms with subjectivity, not just because we have been brought up in an ideology that says that ultimately reality must be completely objective, but because our idea of an objectively observable reality presupposes the notion of observation that is itself ineliminably subjective, and that cannot itself be made the object of observation in a way that objectively existing objects and states of affairs in the world can. There is, in short, no way for us to picture subjectivity as part of our world view because, so to speak, the subjectivity in question is the picturing. The solution is not to try to develop a special mode of picturing, a kind of super-introspection, but rather to stop picturing altogether at this point and just acknowledge the facts. The facts are that biological processes produce conscious mental phenomena, and these are irreducibly subjective.

Philosophers have invented another metaphor for describing certain features of subjectivity that seems to me even more confused than the commonsense metaphor of introspection, and that is "privileged access." For the *visual* metaphor of introspection, we are tempted to substitute the *spatial* metaphor of privileged access, a model that suggests that consciousness is like a private room into which only we are allowed to enter. Only I can go inside the space of my own consciousness. But this metaphor doesn't work either, because for there to be something to which I have privileged access, I would have to be different from the space in which I enter. But just as the metaphor of introspection broke down when the only thing to be observed was the observing itself, so the metaphor of a private inner space breaks down when we understand that there isn't anything like a space into which I can enter, because I cannot make the necessary distinctions between the three elements of myself, the act of entering, and the space in which I am supposed to enter.

We might summarize these points by saying that our modern model of reality and of the relation between reality and observation cannot accommodate the phenomenon of subjectivity. The model is one of objective (in the epistemic sense) observers observing an objectively (in the ontological sense) existing reality. But there is no way on that model to observe the act of observing itself. For the act of observing is the subjective (ontological sense) access to objective reality. Though I can easily observe another person, I cannot observe his or her *subjectivity*. And worse yet, I cannot *observe* my own subjectivity, for any observation that I might care to make is itself that which was supposed to be observed. The whole idea of there being an observation of reality is precisely the idea of (ontologically) subjective representations of reality. The ontology of observation—as opposed to its epistemology—is precisely the ontology of subjectivity. Observation is always someone's observation; it is in general conscious; it is always from a point of view; it has a subjective feel to it; etc.

I want to make clear exactly what I am saying and what I am not saying. I am not making the old muddled point to the effect that there is a self-referential paradox involved in studying subjectivity. Such paradoxes do not worry me at all. We can use the eye to study the eye, the brain to study the brain, consciousness to study consciousness, language to study language, observation to study observation, and subjectivity to study subjectivity. There is no problem in any of these. The point is rather that because of the ontology of subjectivity, our models of "studying," models that rely on the distinction between observation and thing observed, do not work for subjectivity itself.

There is a sense, then, in which we find subjectivity difficult to conceive. Given our concept as to what reality must be like and what it would be like to find out about that reality, it seems inconceivable to us that there should be anything irreducibly subjective in the universe. Yet we all know that subjectivity exists.

I hope we can now see a little more clearly what happens if we try to describe the universe leaving out subjectivity. Suppose we insist on giving an account of the world that is completely objective, not just in the epistemic sense that its claims are independently checkable, but in the ontological sense that the phenomena it describes have an existence independent of any form of subjectivity. Once you adopt this strategy (the principal strategy in the philosophy of mind of the past fifty years), it then becomes impossible to describe consciousness, because it becomes literally impossible to acknowledge the subjectivity of consciousness. Examples of this are really too numerous to mention, but I will cite two authors who explicitly address the problem of consciousness. Armstrong (1980) tacitly eliminates subjectivity by treating consciousness simply as a capacity for making discriminations about one's own inner states, and Changeux, the French neurobiologist, defines consciousness simply as a "global regulatory system dealing with mental objects and computations using these objects" (1985, p. 145). Both of these accounts presuppose a third-person conception of reality, a conception of a reality that is not merely epistemically objective but ontologically objective as well; and such a reality has no place for consciousness, because it has no place for ontological subjectivity.

## III. Consciousness and the Mind-Body Problem

I have said repeatedly that I think the mind-body problem has a rather simple solution, at least in broad outline, and that the only obstacles to our having a full understanding of mind-body relations are our philosophical prejudice in supposing that the mental and the physical are two distinct realms, and our ignorance of the workings of the brain. If we had an adequate science of the brain, an account of the brain that would give causal explanations of consciousness in all its forms and varieties, and if we overcame our conceptual mistakes, no mind-body problem would remain. However, the possibility of any solution to the mind-body problem has been very powerfully challenged over the years by the writings of Thomas Nagel (1974, 1986). He argues as follows: At present, we simply do not have the conceptual apparatus even to conceive of a solution to the mind-body problem. This is for the following reason: Causal explanations in the natural sciences have a kind of causal necessity. We understand, for example, how the behavior of $H_2O$ molecules causes water to be in a liquid form, because we see that the liquidity is a necessary consequence of the molecular behavior. The molecular theory does more than show that systems of $H_2O$ molecules will be liquid under certain conditions; rather it shows why the system *has to be* in a liquid form. Given that we understand the physics in question, it is inconceivable that the molecules should behave in that fashion and the water not be in a liquid state. In short, Nagel argues that explanations in science imply necessity, and necessity implies inconceivability of the opposite.

Now, says Nagel, we cannot achieve this type of necessity for the relationship between matter and consciousness. No possible account of neuronal behavior would explain why, given that behavior, we *have to be*, for example, in pain. No account could explain why pain was a necessary consequence of certain sorts of neuron firings. The proof that the account does not give us causal necessity is that we can always conceive the opposite. We can always conceive of a state of affairs in which the neurophysiology behaves in whatever way you like to specify, but all the same, the system is not in pain. If adequate scientific explanation implies necessity and necessity implies inconceivability of the opposite, then by contraposition the conceivability of the opposite implies that we do not have necessity, and that in turn implies that we do not have an explanation. Nagel's despairing conclusion is that we would need a major overhaul of our conceptual apparatus if we were ever to be able to solve the mind-body problem.

I am not convinced by this argument. First we should note that not all explanations in science have the kind of necessity that we found in the relation between molecule movement and liquidity. For example the inverse square law is an account of gravity, but it does not show why bodies *have to have* gravitational attraction. Secondly, the apparent "necessity" of any scientific explanation may be just a function of the fact that we find the explanation so convincing that we cannot, for example, conceive of the molecules moving in a particular way and the $H_2O$ not being liquid. A person in antiquity or the Middle Ages might not have found the explanation a matter of "necessity." The "mystery" of consciousness today is in roughly the same shape that the mystery of life was before the development of molecular biology or the mystery of electromagnetism was before Clerk-Maxwell's equations. It seems mysterious because we do not know how the system of neurophysiology/consciousness works, and an adequate knowledge of how it works would remove the mystery. Furthermore, the claim that we could always conceive of the possibility that certain brain states *may not* cause the appropriate conscious states might simply depend on our ignorance of how the brain works. Given a full understanding of the brain, it seems to me likely that we would think it obvious that if the brain was in a certain sort of state, it had to be conscious. Notice that we already accept this form of causal necessity of conscious states for gross molar phenomena. For example, if I see a screaming man with his foot caught in a punch press, then I know the man must be in terrible pain. It is, in a sense, inconceivable to me that a normal human being should be in such a situation and not feel a terrible pain. The physical causes necessitate the pain.

However, let us grant Nagel's point for the sake of argument. Nothing follows about how the world works in fact. The limitation that Nagel points out is only a limitation of our powers of conception. Even assuming he is right, what his argument shows is only that in the case of the relations between material and material phenomena, we can subjectively picture both sides of the relation; but in the case of the relations between material and mental phenomena, one side of the relation is already subjective, and hence we cannot picture its relation to the material in the way that we can picture the relations between liquidity and molecule movement, for example. Nagel's argument, in short, only shows that we cannot get out of the subjectivity of our consciousness to see its necessary relation to its material basis. We form a picture of necessity based on our subjectivity, but we cannot in that way form a picture of the necessity of the relation between subjectivity and neurophysiological phenomena, because we are already in the subjectivity, and the picturing relation would require that we get outside it. (If solidity were conscious, it would seem to it mysterious that it was caused by vibratory movements of molecules in lattice structures, but all the same those movements explain solidity.)

You can appreciate this objection to Nagel if you imagine other ways of detecting causally necessary relations. Suppose God or a machine could simply detect causally necessary relations, then for God or the machine there would be no difference between matter/matter forms of necessity and matter/mind forms of necessity. Furthermore, even if we grant that we cannot picture both sides of the relation for consciousness and the brain in a way that we can picture both sides of the relation for liquidity and molecule movement, we could nonetheless get at the causal relations involved in the production of consciousness by indirect means. Suppose we actually had an account of the neurophysiological processes in the brain that cause consciousness. It is not at all impossible that we should get such an account, because the usual tests for causal relations can be performed on brain/consciousness relations as they can on any natural phenomena. The knowledge of lawlike causal relations will give us all of the causal necessity we need. Indeed, we already have the beginnings of such lawlike relations. As I mentioned in chapter 3, standard textbooks of neurophysiology routinely explain, for example, the similarities and differences between how cats see things and how humans see things. There is no question that certain sorts of neurophysiological similarities and differences are causally sufficient for certain sorts of similarities and differences in visual experiences. Furthermore we can and will break down the big question—How does the brain cause consciousness?—into a lot of smaller questions (for example, How does cocaine produce certain characteristic experiences?). And the detailed answers we are already starting to give (for example, Cocaine impedes the capacity of certain synaptic receptors to reabsorb norepenephrine) already allow for the characteristic inferences that go with causal necessity (for example, If you increase the dose of cocaine, you increase the effect). I conclude that Nagel has not shown the mind-body problem to be insoluble, even within our current conceptual apparatus and world view.

Colin McGinn (1991) carries Nagel's argument a step further and argues that it is impossible *in principle* that we should ever be able to understand the solution to the mind-body problem. His argument goes beyond Nagel's and involves assumptions that Nagel does not make, at least not explicitly. Because McGinn's assumptions are widely shared in the philosophical tradition of dualism, and because in this book I am—among other things—trying to overcome these assumptions, I will state them explicitly and try to show that they are false. McGinn assumes:

1. Consciousness is a kind of "stuff."[6]
2. This stuff is known by "the faculty of introspection." Consciousness is the "object" of the introspective faculty, just as the physical world is the object of the perceptual faculty (p. 14ff. and p. 61ff.).

It is a consequence of 1 and 2, though I am not sure if McGinn endorses it, that consciousness, as such, as known by introspection, is not spatial; in contrast to the physical world, which, as such, as known by perception, is spatial.

3. In order that we have an understanding of mind-body relations, we would have to understand "the link" between consciousness and the brain (passim).

McGinn does not doubt that there is such a "link," but he believes that it is impossible in principle for us to understand it. He says, using Kant's term, that for us the relation is "noumenal." It is impossible for us to understand this link, and therefore impossible to understand mind-body relations. McGinn's guess is that the link is provided by a hidden structure of consciousness that is inaccessible to introspection.

These three are Cartesian assumptions and the proposed "solution" is a Cartesian-style solution (with the added disadvantage that the hidden structure of consciousness is unknowable in principle. At least the pineal gland was accessible!). However, as with the pineal gland, the solution is no solution.

If you need a link between consciousness and the brain, then you need a link between the hidden structure of consciousness and the brain. The postulation of a hidden structure—even if it were intelligible—gets us nowhere.

The real problem is with the three assumptions; indeed, I believe that they embody most of the mistakes of traditional dualism over the past three hundred years. Specifically,

1. Consciousness is not a "stuff," it is a *feature* or *property* of the brain in the sense, for example, that liquidity is a feature of water.

2. Consciousness is not known by introspection in a way analogous to the way objects in the world are known by perception. I develop this point in the next chapter, and have already begun to discuss it in this one, so here I will state it very simply: The model of "specting intro," that is, the model of an inner inspection, requires a distinction between the act of inspecting and the object inspected, and we cannot make any such distinction for consciousness. The doctrine of introspection is a good example of what Wittgenstein calls the bewitchment of our intelligence by means of language.

Furthermore, once you get rid of the idea that consciousness is a stuff that is the "object" of introspection, it is easy to see that it is spatial, because it is located in the brain. We are not aware in conscious experience of either the spatial location or the dimensions of our conscious experience, but why should we be? It is an extremely tricky neurophysiological question, one we are a long way from solving, to figure out exactly what the locus of conscious experience in our brains is. It might, for all we know, be distributed over very large portions of the brain.

3. There is no "link" between consciousness and the brain, any more than there is a link between the liquidity of water and $H_2O$ molecules. If consciousness is a higher-level feature of the brain, then there cannot be any question of there being a link between the feature and the system of which it is a feature.

*IV. Consciousness and Selectional Advantage*

My approach to the philosophy of mind, biological naturalism, is sometimes confronted with the following challenge: If we could imagine the same or similar behavior being produced by an unconscious zombie, then why did evolution produce consciousness at all? Indeed, this is often presented by way of suggesting that maybe consciousness does not even exist. I am, of course, not going to attempt to demonstrate the existence of consciousness. If somebody is not conscious, there is no way I can demonstrate the existence of consciousness to him, if he is conscious, it is pretty much inconceivable that he could seriously doubt that he was conscious. I do not say there are no people who are so muddled philosophically that they *say* they doubt that they are conscious, but I do find it hard to take such statements very seriously.

In answering the question as to the evolutionary role of consciousness, I want to reject the implicit assumption that every biologically inherited trait must give some evolutionary advantage to the organism. This seems to me excessively crude Darwinism, and we now have all sorts of good reasons for abandoning it. If it were true that every innate predisposition of an organism were the result of some selectional pressure, then I would have to conclude that my dog has been selected for chasing tennis balls. He has a passion for chasing tennis balls, and it is obviously not something he has learned, but that is no reason for supposing it must have some biological payoff. Or, closer to home, the passion that human beings have for alpine skiing, I believe, has a biological basis that is not the result of training or conditioning. The spread of skiing has been simply phenomenal; and the sacrifices that people are willing to make in money, comfort, and time for the sake of a few hours on a ski slope is at least pretty good evidence that they derive satisfactions from it that are inherent to their biological nature. But it's simply not the case that we were selected by evolution for our predilection for alpine skiing.[7]

With these qualifications we can still address the question "What is the evolutionary advantage to consciousness?" And the answer is that consciousness does all sorts of things. To begin with, there are all sorts of forms of consciousness such as vision, hearing, taste, smell, thirst, pains, tickles, itches, and voluntary actions. Second, within each of these areas there may be a variety of functions served by the conscious forms of these different modalities. However, speaking in the most general terms, it seems clear that consciousness serves to organize a certain set of relationships between the organism and both its environment and its own states. And, again speaking in very general terms, the form of organization might be described as "representation." By way of the sensory modalities, for example, the organism gets conscious information about the state of the world. It hears sounds in its vicinity; it sees objects and states of affairs in its field of vision; it smells the specific odors of distinct features of its environment; etc. In addition to its conscious sensory experience, the organism will also characteristically have experiences of acting. It will run, walk, eat, fight, etc. These forms of consciousness are not primarily for the purpose of getting information about the world; rather, they are cases in which consciousness enables the organism to act on the world, to produce effects in the world. Speaking again very roughly—and we will discuss these points in more refined terms later—we can say that in conscious perception the organism has representations caused by states of affairs in the world, and in the case of intentional actions, the organism causes states of affairs in the world by way of its conscious representations.

If this hypothesis is correct, we can make a general claim about the selectional advantage of consciousness: Consciousness gives us much greater powers of discrimination than unconscious mechanisms would have.

Penfield's (1975) case studies bear this out. Some of Penfield's patients suffered from a form of epilepsy known as *petit mal*. In certain of these cases, the epileptic seizure rendered the patient totally unconscious, yet the patient continued to exhibit what would normally be called goal-directed behavior. Here are some examples:

One patient, whom I shall call A., was a serious student of the piano and subject to automatisms of the type called *petit mal*. He was apt to make a slight interruption in his practicing, which his mother recognized as the beginning of an "absence." Then he would continue to play for a time with considerable dexterity. Patient B was subject to epileptic automatism that began with discharge in the temporal lobe. Sometimes the attack would come on him while walking home from work. He would continue to walk and to thread his way through the busy streets on his way home. He might realize later that he had had an attack because there was a blank in his memory for a part of the journey, as from Avenue X to Street Y. If patient C was driving a car, he would continue to drive, although he might discover later that he had driven through one or more red lights. (p. 39)

In all these cases, we have complex forms of apparently goal-directed behavior without any consciousness. Now why could all behavior not be like that? What does consciousness add? Notice that in the cases, the patients were performing types of actions that were habitual, routine, and memorized. There were presumably well-established neural pathways in the man's brain corresponding to his knowledge of the route home, and similarly, the pianist presumably had the knowledge of how to play the particular piano piece realized in neural pathways in his brain. Complex behavior can be preprogrammed in the structure of the brain, at least as far as we know anything about how the brain works in such cases. Apparently, once started, the activity can run its course even in a *petit mal* seizure. But normal, human, conscious behavior has a degree of flexibility and creativity that is absent from the Penfield cases of the unconscious driver and the unconscious pianist. Consciousness adds powers of discrimination and flexibility even to memorized routine activities.

Apparently, it is just a fact of biology that organisms that have consciousness have, in general, much greater powers of discrimination than those that do not. Plant tropisms, for example, which are light-sensitive, are much less capable of making fine discriminations and much less flexible than, for example, the human visual system. The hypothesis I am suggesting then is that one of the evolutionary advantages conferred on us by consciousness is the much greater flexibility, sensitivity, and creativity we derive from being conscious.

The behaviorist and mechanist traditions we have inherited blind us to these facts; indeed, they make it impossible even to pose the questions appropriately, because they constantly seek forms of explanation that treat the mental-neurophysiological as simply providing an input-output mechanism, a function for mapping input stimuli onto output behaviors. The very terms in which the questions are posed preclude the introduction of topics that are crucial for understanding consciousness, such as creativity, for example.

# Chapter 5

# Reductionism and the
# Irreducibility of Consciousness

---

The view of the relation between mind and body that I have been putting forward is sometimes called "reductionist," sometimes "antireductionist." It is often called "emergentism," and is generally regarded as a form of "supervenience." I am not sure that any one of these attributions is at all clear, but a number of issues surround these mysterious terms, and in this chapter I will explore some of them.

## I. Emergent Properties

Suppose we have a system, $S$, made up of elements $a, b, c \ldots$ For example, $S$ might be a stone and the elements might be molecules. In general, there will be features of $S$ that are not, or not necessarily, features of $a, b, c \ldots$ For example, $S$ might weigh ten pounds, but the molecules individually do not weigh ten pounds. Let us call such features "system features." The shape and the weight of the stone are system features. Some system features can be deduced or figured out or calculated from the features of $a, b, c \ldots$ just from the way these are composed and arranged (and sometimes from their relations to the rest of the environment). Examples of these would be shape, weight, and velocity. But some other system features cannot be figured out just from the composition of the elements and environmental relations; they have to be explained in terms of the causal interactions among the elements. Let's call these "causally emergent system features." Solidity, liquidity, and transparency are examples of causally emergent system features.

On these definitions, consciousness is a causally emergent property of systems. It is an emergent feature of certain systems of neurons in the same way that solidity and liquidity are emergent features of systems of molecules. The existence of consciousness can be explained by the causal interactions between elements of the brain at the micro level, but consciousness cannot itself be deduced or calculated from the sheer physical structure of the neurons without some additional account of the causal relations between them.

This conception of causal emergence, call it "emergent1," has to be distinguished from a much more adventurous conception, call it "emergent2." A feature F is emergent2 iff F is emergent1 and F has causal powers that cannot be explained by the causal interactions of a, b, c. . . If consciousness were emergent2, then consciousness could cause things that could not be explained by the causal behavior of the neurons. The naive idea here is that consciousness gets squirted out by the behavior of the neurons in the brain, but once it has been squirted out, it then has a life of its own.

It should be obvious from the previous chapter that on my view consciousness is emergent1, but not emergent2. In fact, I cannot think of anything that is emergent2, and it seems unlikely that we will be able to find any features that are emergent2, because the existence of any such features would seem to violate even the weakest principle of the transitivity of causation.

## II. Reductionism

Most discussions of reductionism are extremely confusing. Reductionism as an ideal seems to have been a feature of positivist philosophy of science, a philosophy now in many respects discredited. However, discussions of reductionism still survive, and the basic intuition that underlies the concept of reductionism seems to be the idea that certain things might be shown to be *nothing but* certain other sorts of things. Reductionism, then, leads to a peculiar form of the identity relation that we might as well call the "nothing-but" relation: in general, $A$'s can be reduced to $B$'s, iff $A$'s are nothing but $B$'s.

However, even within the nothing-but relation, people mean so many different things by the notion of "reduction" that we need to begin by making several distinctions. At the very outset it is important to be clear about what the relata of the relation are. What is its domain supposed to be: objects, properties, theories, or what? I find at least five different senses of "reduction"—or perhaps I should say five different kinds of reduction—in the theoretical literature, and I want to mention each of them so that we can see which are relevant to our discussion of the mind-body problem.

### 1. Ontological Reduction

The most important form of reduction is ontological reduction. It is the form in which objects of certain types can be shown to consist in nothing but objects of other types. For example, chairs are shown to be nothing but collections of molecules. This form is clearly important in the history of science. For example, material objects in general can be shown to be nothing but collections of molecules, genes can be shown to consist in nothing but DNA molecules. It seems to me this form of reduction is what the other forms are aiming at.

### 2. Property Ontological Reduction

This is a form of ontological reduction, but it concerns properties. For example, heat (of a gas) is nothing but the mean kinetic energy of molecule movements. Property reductions for properties corresponding to theoretical terms, such as "heat," "light," etc., are often a result of theoretical reductions.

### 3. Theoretical Reduction

Theoretical reductions are the favorite of theorists in the literature, but they seem to me rather rare in the actual practice of science, and it is perhaps not surprising that the same half dozen examples are given over and over in the standard textbooks. From the point of view of scientific explanation, theoretical reductions are mostly interesting if they enable us to carry out ontological reductions. In any case, theoretical reduction is primarily a relation between theories, where the laws of the reduced theory can (more or less) be deduced from the laws of the reducing theory. This demonstrates that the reduced theory is nothing but a special case of the reducing theory. The classical example that is usually given in textbooks is the reduction of the gas laws to the laws of statistical thermodynamics.

*4. Logical or Definitional Reduction*
This form of reduction used to be a great favorite among philosophers, but in recent decades it has fallen out of fashion. It is a relation between words and sentences, where words and sentences referring to one type of entity can be translated without any residue into those referring to another type of entity. For example, sentences about the average plumber in Berkeley are reducible to sentences about specific individual plumbers in Berkeley; sentences about numbers, according to one theory, can be translated into, and hence are reducible to, sentences about sets. Since the words and sentences are *logically* or *definitionally* reducible, the corresponding entities referred to by the words and sentences are *ontologically* reducible. For example, numbers are nothing but sets of sets.

*5. Causal Reduction*
This is a relation between any two types of things that can have causal powers, where the existence and a fortiori the causal powers of the reduced entity are shown to be entirely explainable in terms of the causal powers of the reducing phenomena. Thus, for example, some objects are solid and this has causal consequences: solid objects are impenetrable by other objects, they are resistant to pressure, etc. But these causal powers can be causally explained by the causal powers of vibratory movements of molecules in lattice structures.

Now when the views I have urged are accused of being reductionist—or sometimes insufficiently reductionist—which of these various senses do the accusers have in mind? I think that theoretical reduction and logical reduction are not intended. Apparently the question is whether the causal reductionism of my view leads—or fails to lead—to ontological reduction. I hold a view of mind/brain relations that is a form of causal reduction, as I have defined the notion: Mental features are caused by neurobiological processes. Does this imply ontological reduction?

In general in the history of science, successful causal reductions tend to lead to ontological reductions. Because where we have a successful causal reduction, we simply redefine the expression that denotes the reduced phenomena in such a way that the phenomena in question can now be identified with their causes. Thus, for example, color terms were once (tacitly) defined in terms of the subjective experience of color perceivers; for example, "red" was defined ostensively by pointing to examples, and then real red was defined as whatever seemed red to "normal" observers under "normal" conditions. But once we have a causal reduction of color phenomena to light reflectances, then, according to many thinkers, it becomes possible to redefine color expressions in terms of light reflectances. We thus carve off and eliminate the subjective experience of color from the "real" color. Real color has undergone a property ontological reduction to light reflectances. Similar remarks could be made about the reduction of heat to molecular motion, the reduction of solidity to molecular movements in lattice structures, and the reduction of sound to air waves. In each case, the causal reduction leads naturally to an ontological reduction by way of a redefinition of the expression that names the reduced phenomenon. Thus, to continue with the example of "red," once we know that the color experiences are caused by a certain sort of photon emission, we then redefine the word in terms of the specific features of the photon emission. "Red," according to some theorists, now refers to photon emissions of 600 nanometers. It thus follows trivially that the color red is nothing but photon emissions of 600 nanometers.

The general principle in such cases appears to be this: Once a property is seen to be *emergent1*, we automatically get a causal reduction, and that leads to an ontological reduction, by redefinition if necessary. The general trend in ontological reductions that have a scientific basis is toward greater generality, objectivity, and redefinition in terms of underlying causation.

So far so good. But now we come to an apparently shocking asymmetry. When we come to consciousness, we cannot perform the ontological reduction. Consciousness is a causally emergent property of the behavior of neurons, and so consciousness is causally reducible to the brain processes. But—and this is what seems so shocking—a perfect science of the brain would still not lead to an ontological reduction of consciousness in the way that our present science can reduce heat, solidity, color, or sound. It seems to many people whose opinions I respect that the irreducibility of consciousness is a primary reason why the mind-body problem continues to seem so intractable. Dualists treat the irreducibility of consciousness as incontrovertible proof of the truth of dualism. Materialists insist that consciousness must be reducible to material reality, and that the price of denying the reducibility of consciousness would be the abandonment of our overall scientific world view.

I will briefly discuss two questions: First, I want to show why consciousness is irreducible, and second, I want to show why it does not make any difference at all to our scientific world view that it should be irreducible. It does not force us to property dualism or anything of the sort. It is a trivial consequence of certain more general phenomena.

### III. Why Consciousness Is an Irreducible Feature of Physical Reality

There is a standard argument to show that consciousness is not reducible in the way that heat, etc., are. In different ways the argument occurs in the work of Thomas Nagel (1974), Saul

Kripke (1971), and Frank Jackson (1982). I think the argument is decisive, though it is frequently misunderstood in ways that treat it as merely epistemic and not ontological. It is sometimes treated as an epistemic argument to the effect that, for example, the sort of third-person, objective knowledge we might possibly have of a bat's neurophysiology would still not include the first-person, subjective experience of what it feels like to be a bat. But for our present purposes, the point of the argument is ontological and not epistemic. It is a point about what real features exist in the world and not, except derivatively, about how we know about those features.

Here is how it goes: Consider what facts in the world make it the case that you are now in a certain conscious state such as pain. What fact in the world corresponds to your true statement, "I am now in pain"? Naively, there seem to be at least two sorts of facts. First and most important, there is the fact that you are now having certain unpleasant conscious sensations, and you are experiencing these sensations from your subjective, first-person point of view. It is these sensations that are constitutive of your present pain. But the pain is also caused by certain underlying neurophysiological processes consisting in large part of patterns of neuron firing in your thalamus and other regions of your brain. Now suppose we tried to reduce the subjective, conscious, first-person sensation of pain to the objective, third-person patterns of neuron firings. Suppose we tried to say the pain is really "nothing but" the patterns of neuron firings. Well, if we tried such an ontological reduction, the essential features of the pain would be left out. No description of the third-person, objective, physiological facts would convey the subjective, first-person character of the pain, simply because the first-person features are different from the third-person features. Nagel states this point by contrasting the objectivity of the third-person features with the what-it-is-like features of the subjective states of consciousness. Jackson states the same point by calling attention to the fact that someone who had a complete knowledge of the neurophysiology of a mental phenomenon such as pain would still not know what a pain was if he or she did not know what it felt like. Kripke makes the same point when he says that pains could not be identical with neurophysiological states such as neuron firings in the thalamus and elsewhere, because any such identity would have to be necessary, because both sides of the identity statement are rigid designators, and yet we know that the identity could not be necessary.[1] This fact has obvious epistemic consequences: my knowledge that I am in pain has a different sort of basis than my knowledge that you are in pain. But the antireductionist point of the argument is ontological and not epistemic.

So much for the antireductionist argument. It is ludicrously simple and quite decisive. An enormous amount of ink has been shed trying to answer it, but the answers are all so much wasted ink. But to many people it seems that such an argument paints us into a corner. To them it seems that if we accept that argument, we have abandoned our scientific world view and adopted property dualism. Indeed, they would ask, what is property dualism but the view that there are irreducible mental properties? In fact, doesn't Nagel accept property dualism and Jackson reject physicalism precisely because of this argument? And what is the point of scientific reductionism if it stops at the very door of the mind? So I now turn to the main point of this discussion.

### IV. Why the Irreducibility of Consciousness Has No Deep Consequences

To understand fully why consciousness is irreducible, we have to consider in a little more detail the pattern of reduction that we found for perceivable properties such as heat, sound, color, solidity, liquidity, etc., and we have to show how the attempt to reduce consciousness differs from the other cases. In every case the ontological reduction was based on a prior causal reduction. We discovered that a surface feature of a phenomenon was caused by the behavior of the elements of an underlying microstructure. This is true both in the cases in which the reduced phenomenon was a matter of subjective appearances, such as the "secondary qualities" of heat or color; and in the cases of the "primary qualities" such as solidity, in which there was both an element of subjective appearance (solid things feel solid), and also many features independent of subjective appearances (solid things, e.g., are resistant to pressure and impenetrable by other solid objects). But in each case, for both the primary and secondary qualities, the point of the reduction was to carve off the surface features and redefine the original notion in terms of the causes that produce those surface features.

Thus, where the surface feature is a subjective appearance, we redefine the original notion in such a way as to exclude the appearance from its definition. For example, pretheoretically our notion of heat has something to do with perceived temperatures: Other things being equal, hot is what feels hot to us, cold is what feels cold. Similarly with colors: Red is what looks red to normal observers under normal conditions. But when we have a theory of what causes these and other phenomena, we discover that it is molecular movements causing sensations of heat and cold (as well as other phenomena such as increases in pressure), and light reflectances causing visual experiences of certain sorts (as well as other phenomena such as movements of light meters). We then *redefine* heat and color in terms of the underlying causes of both the subjective experiences and the other surface phenomena. And in the redefinition we eliminate any reference to the subjective appearances and other surface effects of the underlying causes. "Real" heat is now defined in terms of the kinetic energy of the molecular movements, and the subjective feel of heat that we get when we touch a hot object is now treated as just a subjective appearance caused by heat, as an effect of heat. It is no longer part of real heat. A similar distinction is made between real color and the subjective experience of color. The same pattern works for the primary qualities: Solidity is defined in terms of the vibratory movements of molecules in lattice structures, and objective, observer-independent features, such as impenetrability by other objects, are now seen as surface effects of the underlying reality. Such redefinitions are achieved by way of carving off all of the surface features of the phenomenon, whether subjective or objective, and treating them as effects of the real thing.

But now notice: The actual pattern of the facts in the world that correspond to statements about particular forms of heat such as specific temperatures are quite similar to the pattern of facts in the world that correspond to statements about particular forms of consciousness, such as pain. If I now say, "It's hot in this room," what are the facts? Well, first there is a set of "physical" facts involving the movement of molecules, and second there is a set of "mental" facts involving my subjective experience of heat, as caused by the impact of the moving air molecules on my nervous system. But similarly with pain. If I now say , "I am in pain," what are the facts? Well, first there is a set of "physical" facts involving my thalamus and other regions of the brain, and second there is a set of "mental" facts involving my subjective experience of pain. So why do we regard heat as reducible and pain as irreducible? The answer is that what interests us about heat is not the subjective appearance but the underlying physical causes. Once we get a causal reduction, we simply redefine the notion to enable us to get an ontological reduction. Once you know all the facts about heat—facts about molecule movements, impact on sensory nerve endings, subjective feelings, etc.—the reduction of heat to molecule movements involves no new *fact* whatever. It is simply a trivial consequence of the redefinition. We don't first discover all the facts and then discover a new fact, the fact that heat is reducible; rather, we simply redefine heat so that the reduction follows from the definition. But this redefinition does not eliminate, and was not intended to eliminate, the subjective experiences of heat (or color, etc.) from the world. They exist the same as ever.

We might not have made the redefinition. Bishop Berkeley, for example, refused to accept such redefinitions. But it is easy to see why it is rational to make such redefinitions and accept their consequences: To get a greater understanding and control of reality, we want to know how it works causally, and we want our concepts to fit nature at its causal joints. We simply redefine phenomena with surface features in terms of the underlying causes. It then looks like a new discovery that heat is *nothing but* mean kinetic energy of molecule movement, and that if all subjective experiences disappeared from the world, real heat would still remain. But this is not a new discovery, it is a trivial consequence of a new definition. Such reductions do not show that heat, solidity, etc., do not really exist in the way that, for example, new knowledge showed that mermaids and unicorns do not exist.

Couldn't we say the same thing about consciousness? In the case of consciousness, we do have the distinction between the "physical" processes and the subjective "mental" experiences, so why can't consciousness be redefined in terms of the neuro-physiological processes in the way that we redefined heat in terms of underlying physical processes? Well, of course, if we insisted on making the redefinition, we could. We could simply define, for example, "pain" as patterns of neuronal activity that cause subjective sensations of pain. And if such a redefinition took place, we would have achieved the same sort of reduction for pain that we have for heat. But of course, the reduction of pain to its physical reality still leaves the subjective experience of pain unreduced, just as the reduction of heat left the subjective experience of heat unreduced. Part of the point of the reductions was to carve off the subjective experiences and exclude them from the definition of the real phenomena, which are now defined in terms of those features that interest us most. But where the phenomena that interest us most are the subjective experiences themselves, there is no way to carve anything off. Part of the point of the reduction in the case of heat was to distinguish between the subjective appearance on the one hand and the underlying physical reality on the other. Indeed, it is a general feature of such reductions that the phencmenon is defined in terms of the "reality" and not in terms of the "appearance." But we can't make that sort of appearance-reality distinction for consciousness because consciousness consists in the appearances themselves. *Where appearance is concerned we cannot make the appearance-reality distinction because the appearance is the reality.*

For our present purposes, we can summarize this point by saying that consciousness is not reducible in the way that other phenomena are reducible, not because the pattern of facts in the real world involves anything special, but because the reduction of other phenomena depended in part on distinguishing between "objective physical reality," on the one hand, and mere "subjective appearance," on the other; and eliminating the appearance from the phenomena that have been reduced. But in the case of consciousness, its reality is the appearance; hence, the point of the reduction would be lost if we tried to carve off the appearance and simply defined consciousness in terms of the underlying physical reality. In general, the pattern of our reductions rests on rejecting the subjective epistemic basis for the presence of a property as part of the ultimate constituent of that property. We find out about heat or light by feeling and seeing, but we then define the phenomenon in a way that is independent of the epistemology. Consciousness is an exception to this pattern for a trivial reason. The reason, to repeat, is that the reductions that leave out the epistemic bases, the appearances, cannot work for the epistemic bases themselves. In such cases, the appearance is the reality.

But this shows that the irreducibility of consciousness is a trivial consequence of the pragmatics of our definitional practices. A trivial result such as this has only trivial consequences. It has no deep metaphysical consequences for the unity of our overall scientific world view. It does not show that consciousness is not part of the ultimate furniture of reality or cannot be a subject of scientific investigation or cannot be brought into our overall physical conception of the universe; it merely shows that in the way that we have decided to carry out reductions, consciousness, by definition, is excluded from a certain pattern of reduction. Consciousness fails to be reducible, not because of some mysterious feature, but simply because by definition it falls outside the pattern of reduction that we have chosen to use for pragmatic reasons. Pretheoretically, consciousness, like solidity, is a surface feature of certain physical systems. But unlike solidity, consciousness cannot be redefined in terms of an underlying microstructure, and the surface features then treated as mere effects of real consciousness, without losing the point of having the concept of consciousness in the first place.

So far, the argument of this chapter has been conducted, so to speak, from the point of view of the materialist. We can summarize the point I have been making as follows: The contrast between the reducibility of heat, color, solidity, etc., on the one hand, and the irreducibility of conscious states, on the other hand, does not reflect any distinction in the structure of reality, but a distinction in our definitional practices. We could put the same point from the point of view of the property dualist as follows: The apparent contrast between the irreducibility of consciousness and the reducibility of color, heat, solidity, etc., really was *only* apparent. We did not really eliminate the subjectivity of red, for example, when we reduced red to light reflectances; we simply stopped calling the subjective part "red." We did not eliminate any subjective phenomena whatever with these "reductions"; we simply stopped calling them by their old names. Whether we treat the irreducibility from the materialist or from the dualist point of view, we are still left with a universe that contains an irreducibly subjective physical component as a component of physical reality.

To conclude this part of the discussion, I want to make clear what I am saying and what I am not saying. I am not saying that consciousness is not a strange and wonderful phenomenon. I think, on the contrary, that we ought to be amazed by the fact that evolutionary processes produced nervous systems capable of causing and sustaining subjective conscious states. As I remarked in chapter 4, consciousness is as empirically mysterious to us now as electromagnetism was previously, when people thought the universe must operate entirely on Newtonian principles. But I am saying that once the existence of (subjective, qualitative) consciousness is granted (and no sane person can deny its existence, though many pretend to do so), then there is nothing strange, wonderful, or mysterious about its *irreducibility*. Given its existence, its irreducibility is a trivial consequence of our definitional practices. Its irreducibility has no untoward scientific consequences whatever. Furthermore, when I speak of the irreducibility of consciousness, I am speaking of its *irreducibility according to standard patterns of reduction*. No one can rule out a priori the possibility of a major intellectual revolution that would give us a new—and at present unimaginable—conception of reduction, according to which consciousness would be reducible.

## V. Supervenience

In recent years there has been a lot of heavy going about a relationship between properties called "supervenience" (e.g., Kim 1979, 1982; Haugeland 1982). It is frequently said in discussions in the philosophy of mind that the mental is supervenient on the physical. Intuitively, what is meant by this claim is that mental states are totally dependent on corresponding neurophysiological states in the sense that a difference in mental states would necessarily involve a corresponding difference in neurophysiological states. If, for example, I go from a state of being thirsty to a state of no longer being thirsty, then there must have been some change in my brain states corresponding to the change in my mental states.

On the account that I have been proposing, mental states are supervenient on neurophysiological states in the following respect: Type-identical neurophysiological causes would have type-identical mentalistic effects. Thus, to take the famous brain-in-the-vat example, if you had two brains that were type-identical down to the last molecule, then the causal basis of the mental would guarantee that they would have the same mental phenomena. On this characterization of the supervenience relation, the supervenience of the mental on the physical is marked by the fact that physical states are causally sufficient, though not necessarily causally necessary, for the corresponding mental states. That is just another way of saying that as far as this definition of supervenience is concerned, sameness of neurophysiology guarantees sameness of mentality; but sameness of mentality does not guarantee sameness of neurophysiology.

It is worth emphasizing that this sort of supervenience is *causal* supervenience. Discussions of supervenience were originally introduced in connection with ethics, and the notion in question was not a causal notion. In the early writings of Moore (1922) and Hare (1952), the idea was that moral properties are supervenient on natural properties, that two objects cannot differ solely with respect to, for example, their goodness. If one object is better than another, there must be some other feature in virtue of which the former is better than the latter. But this notion of moral supervenience is not a causal notion. That is, the features of an object that make it good do not *cause* it to be good, they rather *constitute* its goodness. But in the case of mind/brain supervenience, the neural phenomena cause the mental phenomena.

So there are at least two notions of supervenience: a constitutive notion and a causal notion. I believe that only the causal notion is important for discussions of the mind-body problem. In this respect my account differs from the usual accounts of the supervenience of the mental on the physical. Thus Kim (1979, especially p. 45ff.) claims that we should not think of the relation of neural events to their supervening mental events as causal, and indeed he claims that supervening mental events have no causal status apart from their supervenience on neurophysiological events that have "a more direct causal role." "If this be epiphenomenalism, let us make the most of it," he says cheerfully (p. 47).

I disagree with both of these claims. It seems to me obvious from everything we know about the brain that macro mental phenomena are all caused by lower-level micro phenomena.

There is nothing mysterious about such bottom-up causation; it is quite common in the physical world. Furthermore, the fact that the mental features are supervenient on neuronal features in no way diminishes their causal efficacy. The solidity of the piston is causally supervenient on its molecular structure, but this does not make solidity epiphenomenal; and similarly, the causal supervenience of my present back pain on micro events in my brain does not make the pain epiphenomenal.

My conclusion is that once you recognize the existence of bottom-up, micro to macro forms of causation, the notion of supervenience no longer does any work in philosophy. The formal features of the relation are already present in the causal sufficiency of the micro-macro forms of causation. And the analogy with ethics is just a source of confusion. The relation of macro mental features of the brain to its micro neuronal features is totally unlike the relation of goodness to good-making features, and it is confusing to lump them together. As Wittgenstein says somewhere, "If you wrap up different kinds of furniture in enough wrapping paper, you can make them all look the same shape."

# Chapter 6
# The Structure of Consciousness:
# An Introduction

I have made in passing various claims about the nature of consciousness, and it is now time to attempt a more general account. Such a task can seem both impossibly difficult and ludicrously easy. Difficult because, after all, is not the story of our consciousness the story of our whole life? And easy because, after all, are we not closer to consciousness than to anything else? According to the Cartesian tradition, we have immediate and certain knowledge of our own conscious states, so the job ought to be easy. But it is not. For example, I find it easy to describe the objects on the table in front of me, but how, separately and in addition, would I describe my conscious experience of those objects?

Two subjects are crucial to consciousness, but I will have little to say about them because I do not yet understand them well enough. The first is temporality. Since Kant we have been aware of an asymmetry in the way that consciousness relates to space and to time. Although we experience objects and events as both spatially extended and of temporal duration, our consciousness itself is not experienced as spatial, though it is experienced as temporally extended. Indeed, the spatial metaphors for describing time seem almost inevitable for consciousness as well, as when we speak for example of the "stream of consciousness." Notoriously, phenomenological time does not exactly match real time, but I do not know how to account for the systematic character of the disparities.[1]

The second neglected topic is society. I am convinced that the category of "other people" plays a special role in the *structure* of our conscious experiences, a role unlike that of objects and states of affairs; and I believe that this capacity for assigning a special status to other loci of consciousness is both biologically based and is a Background presupposition for all forms of collective intentionality (Searle 1990). But I do not yet know how to demonstrate these claims, nor how to analyze the structure of the social element in individual consciousness.

## I. A Dozen Structural Features

In what follows, I will attempt to describe gross structural features of normal, everyday consciousness. Often the argument I will use for identifying a feature is the absence of the feature in pathological forms.

### 1. Finite Modalities

Human consciousness is manifested in a strictly limited number of modalities. In addition to the five senses of sight, touch, smell, taste, and hearing, and the sixth, the "sense of balance," there are also bodily sensations ("proprioception") and the stream of thought. By bodily sensations, I mean not only obvious physical sensations, such as pains, but also my sensory awareness, for example, of the position of my arms and legs or the feeling in my right knee. The stream of thought contains not only words and images, both visual and otherwise, but other elements as well, which are neither verbal nor imagistic. For example, a thought sometimes occurs to one suddenly, "in a flash," in a form that is neither in words nor images. Furthermore, the stream of thought, as I am using this expression, includes feelings, such as those generally called "emotions." For example, in the stream of thought I might feel a sudden surge of anger or a desire to hit someone or a strong thirst for a glass of water.

There is no a priori reason why consciousness should be limited to these forms. It just seems to be a fact about human evolutionary history that these are the forms that our species has developed. There is good evidence that certain other species have other sensory modalities. Vision is especially important in human beings, and according to some neurophysiological accounts, over half of our cortex is dedicated to visual functions.

Another general feature of each modality is that it can occur under the aspect of pleasant or unpleasant, and the way in which it is pleasant/unpleasant is in general specific to the modality. For example, pleasant smells are not pleasant in way that pleasant thoughts are pleasant, even pleasant thoughts about pleasant smells. Often but not always, the pleasure/unpleasure aspect of conscious modalities is associated with a form of intentionality. Thus, in the case of visual experiences, it is in general the intentionality internal to the visual experiences rather than their purely sensory aspects that is pleasant or unpleasant. We find it unpleasant to see something disgusting, such as a man throwing up; and we find it pleasant to see something impressive, such as the stars on a clear night. But in each case, it is more than the purely visual aspects of the scene that are the source of the pleasant or unpleasant character. This is not always the case with bodily sensations. Pain can be simply experienced as painful, without any correlated intentionality. However, the unpleasantness of the pain will vary with certain sorts of associated intentionality. If one believes the pain is being inflicted unjustly, it is more unpleasant than if one believes it is being inflicted, for example, as part of a necessary medical treatment. Orgasms are similarly colored by intentionality. One could easily imagine an orgasm occurring without any erotic thoughts whatever— suppose, for example, it was induced by electrical means—but in general, the pleasure of an orgasm is internally related to its intentionality, even though orgasms are bodily sensations. In this section I am concerned only with the pleasure/unpleasure of each modality. I shall discuss the pleasure/unpleasure of total conscious states as feature 12.

## 2. Unity

It is characteristic of nonpathological conscious states that they come to us as part of a unified sequence. I do not just have an experience of a toothache and also a visual experience of the couch that is situated a few feet from me and of roses that are sticking out from the vase on my right, in the way that I happen to have on a striped shirt at the same time as I have on dark blue socks. The crucial difference is this: I have my experiences of the rose, the couch, and the toothache all as experiences that are part of one and the same conscious event. Unity exists in at least two dimensions, which, continuing the spatial metaphors, I will call "horizontal" and "vertical." Horizontal unity is the organization of conscious experiences through short stretches of time. For example, when I speak or think a sentence, even a long one, my awareness of the beginning of what I said or thought continues even when that part is no longer being thought or spoken. Iconic memory of this sort is essential to the unity of consciousness, and perhaps even short-term memory is essential. Vertical unity is a matter of the simultaneous awareness of all the diverse features of any conscious state, as illustrated by my example of the couch, the toothache, and the rose. We have little understanding of how the brain achieves this unity. In neurophysiology it is called "the binding problem," and Kant called the same phenomenon "the transcendental unity of apperception."

Without these two features—the horizontal unity of the remembered present[2] and the vertical unity of the binding of the elements into a unified column—we could not make normal sense of our experiences. This is illustrated by the various forms of pathology such as the split-brain phenomena (Gazzaniga 1970) and Korsakov's syndrome (Sacks 1985).

### 3. Intentionality

Most, but not all, consciousness is intentional. I may, for example, simply be in a mood of depression or elation without being depressed or elated about anything in particular. In these cases, my mood, as such, is not intentional. But in general in any conscious state, the state is directed at something or other, even if the thing it is directed at does not exist, and in that sense it has intentionality. For a very large number of cases, consciousness is indeed consciousness of something, and the "of" in "consciousness of" is the "of" of intentionality.

The reason we find it difficult to distinguish between my description of the objects on the table and my description of my experience of the objects is that the features of the objects are precisely the conditions of satisfaction of my conscious experiences of them. So the vocabulary I use to describe the table—"There's a lamp on the right and a vase on the left and a small statue in the middle"—is precisely that which I use to describe my conscious visual experiences of the table. To describe the experiences I have to say, for example, "It seems to me visually that there is a lamp on the right, a vase on the left, and a small statue in the middle."

My conscious experiences, unlike the objects of the experiences, are always perspectival. They are always from a point of view. But the objects themselves have no point of view. Perspective and point of view are most obvious for vision, but of course they are features of our other sensory experiences as well. If I touch the table, I experience it only under certain aspects and from a certain spatial location. If I hear a sound, I hear it only from a certain direction and hear certain aspects of it. And so on.

Noticing the perspectival character of conscious experience is a good way to remind ourselves that *all intentionality is aspectual.* Seeing an object from a point of view, for example, is seeing it under certain aspects and not others. In this sense, all seeing is "seeing as." And what goes for seeing goes for all forms of intentionality, conscious and unconscious. All representations represent their objects, or other conditions of satisfaction, under aspects. Every intentional state has what I call *an aspectual shape.*

### 4. Subjective Feeling

The discussion of intentionality naturally leads into the subjective feel of our conscious states. I had occasion, in earlier chapters, to discuss subjectivity at some length, so I will not belabor the point here. Suffice it to say here that the subjectivity necessarily involves the what-it-feels-like aspect of conscious states. So, for example, I can reasonably wonder what it feels like to be a dolphin and swim around all day, frolicking in the ocean, because I assume dolphins have conscious experiences. But I cannot in that sense wonder what it feels like to be a shingle nailed to a roof year in and year out, because in the sense in which we are using this expression, there isn't anything at all that it feels like to be a shingle, because shingles are not conscious.

As I pointed out earlier, subjectivity is responsible, more than anything else, for the philosophical puzzlement concerning consciousness.

### 5. The Connection between Consciousness and Intentionality
I hope most of what I have said so far seems obvious. I now want to make a very strong claim, one that I will not fully substantiate until the next chapter. The claim is this: Only a being that could have conscious intentional states could have intentional states at all, and every unconscious intentional state is at least potentially conscious. This thesis has enormous consequences for the study of the mind. It implies, for example, that any discussion of intentionality that leaves out the question of consciousness will be incomplete. It is possible to describe the logical structure of intentional phenomena without discussing consciousness—indeed, for the most part, I did so in *Intentionality* (Searle 1983), but there is a conceptual connection between consciousness and intentionality that has the consequence that a complete theory of intentionality requires an account of consciousness.

### 6. The Figure-Ground, Gestalt Structure of Conscious Experience
It is a familiar point from Gestalt psychology that our perceptual experiences come to us as a figure against a background. For example, if I see the sweater on the table in front of me, I see the sweater against the background of the table. If I see the

table, I see it against the background of the floor. If I see the floor, I see it against the background of the whole room, until finally we reach the limits of my visual field. But what is characteristic of perception seems to be characteristic of consciousness generally: that whatever I focus my attention on will be against a background that is not the center of attention; and the larger the scope of the attention, the nearer we reach the limits of my consciousness where the background will simply be the boundary conditions that I will discuss further as feature number 10.

Related to the figure-ground structure of conscious experiences is the fact that our normal perceptions are always structured; that I perceive not just undifferentiated shapes, but that my perceptions are organized into objects and features of objects. This has the consequence that all (normal) seeing is *seeing as*, all (normal) perceiving is *perceiving as*, and indeed, all consciousness is *consciousness of something as such and such*.

There are two different but related features here. One is the figure-ground structure of perception and consciousness generally, and the second is the organization of our perceptual and other conscious experiences. The figure-ground structure is a special, though pervasive, case of the more general feature of structuredness. Another related feature, which I will discuss shortly as feature number 10, is the general boundary conditions that seem applicable to any conscious state at all.

### 7. The Aspect of Familiarity

Given the temporality, sociality, unity, intentionality, subjectivity, and structuredness of consciousness, it seems to me the most pervasive feature of ordinary, nonpathological states of conscious awareness is what I will call "the aspect of familiarity." As all conscious intentionality is aspectual (feature 3), and because nonpathological forms of consciousness are structured or organized (feature 6), the prior possession of an apparatus sufficient to generate aspectual and organized consciousness automatically guarantees that the aspectual features of con-

scious experience and the occurring structures and organization of consciousness will be more or less familiar, in ways I
will now try to explain.

One can best get at the aspect of familiarity by contrasting
my account with Wittgenstein's. Wittgenstein asks us (1953)
whether when I enter my room, I experience an "act of recognition," and he reminds us that there is in fact no such act. I
believe he is right about this. Nonetheless, when I enter my
room, *it does look familiar to me*. You can see this if you imagine
that something was radically unfamiliar, if there were a large
elephant in the middle of the room, or if the ceiling had collapsed, or if somebody had put in completely different furniture, for example. But in the normal everyday case, the room
looks familiar to me. Now, what is true of my experience of
the room, I suggest, is in greater or lesser degree true of my
experiences of the world. When I walk down the street, these
objects are familiar to me as houses, and these other objects are
familiar to me as people. I experience the trees, the sidewalk,
the streets as part of the familiar. And even when I am in a
strange city and am struck by the oddity of the dress of the
people or the strangeness of the architecture of their houses,
there is nonetheless the aspect of familiarity. These are still
people; those are still houses; I am still an embodied being,
with a conscious sense of my own weight, a sense of the forces
of gravity acting on me and on other objects; I have an inner
sense of my bodily parts and their positions. Perhaps most
important of all, I have an inner sense of what it feels like to be
me, a feeling of myself.[3]

It takes an intellectual effort to break this aspect of familiarity. So, for example, surrealist painters draw landscapes in
which there are no familiar objects. But even in such cases, we
still sense objects in an environment, a horizon of the earth,
gravitational attraction of the objects to the earth, light coming
from a source, a point of view from which the picture is
painted, ourselves looking at the picture—and all of these
sensings are parts of the aspect of familiarity of our consciousness. The drooping watch is still a watch, the three-headed

woman is still a woman. It is this aspect of familiarity—more than, for example, inductive predictability—that prevents conscious states from being the "blooming, buzzing confusion" described by William James.

I have been deliberately using the expression "aspect of familiarity" rather than the more colloquial "feeling of familiarity" because I want to emphasize that the phenomenon I am discussing is not a separate feeling. When I see my shoes, for example, I do not have both a visual experience of the shoes, and a feeling of familiarity, but rather I *see* the shoes at once *as* shoes and *as* mine. The aspect of familiarity is not a separate experience, and that is why Wittgenstein is right in saying there is no act of recognition when I see my room. Nonetheless, it does look to me like my room, and I do perceive it under this aspect of familiarity.

The aspect of familiarity comes in varying degrees; it is a scalar phenomenon. At the top of the familiarity scale are the objects, scenes, people, and sights of my ordinary, everyday life. Lower down are strange scenes in which the objects and people are nonetheless easily recognizable and categorizable by me. Yet further down are scenes in which I find little that is recognizable or categorizable. These are the sorts of scenes depicted by surrealist painters. It is possible to imagine a limiting case in which absolutely nothing was perceived as familiar, in which nothing was recognizable and categorizable, not even as objects, where even my own body was no longer categorizable as mine or even as a body. Such a case would be pathological in the extreme. Less extreme forms of pathology occur when familiar scenes suddenly lose their familiarity—when, for example, in states of neurotic desperation one stares at the texture of the wood in the table and becomes totally lost in it, as if one had never seen such a thing before.

It is the aspect of familiarity that makes possible much of the organization and order of my conscious experiences. Even if I find an elephant in my room or a collapsed ceiling, nonetheless, the object is still familiar to me as an elephant or a collapsed ceiling and the room as my room. Psychologists have a lot of evidence to show that perception is a function of expectation (e.g., Postman, Bruner, and Walk 1951). A natural corollary of this claim is that the organization of perception is only possible given a set of categories that identify entities within the familiar.

I think the feature of experience that I am alluding to will be recognizable by anyone who thinks about it, but to describe the structure of the intentionality involved is fairly tricky. Objects and states of affairs are experienced by me as familiar, but the familiarity is not in general a separate condition of satisfaction. Rather, consciousness involves categorization—I see things, for example, as trees, people, houses, cars, etc.—but the categories have to exist prior to the experience, because they are the conditions of possibility of having just these experiences. To see this as a duck or a rabbit, I have to have the categories "duck" or "rabbit" prior to the perception. So the perception will be under the aspect of familiarity, because the categories that make it possible are themselves familiar categories. The argument in a nutshell is: All perceiving is perceiving as, and more generally, all consciousness *of* is consciousness *as*. To be conscious of something you have to be conscious of it as something ( again, barring pathology and the like), but perceiving as, and other forms of consciousness as, require categories. But preexisting categories imply prior familiarity with the categories, hence the perceptions are under the aspect of the familiar. *So these features hang together: structuredness, perception as, the aspectual shape of all intentionality, categories, and the aspect of familiarity. Conscious experiences come to us as structured, those structures enable us to perceive things under aspects, but those aspects are constrained by our mastery of a set of categories, and those categories, being familiar, enable us, in varying degrees, to assimilate our experiences, however novel, to the familiar.*

I am not here making the fallacious argument that because we experience under familiar aspects, we therefore experience an aspect of familiarity. That is not the point at all. The point rather is that nonpathological forms of consciousness do in fact have an aspect of familiarity; and this is accounted for by the fact that we have Background capacities, realized neurobiologically, to generate experiences that are both structured and aspectual, where specific structures and aspects are more or less familiar. The capacities in question are not part of consciousness but are part of the Background (more about the Background in chapter 8).

### 8. Overflow

Conscious states in general refer beyond their immediate content. I call this phenomenon, "overflow." Consider an extreme sort of case. Sally looks at Sam and suddenly has a thought in a flash: "That's it!" If asked to state the thought, she might begin, "Well, I suddenly realized that for the past eighteen months I have been wasting my time in a relationship with someone who is totally inappropriate for me, that whatever its other merits, my relationship with Sam was founded on a false premise on my part. It suddenly occurred to me that I could never have an enduring relationship with the head of a motorcycle gang like the Hell's Angels because. . ." And so on.

In such a case the immediate content tends to spill over, to connect with other thoughts that in a sense were part of the content but in a sense were not. Though it is best illustrated with an extreme case like this, I think the phenomenon is general. For example, as I look out the window now at the trees and the lake, if asked to describe what I see, the answer would have an indefinite extendability. I don't just see these as trees, but as pines, as like the pines of California, but in some ways different, as like in these respects but unlike in those, etc.

### 9. The Center and the Periphery

Within the field of consciousness, we need to distinguish between those things that are at the center of our attention and those that are at the periphery. We are conscious of a very large number of things that we are not attending to or focusing our attention upon. For example, up to this moment I have been focusing my attention on the philosophical problem of describing consciousness, and I have not been paying any attention to the feeling of the chair against my back, the tightness of my shoes, or the slight headache I have from drinking too much wine last night. Nonetheless, all of these phenomena are part of my conscious awareness. In colloquial speech, we often talk of such features of our conscious life as being unconscious, but it is a mistake to say that, for example, I am unconscious of the feeling of my shirt against my skin in the sense in which I am unconscious of the growth of my toenails. In short, we need to distinguish the conscious/unconscious distinction from the center of attention/periphery distinction.

Consider another example. When I drove to my office today, most of my attention was on philosophical thoughts. However, it is not true to say that I drove unconsciously. Unconscious driving would have led to automotive disaster. I was conscious throughout the journey, but the center of my concern was not with the traffic and the route, rather it was with thoughts of philosophical problems. This example illustrates that it is essential to distinguish between different levels of attention within conscious states. When I drove to the office this morning, my highest level of attention was on philosophical problems that are bothering me. At a lower level of attention, but still a level that can literally be described as *attention*, I was paying attention to the driving. And indeed, on occasion things would happen that would require my *full attention*, such that I would stop thinking about philosophy and focus all of my attention on the road. In addition to these two levels of attention, there were also many things that I was peripherally aware of, but that were nowhere near the center of my attention. These would include such things as the trees and houses on the side of the road as I passed, the feeling of the seatback of the car against my back and the steering wheel in my hands, and the music playing from the car radio.

It is important to try to get these distinctions right because the temptation is often to say that many things that are on the periphery of our consciousness are really unconscious. And that is wrong. Dreyfus (1991) frequently quotes Heidegger's example of the skilled carpenter hammering. The carpenter, as he hammers the nails, may be thinking about his girlfriend, or about lunch, and not focusing all of his attention on the hammering. But it is still totally wrong to suggest that he is unconscious of hammering. Unless he is a total zombie or an unconscious machine, he is fully conscious of his hammering, though it is not at the center of his attention.

William James formulated a law of which it is useful to remind ourselves: He expressed it as, "Consciousness goes away from where it is not needed." I think it is better expressed as, "Attention goes away from where it is not needed." When, for example, I first put on my shoes, the pressure and the feel of the shoes are at the center of my consciousness; or when I sit down in a chair, the feeling of the chair is at the center of my consciousness. But these focusings really are not necessary to enable me to cope with the world, and after a while the features of shoes and chair retreat to the periphery of my consciousness; they are no longer at the center. If I get a nail in my shoe or if I fall off the chair, then such experiences move to the center of my consciousness. I believe that James's point is about the center and periphery of consciousness, rather than about consciousness as such.

## 10. Boundary Conditions

In the course of reflecting about the present, I have at no point had any thoughts concerning where I am located, what day of the month it is, what time of year it is, how long it is since I had breakfast, what my name and past history are, which country I am a citizen of, and so on. Yet it seems to me, all of these are part of the situatedness, part of the spatio-temporal-socio-biological location of my present conscious states. Any state of consciousness is in that way characteristically located. But the location may itself not be at all the object of consciousness, not even at the periphery.

One way to notice the pervasiveness of the boundary of consciousness is in cases of its breakdown. There is, for example, a sense of disorientation that comes over one when one suddenly is unable to recall what month it is, or where one is, or what time of day it is.

## 11. Mood

I mentioned earlier that often we have moods that are not themselves intentional, though they are conscious. I can be in an elated mood or a depressed mood, a cheerful mood or a downcast mood, and these need not be consciously directed at any intentional conditions of satisfaction. A mood, by itself, never constitutes the whole content of a conscious state. Rather, the mood provides the tone or color that characterizes the whole of a conscious state or sequence of conscious states.

Are we always in some mood or other? The answer depends on how broadly we want to construe the notion of mood. We certainly are not always in a mood that has a name in a language like English. At present, I am neither especially elated nor especially depressed; I am neither ecstatic nor in despair; nor indeed am I simply blah. Yet is seems to me there is what one might call a "tone" to my present experiences. And this seems to me to be properly assimilable to the general notion of mood. The fact that my present experiences have a somewhat neutral tone does not mean they have no tone to them at all. It is characteristic of moods that they pervade all of our conscious experiences. For the man who is elated, the sight of the tree and the landscape and the sky is a source of great joy; for the man in despair, the very same sight produces only further depression. It seems to me it is characteristic of normal human conscious life that we are always in some mood or other, and that this mood pervades all of our conscious forms of intentionality, even though it is not itself, or need not itself be, intentional.

Nothing makes one more aware of the pervasiveness of mood than a dramatic shift. When one's normal mood is radically shifted either up or down, either into an unexpected elation or depression, one suddenly becomes aware of the fact that one is always in some mood and that one's mood pervades one's conscious states. For many people depression, alas, is much more common than elation.

My guess is that we will get a good neurobiological account of mood rather more easily than of, say, the emotions. Moods are pervasive, they are rather simple, especially because they have no essential intentionality, and it looks like there ought even to be a biochemical account of some moods. We already have drugs that are used to alleviate clinical depression.

## 12. The Pleasure/Unpleasure Dimension

Remember that we are considering the whole of a conscious state, a slice out of the stream of consciousness big enough to have the unity and coherence I am trying to describe. For such a chunk, it seems to me there is always a dimension of pleasure and unpleasure. One can always ask at least some questions in the inventory that includes, "Was is fun or not?" "Did you enjoy it or not?" "Were you in pain, exasperated, annoyed, amused, bored, ecstatic, nauseous, disgusted, enthusiastic, terrified, irritated, enchanted, happy, unhappy, etc. ?" Furthermore, within the pleasure/unpleasure dimension there are many subdimensions. It is possible, though eccentric, to be bored during sexual ecstasy and exultant during physical pain. As with mood, we must avoid the mistake of supposing that the intermediate and therefore nameless positions on the scale are not on the scale at all.

## II. Three Traditional Mistakes

I now turn to three theses about conscious states, which, though they are quite widely accepted, seem to me, on a natural interpretation, false. They are:

1. All conscious states are self-conscious.
2. Consciousness is known by a special faculty of introspection.
3. Knowledge of our own conscious states is incorrigible. We cannot be mistaken about such matters.

Let us consider each in turn.

## 1. Self-Consciousness

It is sometimes argued[4] that every state of consciousness is also a state of self-consciousness; that it is characteristic of conscious mental states that they are, so to speak, conscious of themselves. I am not quite sure what to make of this claim, but I suspect that if we examine it, we will find that it is either trivially true or simply false.

To begin, we need to distinguish the ordinary unproblematic notion of self-consciousness from the technical philosopher's notion. In the ordinary sense, there clearly are states of consciousness in which I am conscious of my own person, perhaps, but not necessarily conscious of my own conscious states. We can illustrate these points with examples.

First, suppose I am sitting in a restaurant eating a steak. In the ordinary sense, I would characteristically not be *self*-conscious at all. I might be conscious that the steak tastes good, that the wine I am washing it down with is too young, that the potatoes are overcooked, etc. But there is no self-consciousness.

Second, suppose that I suddenly notice that everyone in the restaurant is staring at me. I might wonder why they are all gaping in that way until I discover that in fit of absentmindedness, I have forgotten to wear my trousers. I am sitting there in my underwear. Such a circumstance might produce feelings that we would normally describe as "acute self-consciousness." I am aware of my own person and the effect I am having on others. But even here my self-consciousness is not directed at my own conscious states.

Third, imagine that I am now in the restaurant fully clothed, and I suddenly focus all my attention on the conscious experiences I am having in the restaurant eating the meal and drinking the wine. Suddenly, for example, it seems to me that I have been inexcusably wallowing in a kind of hyperesthetic self-indulgence to have put so much time, effort, and money into securing *these* gastronomic experiences. Suddenly it all seems *de trop*.

This case also seems one of self-consciousness in the ordinary sense, but it differs from the second in that the self-consciousness is directed at the states of consciousness of the agent himself and not at his public persona.

Now in the ordinary sense of self-consciousness, as exemplified by cases two and three, it just seems false that every case of consciousness is a case of self-consciousness. In the ordinary sense, self-consciousness is an extremely sophisticated form of sensibility and is probably possessed only by humans and perhaps a few other species.

So it must be that the claim that all consciousness involves self-consciousness is intended in a technical sense. What is that sense? We saw in our discussion of the distinction between the center and the periphery that we can always shift our attention from the objects at the center of consciousness to those at the periphery, so that what was previously peripheral becomes central. Similarly, it seems that we can always shift our attention from the *object* of the conscious experience to the *experience* itself. We can always, for example, make the move made by the impressionist painters. Impressionist painters produced a revolution in painting by shifting their attention from the object to the actual visual experience they had when they looked at the object. This is a case of self-consciousness about the character of experiences. It seems to me that we could get a sense of "self-consciousness" where it is trivially true that any conscious state is self-conscious: In any conscious state, we can shift our attention to the state itself. I can focus my attention, for example, not on the scene in front of me but on the experience of my seeing this very scene. And because the possibility of that shift of attention was present in the state itself, we can say, in this very special technical sense, that every conscious state is self-conscious.

But I doubt very much that this is the sense intended by those who claim that all consciousness is self-consciousness. Except for this very special sense, it seems just false to make that claim.

## 2. Introspection
Are conscious mental states known by a special capacity, the capacity for introspecting? In earlier chapters I have tried to cast doubt on this view, which is prevalent both in philosophy and in common sense. As in the case of self-consciousness, there is both a technical and a commonsense notion of introspection. In the ordinary sense, we often introspect our own

conscious states. Suppose, for example, that Sally wants to know whether or not she should marry Jimmy, who has just proposed. Well, one of her procedures might reasonably be to examine her feelings very closely. And this, in ordinary English, we would call a form of introspection. She asks herself such questions as, "Do I really love him, and if so, how much?," "What are my deepest feelings about him?," etc. The problem, I believe, is not with the ordinary use of the notion of introspection, but with our urge as philosophers to take the metaphor literally. The metaphor suggests that we have a capacity to examine our own conscious states, a capacity modeled on vision. But that model or analogy is surely wrong. In the case of vision, we have a clear distinction between the object seen and the visual experience that the perceiver has when he perceives the object. But we can't make that distinction for the act of introspection of one's own conscious mental states. When Sally turns her attention inward to introspect her deepest feelings about Jimmy, she can't step back to get a good view and direct her gaze at the independently existing object of her feelings for Jimmy. In short, if by "introspection" we mean simply thinking about our own mental states, then there is no objection to introspection. It happens all the time, and is crucial for any form of self-knowledge. But if by "introspection" we mean a special capacity, just like vision only less colorful, that we have to *spect intro*, then it seems to me there is no such capacity. There could not be, because the model of specting intro requires a distinction between the object spected and the specting of it, and we cannot make this distinction for conscious states. We can direct one mental state at another; we can think about our thoughts and feelings; and we can have feelings about our thoughts and feelings; but none of these involves a special faculty of introspection.

### 3. Incorrigibility
It is often said that we can't be mistaken about the contents of our own minds. On the traditional Cartesian conception of the

mind, first-person reports of mental states are somehow *incorrigible*. According to this view, we have a certain kind of *first-person authority* in reports of our mental states. It has even been maintained that this incorrigibility is a sure sign that something is mental (Rorty 1970). But if you think about it for a moment, the claim of incorrigibility seems obviously false. Consider Sally and Jimmy. Sally might later come to realize that she was simply mistaken when she thought she was in love with Jimmy; that the feeling was incorrectly ascribed; it was in fact only a form of infatuation. And someone who knew her well might know from the beginning that she was mistaken.

Given such facts, why would anyone think that it was impossible for one to be mistaken about the contents of one's own mental states? Why would one ever suppose they were "incorrigible" to begin with? Perhaps the answer has to do with confusing the subjective ontology of the mental with epistemic certainty. It is indeed the case that conscious mental states have a subjective ontology, as I have said repeatedly in the course of this book. But from the fact of subjective ontology it does not follow that one cannot be mistaken about one's mental states. All that follows is that the standard models of mistake, models based on the appearance-reality distinction, don't work for the existence or characterization of mental states. But these are not the only possible forms of being mistaken about a phenomenon. We all know from our own experiences that it often happens that someone else is in a better position than we are to determine whether or not we are really, for example, jealous, angry, or feeling generous. It is true that the way that I stand to my mental states, and therefore the way that I stand to my reports of my mental states, is different from the way that other people stand to my mental states. And this affects the status of their reports of my mental states. Nevertheless, their reports may be more accurate than mine.

In what sense exactly am I supposed to have first-person authority about the contents of my own mind and why? Wittgenstein, in *Philosophical Investigations* (1953), tried valiantly to eliminate the idea that we should think of my first-person mental utterances as *reports or descriptions at all*. If we could, as Wittgenstein suggested, think of them rather as expressions (*Aeusserungen*), then they would not be reports or descriptions at all, and hence there would be no question of any authority. When I simply cry out in pain, there isn't any question about authority, because my pain behavior was simply a natural reaction caused by the pain, and not any sort of claim. If my saying "I am in pain" could similarly be treated as a kind of ritualized cry, a conventionalized form of pain behavior, then there wouldn't be any question about my authority. I think that it is fair to say that Wittgenstein's attempted solution to this problem has failed. There are indeed some cases where one's verbal behavior regarding one's mental states is more naturally regarded as a form of expression of the mental phenomenon rather than a description of it (e.g., Ouch!), but there are still many cases in which one is attempting to give a careful statement or description of one's mental state and not simply give expression to that state. Now what sort of "authority" does one have in such utterances, and why?

I think the way to get at what is special about first-person reports is to ask why we do not think we have the same special authority about objects and states of affairs in the world *other* than our mental states. The reason is that in our reports of the world at large, there is a distinction between how things seem to us and how they really are. It can seem to me that there is a man hiding in the bushes outside my window, when in fact the appearance was simply caused by the peculiar pattern of light and shadow on the shrubbery. But for how things seem to me, there is no reality/appearance distinction to be made. It really does seem to me there is a man hiding in the bushes. Where intentional mental states are concerned, the states themselves are constitutive of the seeming. The origin, in short, of our conviction of a special first-person authority lies simply in the fact that we cannot make the conventional reality/appearance distinction for appearances themselves. This leaves us with two questions. First, how is it possible that we can be mistaken about our own mental states? What, so to speak, is the *form* of the mistake that we make, if it is not the same as the appearance/reality mistakes we make about the world at large? And second, as appearances are themselves part of reality, why shouldn't we be able to make the reality/appearance distinction for appearances? We can begin to answer the first question if we explore some of the ways one can be mistaken about whether or not one, for example, is angry. Leaving out the question of purely linguistic errors—that is, leaving out cases in which a man thinks, for example, that the word "angry" means happy—some typical cases where one gives misdescriptions of one's own mental phenomena are self-deception, misinterpretation, and inattention. I will consider each of these in turn.

It seems easy enough to "prove" the impossibility of self-deception, but self-deception is nonetheless a pervasive psychological phenomenon, and therefore there must be something wrong with the proof. The proof goes as follows: In order that $x$ deceive $y$, $x$ must have a belief that $p$ and must successfully attempt to induce in $y$ the belief that not $p$. But in the case where $x$ is identical with $y$, it looks like $x$ would have to produce in himself the self-contradictory belief that $p$ and not $p$. And this seems impossible.

Yet we know that self-deception is possible. No doubt there are many forms of self-deception, but in one very common form the agent has a motive or reason for not admitting to himself that he is in a certain mental state. He may be ashamed of the fact that he is angry or that he hates a certain person or a certain class of people. In such cases, the agent simply resists consciously thinking about certain of his psychological states. When the thought of these states arises, he immediately thinks of the converse state that he wishes he in fact held. Suppose that he hates the members of a minority group, but is ashamed of this prejudice and consciously wishes that he did not have this hatred. When confronted with the evidence of his prejudice, he simply refuses to admit it, and indeed, vehemently and sincerely denies it. The agent has a hatred together with a desire not to have that hatred, that is, a form of shame about that hatred. To reconcile these two, the agent avoids consciously thinking about his hatred and thus is able sincerely to refuse to admit the existence of this hatred when confronted with evidence. This is surely one common form of self-deception.

A second form of "mistake" that one can make about one's own mental phenomena is misinterpretation. For example, in the heat of a passion a man may think he is in love, indeed, quite sincerely think he is in love, but later come to realize that at the time he simply misinterpreted his feelings. Crucial to this sort of case is the operation of the Network and the Background. Just as a person may misinterpret a text by failing to see how the elements of the text relate to each other, and by failing to understand the operation of the Background circumstances in which the text was composed, so a person may misinterpret his own intentional states by failing to see their interrelationships and by failing to locate them correctly relative to the Background of nonrepresentational mental capacities. In such cases we do not have the traditional epistemic model of making incorrect *inferences* on the basis of insufficient *evidence*. It is not a question of getting from appearance to reality, but rather of locating a piece in a puzzle relative to a whole lot of other pieces.

A final and indeed obvious case of "mistake" about one's own mental states is simple inattention. In the sheer chaotic busyness of life we often do not pay close attention to our conscious states. For example, a famous politician recently announced in the press that she had been mistaken in thinking that she was sympathetic to the Democrats. Without her noticing it, her sympathies had shifted to the Republicans. What we have in her case is a whole Network of intentionality—such things as attitudes toward legislation, sympathy with certain classes of politicians and hostility toward others, reactions to certain events in foreign policy, etc.—and this Network had shifted without her being aware of it. In such cases our mistakes are a matter of the focusing of attention, rather than the traditional distinction between appearance and reality.

### III. Conclusion

I believe that at least two, and perhaps all three, mistakes have a common origin in Cartesianism. Philosophers in the Cartesian tradition in epistemology wanted consciousness to provide a foundation for all knowledge. But for consciousness to give us a certain foundation for knowledge, we must first have certain knowledge of conscious states; hence the doctrine of incorrigibility. To know consciousness with certainty, we must know it by means of some special faculty that gives us direct access to it; hence the doctrine of introspection. And—though I am less confident about this as a historical diagnosis—if the self is to be the source of all knowledge and meaning, and these are to be based on its own consciousness, then it is natural to think that there is a necessary connection between consciousness and self-consciousness; hence the doctrine of self-consciousness.

In any case, several recent attacks on consciousness, such as Dennett's (1991), are based on the mistaken assumption that if we can show that there is something wrong with the doctrine of incorrigibility or introspection, we have shown that there is something wrong with consciousness. But nothing could be further from the truth. Incorrigibility and introspection have nothing to do with the essential features of consciousness. They are simply elements of mistaken philosophical theories about it.

# Chapter 7

# The Unconscious and
# Its Relation to Consciousness

The aim of this chapter is to explain the relations between unconscious mental states and consciousness. The explanatory power of the notion of the unconscious is so great that we cannot do without it, but the notion is far from clear. This unclarity has had some unfortunate consequences, as we will see. I will also say something about the Freudian conception of the relation between consciousness and the unconscious, because I believe that at base it is incoherent. I will make heavy use of the distinctions between epistemology, causation, and ontology that I explained in chapter 1.

## I. The Unconscious

Earlier generations—prior to the twentieth century, roughly speaking—found the notion of consciousness unproblematic and the notion of the unconscious mind puzzling, perhaps even self-contradictory. We have reversed the roles. After Freud, we routinely invoke unconscious mental phenomena to explain human beings, and we find the notion of consciousness puzzling and perhaps even unscientific. This shift in explanatory emphasis has taken different forms, but the general tendency in cognitive science has been to drive a wedge between conscious, subjective mental processes, which are not regarded as a proper subject of scientific investigation, and those processes that are regarded as the genuine subject matter of cognitive science—and which, therefore, must be objective. The general theme is that unconscious mental processes are more important than conscious ones. Perhaps the strongest statement is in Lashley's claim, *"No activity of mind is ever con-*

*scious*" (Lashley's italics).[1] Another extreme version of this approach is to be found in Ray Jackendoff's claim (1987) that in fact there are two "notions of mind," the "computational mind" and the "phenomenological mind."

I believe that in spite of our complacency in using the concept of the unconscious, we do not have a clear notion of unconscious mental states, and my first task in clarification is to explain the relations between the unconscious and consciousness. The claim I will make can be stated in one sentence: *The notion of an unconscious mental state implies accessibility to consciousness.* We have no notion of the unconscious except as that which is potentially conscious.

Our naive, pretheoretical notion of an *unconscious* mental state is the idea of a conscious mental state minus the consciousness. But what exactly does that mean? How could we subtract the consciousness from a mental state and still have a *mental* state left over? Since Freud, we have grown so used to talking about unconscious mental states that we have lost sight of the fact that the answer to this question is by no means obvious. Yet it is clear that we do think of the unconscious on the model of the conscious. Our idea of an unconscious state is the idea of a mental state that just happens then and there to be unconscious; but we still understand it on the model of a conscious state, in the sense that we think of it as being just like a conscious state and as one that in some sense could have been conscious. This is clearly true, for example, in Freud, whose notions of both what he calls "preconscious" and "unconscious" states is built on a rather simple model of conscious states (Freud 1949, esp. pp. 19–25). At its most naive, our picture is something like this: Unconscious mental states in the mind are like fish deep in the sea. The fish that we can't see underneath the surface have exactly the same shape they have when they surface. The fish don't lose their shapes by going under water. Another simile: Unconscious mental states are like objects stored in the dark attic of the mind. These objects have their shapes all along, even when you can't see them. We are tempted to smile at these simple models, but I think something like these pictures underlies our conception of unconscious mental states, and it is important to try to see what is right and what wrong about that conception.

As I mentioned earlier, there has been in recent decades a fairly systematic effort to separate consciousness from intentionality. The connection between the two is being gradually lost, not only in cognitive science but in linguistics and philosophy as well. I think the underlying—and perhaps unconscious—motivation for this urge to separate intentionality from consciousness is that we do not know how to explain consciousness, and we would like to get a theory of the mind that will not be discredited by the fact that it lacks a theory of consciousness. The idea is to treat intentionality "objectively," to treat it as if the subjective features of consciousness did not really matter to it. For example, many functionalists will concede that functionalism can't "handle" consciousness (this is called the problem of *qualia*; see chapter 2), but they think that this issue doesn't matter to their accounts of belief, desire, etc., because these intentional states have no *quale*, no special conscious qualities. They can be treated as if they were completely independent of consciousness. Similarly, both the idea of some linguists that there are rules of syntax that are psychologically real but totally inaccessible to consciousness, and the idea of some psychologists that there are complex inferences in perception that are genuine psychological inferential processes but inaccessible to consciousness, imply a separation between intentionality and consciousness. The idea in both cases is not that there are mental phenomena that just happen to be unconscious, but that somehow, in some way, they are *in principle* inaccessible to consciousness. They are not the sort of thing that could be or could ever have been conscious.

I think these recent developments are mistaken. For deep reasons, our notion of an unconscious mental state is parasitic on our notion of a conscious state. Of course, at any given moment a person may be unconscious; he or she may be asleep, in a coma, etc.; and of course, many mental states are never brought to consciousness. And no doubt there are many that could not be brought to consciousness for one reason or another—they may be too painful and hence too deeply repressed for us to think of them, for example. Nonetheless, not every state of an agent is a mental state, and not even every state of the brain that functions essentially in the *production* of mental phenomena is itself a mental phenomenon. So what makes something mental when it is not conscious? For a state to be a mental state, and a fortiori for it to be an intentional mental state, certain conditions must be met. What are they?

To explore these questions, let us first consider cases that are clearly mental, though unconscious, and contrast them with cases which are "unconscious" because they are not mental at all. Think of the difference, for example, between my belief (when I am not thinking about it) that the Eiffel Tower is in Paris, and the myelination of the axons in my central nervous system. There is a sense in which both are unconscious. But there is a big difference between them in that the structural states of my axons couldn't themselves be conscious states, because there isn't anything mental about them. I assume for the sake of this argument that myelination functions essentially in the production of my mental states, but even if myelinated axons were themselves objects of experiences, even if I could feel inwardly the state of the myelin sheaths, still the actual structures are not themselves mental states. Not every unconscious feature of my brain that (like myelination) functions essentially in my mental life is itself a mental feature. But the belief that the Eiffel Tower is in Paris is a genuine mental state, even though it happens to be a mental state that most of the time is not present to consciousness. So here are two states in me, my belief and my axon myelination: both have something to do with my brain, and neither is conscious. But only one is mental, and we need to get clear about what makes it mental and the connection between that feature—whatever it is—and consciousness. Just to keep this distinction clear, I propose in this chapter to call phenomena like myelination, which are not in the mental line of business at all, "nonconscious" and phenomena like mental states that I am not thinking about or have repressed "unconscious."

There are at least two constraints on our conception of intentionality that any theory of the unconscious must be able to account for: First, it must be able to account for the distinction between phenomena that are genuinely intentional and those that in some respects behave as if they were, but in fact are not. This is the distinction I discussed at the end of chapter 3 between *intrinsic* and *as-if* forms of intentionality.[2] And second, it must be able to account for the fact that intentional states represent their conditions of satisfaction only under certain aspects, and those aspects must matter to the agent. My unconscious belief that the Eiffel Tower is in Paris satisfies both of these conditions. My having that belief is a matter of intrinsic intentionality, and not a matter of what anybody else chooses to say about me or how I behave or what sort of stance someone might adopt toward me. And the belief that the Eiffel Tower is in Paris represents its conditions of satisfaction under certain aspects and not others. It is, for example, distinct from the belief that the tallest iron structure built in France before 1900 is located in the French capital, even assuming that the Eiffel Tower is identical with the tallest iron structure built in France before 1900, and Paris is identical with the French capital. We might say that every intentional state has a certain *aspectual shape*, and this aspectual shape is part of its identity, part of what makes it the state that it is.

## II. The Argument for the Connection Principle

These two features—the fact that an unconscious intentional state must nonetheless be intrinsically mental, and the fact that it must have a certain aspectual shape—have important consequences for our conception of the unconscious. They will provide the basis for an argument to show that we understand the notion of an unconscious mental state only as a possible content of consciousness, only as the sort of thing that, though not conscious, and perhaps impossible to bring to consciousness for various reasons, nonetheless is the *sort of thing* that could be or could have been conscious. This idea, that all unconscious intentional states are in principle accessible to consciousness, I call the connection principle, and I will now spell out the argument for it in more detail. For the sake of clarity I will number the major steps in the argument, though I do not mean to imply that the argument is a simple deduction from axioms.

1. *There is a distinction between* intrinsic *intentionality and* as-if *intentionality; only intrinsic intentionality is genuinely mental.* I have argued at some length for this rather obvious distinction, both in this book and in the writings previously mentioned, and so I will not repeat the arguments here. I believe that the distinction is correct and that the price of giving it up would be that everything would become mental, because relative to some purpose or other anything can be treated *as if* it were mental. For instance, water flowing downhill can be described *as if* it had intentionality: It *tries* to get to the bottom of the hill by ingeniously *seeking* the line of the least resistance, it does *information processing*, it *calculates* the size of rocks, the angle of the slope, the pull of gravity, etc. But if water is mental, then everything is mental.

2. *Unconscious intentional states are intrinsic.* When I say of someone who is asleep that he believes that George Bush is president of the United States, or when I say of someone who is awake that he has an unconscious but repressed hatred of his father, I am speaking quite literally. There is nothing metaphorical or *as-if* about these attributions. Attributions of the unconscious lose their explanatory power if we do not take them literally.

3. *Intrinsic intentional states, whether conscious or unconscious, always have aspectual shapes.* I have been using the term of art, "aspectual shape," to mark a universal feature of intentionality. It can be explained as follows: Whenever we perceive any-

thing or think about anything, we always do so under some aspects and not others. These aspectual features are essential to the intentional state; they are part of what makes it the mental state that it is. Aspectual shape is most obvious in the case of conscious perceptions: think of seeing a car, for example. When you see a car, it is not simply a matter of an object being registered by your perceptual apparatus; rather, you actually have a conscious experience of the object from a certain point of view and with certain features. You see the car as having a certain shape, as having a certain color, etc. And what is true of conscious perceptions is true of intentional states generally. A man may believe, for example, that the star in the sky is the Morning Star without believing that it is the Evening Star. A man may, for example, want to drink a glass of water without wanting to drink a glass of $H_2O$. There is an indefinitely large number of true descriptions of the Evening Star and of a glass of water, but something is believed or desired about them only under certain aspects and not under others. Every belief and every desire, and indeed every intentional phenomenon, has an aspectual shape.

Notice furthermore that the aspectual shape must matter to the agent. It is for example from the agent's point of view that he can want water without wanting $H_2O$. In the case of conscious thoughts, the way that the aspectual shape matters is that it constitutes the way the agent thinks about or experiences a subject matter: I can think about my thirst for a drink of water without thinking at all about its chemical composition. I can think of it *as* water without thinking of it *as* $H_2O$.

It is reasonably clear how this works for conscious thoughts and experiences, but how does it work for unconscious mental states? One way to get at our question is to ask what fact about an unconscious mental state makes it have the particular aspectual shape that it has, that is, what fact about it makes it the mental state that it is?

*4. The aspectual feature cannot be exhaustively or completely characterized solely in terms of third-person, behavioral, or even neuro-*

*physiological predicates. None of these is sufficient to give an exhaustive account of aspectual shape.* Behavioral evidence concerning the existence of mental states, including even evidence concerning the causation of a person's behavior, no matter how complete, always leaves the aspectual character of intentional states underdetermined. There will always be an inferential gulf between the behavioral *epistemic* grounds for the presence of the aspect and the *ontology* of the aspect itself.

A person may indeed exhibit water-seeking behavior, but any water-seeking behavior will also be $H_2O$-seeking behavior. So there is no way the behavior, construed without reference to a mental component, can constitute wanting water rather than wanting $H_2O$. Notice that it is not enough to suggest that we might get the person to respond affirmatively to the question "Do you want water?" and negatively to the question "Do you want $H_2O$?", because the affirmative and negative responses are themselves insufficient to fix the aspectual shape under which the person interprets the question and the answer. There is no way just from the behavior to determine whether the person means by "$H_2O$" what I mean by "$H_2O$" and whether the person means by "water" what I mean by "water." No amount of behavioral facts constitute the fact that the person represents what he wants under one aspect and not under another. This is not an epistemic point.

It is equally true, though less obvious, that no amount of neurophysiological facts under neurophysiological descriptions constitute aspectual facts. Even if we had a perfect science of the brain, and even if such a perfect science of the brain allowed us to put our brain-o-scope on the person's skull and see that he wanted water but not $H_2O$, all the same there would still be an inference—we would still have to have some lawlike connection that would enable us to infer from our observations of the neural architecture and neuron firings that they were realizations of the desire for water and not of the desire for $H_2O$.

Because the neurophysiological facts are always causally sufficient for any set of mental facts,[3] someone with perfect causal knowledge might be able to make the inference from the neurophysiological to the intentional at least in those few cases where there is a lawlike connection between the facts specified in neural terms and the facts specified in intentional terms. But even in these cases, if there are any, there is still an *inference*, and the specification of the neurophysiological in neurophysiological terms is not yet a specification of the intentional.

*5. But the ontology of unconscious mental states, at the time they are unconscious, consists entirely in the existence of purely neurophysiological phenomena.*  Imagine that a man is in a sound dreamless sleep. Now, while he is in such a state it is true to say of him that he has a number of unconscious mental states. For example, he believes that Denver is the capital of Colorado, Washington is the capital of the United States, etc. But *what fact about him makes it the case that he has these unconscious beliefs?* Well, the only facts that could exist while he is completely unconscious are neurophysiological facts. The only things going on in his unconscious brain are sequences of neurophysiological events occurring in neuronal architectures. At the time when the states are totally unconscious, there is simply nothing there except neurophysiological states and processes.

But now we seem to have a contradiction: The ontology of unconscious intentionality consists entirely in third-person, objective, neurophysiological phenomena, but all the same the states have an aspectual shape that cannot be constituted by such facts, because there is no aspectual shape at the level of neurons and synapses.

I believe there is only one solution to this puzzle. The apparent contradiction is resolved by pointing out that:

*6. The notion of an unconscious intentional state is the notion of a state that is a possible conscious thought or experience.*  There are plenty of unconscious mental phenomena, but to the extent that they are genuinely *intentional*, they must in some sense preserve their aspectual shape even when unconscious, but the only sense that we can give to the notion that they preserve their aspectual shape when unconscious is that they are possible contents of consciousness.

This is our first main conclusion. But this answer to our first question immediately gives rise to another question: What is meant by "possible" in the previous two sentences? After all, it might be quite *impossible* for the state to occur consciously, because of brain lesion, repression, or other causes. So in what sense exactly must it be a possible content of a thought or experience? This question leads to our next conclusion, which is really a further explanation of step 6, and is implied by 5 and 6 together:

7. *The ontology of the unconscious consists in objective features of the brain capable of causing subjective conscious thoughts.* When we describe something as an unconscious intentional state, we are characterizing an objective *ontology* in virtue of its *causal* capacity to produce consciousness. But the existence of these causal features is consistent with the fact that in any given case their causal powers may be blocked by some other interfering causes, such as psychological repression or brain damage.

The possibility of interference by various forms of pathology does not alter the fact that any unconscious intentional state is the sort of thing that is in principle accessible to consciousness. It may be unconscious not only in the sense that it does not *happen* to be conscious then and there, but also in the sense that for one reason or another the agent simply *could not* bring it to consciousness, but it must be the *sort of thing* that can be brought to consciousness because its ontology is that of a neurophysiology characterized in terms of its capacity to cause consciousness.

Paradoxically, the naive mentalism of my view of the mind leads to a kind of dispositional analysis of unconscious mental phenomena; only it is not a disposition to "behavior," but a "disposition"—if that is really the right word—to conscious thoughts, including conscious thoughts manifested in behavior. This is paradoxical, even ironic, because the notion of a dispositional account of the mental was introduced precisely to get rid of the appeal to consciousness; and I am in effect trying to turn this tradition on its head by arguing that unconscious beliefs are indeed dispositional states of the brain, but they are dispositions to produce conscious thoughts and conscious behavior. This sort of dispositional ascription of causal capacities is quite familiar to us from common sense. When, for example, we say of a substance that it is bleach or poison, we are ascribing to a chemical ontology a dispositional causal capacity to produce certain effects. Similarly, when we say of the man who is unconscious that he believes that Bush is president, we are ascribing to a neurobiological ontology the dispositional causal capacity to produce certain effects, namely conscious thoughts with specific aspectual shapes. The concept of unconscious intentionality is thus that of a *latency* relative to its *manifestation* in consciousness.

To summarize: The argument for the connection principle was somewhat complex, but its underlying thrust was quite simple. Just ask yourself what fact about the world is supposed to correspond to your claims. When you make a claim about unconscious intentionality, there are no facts that bear on the case except neurophysiological facts. There is nothing else there except neurophysiological states and processes describable in neurophysiological terms. But intentional states, conscious or unconscious, have aspectual shapes, and there is no aspectual shape at the level of the neurons. So the only fact about the neurophysiological structures that corresponds to the ascription of intrinsic aspectual shape is the fact that the system has the causal capacity to produce conscious states and processes where those specific aspectual shapes are manifest.

The overall picture that emerges is this. There is nothing going on in my brain but neurophysiological processes, some conscious, some unconscious. Of the unconscious neurophysiological processes, some are mental and some are not. The difference between them is not in consciousness, because, by hypothesis, neither is conscious; the difference is that the mental processes are candidates for consciousness, because they are capable of causing conscious states. But that's all. All my mental life is lodged in the brain. But what in my brain is my "mental life"? Just two things: conscious states and those neurophysiological states and processes that—given the right circumstances—are capable of generating conscious states. Let's call those states that are in principle accessible to consciousness "shallow unconscious," and those inaccessible even in principle "deep unconscious." The main conclusion of this chapter so far is that there are no deep unconscious intentional states.

### III. Two Objections to the Connection Principle

I want to discuss two objections. The first I thought of myself, though several other people[4] also gave me different versions of it; the second is due to Ned Block.

First objection: Suppose we had a perfect science of the brain. Suppose, for example, that we could put our brain-o-scope on someone's skull and see that he wanted water. Now suppose that the "I-want-water" configuration in the brain was universal. People want water iff they have that configuration. This is a total sci-fi fantasy, of course, but let's pretend. Now let's suppose that we found a subsection of the population that had exactly that configuration but could not "in principle" bring any desire for water to consciousness. They engage in water-seeking behavior, but "in principle" they are unable to become conscious of the desire for water. There is nothing pathological about them; that is just how their brains are constructed. Now if this is possible—and why not?—then we have found a counterexample to the connection principle, because we have found an example of an unconscious desire for water that it is in principle impossible to bring to consciousness.

I like the example, but I do not think it is a counterexample. Characteristically in the sciences we define surface phenomena in terms of their micro causes; we can define colors in terms of wavelengths of a certain number of nanometers, for example. If we had a perfect science of the brain of the sort imagined, we could certainly identify mental states by their micro-causes in the neurophysiology of the brain. But—and this is the crucial point—the redefinition works as an identification of an unconscious mental phenomenon only to the extent that we continue to suppose that the unconscious neurophysiology is still, so to speak, tracking the right conscious mental phenomenon with the right aspectual shape. So the difficulty is with the use of the expression "in principle." In the imagined case, the "I-want-water" neurophysiology is indeed capable of causing the conscious experience. It was only on that supposition that we got the example going in the first place. The cases we have imagined are simply cases where there is a blockage of some sort. They are like Weiskrantz's "blind sight" examples, only without the pathology. But there is nothing "in principle" inaccessible to consciousness about the phenomena in question, and that is why it is not a counterexample to the connection principle.

Second objection: The argument has the consequence that there could not be a totally unconscious intentional zombie. But why could there not be? If such a thing is possible—and why not?—then the connection principle entails a false proposition and is therefore false.

Actually, there could not be an intentional zombie, and Quine's famous argument for the indeterminacy of translation (Quine 1960, ch. 2) has inadvertently supplied us with the proof: For a zombie, unlike a conscious agent, there simply is no fact of the matter as to exactly which aspectual shapes its alleged intentional states have. Suppose we built a "water-seeking" zombie. Now, what fact about the zombie makes it the case that he, she, or it is seeking the stuff under the aspect "water" and not under the aspect "$H_2O$"? Notice that it would not be enough to answer this question to say that we could program the zombie to say, "I sure do want water, but I do not want any $H_2O$" because that only forces the question back a step: What fact about the zombie makes it the case that by "water" it means what we mean by "water," and by "$H_2O$" it means what we mean by "$H_2O$"? And even if we complicated its behavior to try to answer this question, there will always be alternative ways of interpreting its verbal behavior that will be consistent with all the facts about verbal behavior, but that give inconsistent attributions of meaning and intentionality to the zombie. And, as Quine has shown in laborious detail, the problem is not that we could not know for sure that the zombie meant, for example, "rabbit" as opposed to "stage in the life history of a rabbit," or "water" as opposed to "$H_2O$," but there is no fact of the matter at all about which the zombie meant. But where there is no fact of the matter about aspectual shape, there is no aspectual shape, and where there is no aspectual shape, there is no intentionality. Quine, we might say, has a theory of meaning appropriate for verbally behaving zombies. But we are not zombies and our utterances do, on occasion at least, have determinate meanings with determinate aspectual shapes, just as our intentional states often have determinate intentional contents with determinate aspectual shapes (Searle 1987). But all of that presupposes consciousness.

### IV. Could There Be Unconscious Pains?

I want to illustrate the connection principle further by imagining a case in which we would have a use for the notion of "unconscious pain." We don't normally think of unconscious pains, and many people, I believe, would accept the Cartesian notion that for something to be a genuine pain, it has to be conscious. But I think it is easy to invoke contrary intuitions. Consider the following: It is a very common occurrence for people who suffer from chronic pains, say, chronic back pains, that sometimes the pain makes it difficult for them to go to sleep. And indeed, once they have fallen asleep, there sometimes are occasions during the night when *their condition causes them to wake up*. Now, how exactly shall we describe these cases? For the sake of this example, we are assuming that the patients are totally unconscious during sleep; they have no consciousness of any pain whatever. Shall we say then, that during sleep there really was no pain, but that the pain began when they woke up and that they were awakened by neurophysiological processes that normally would cause pain, but didn't cause pain because at the time they were asleep? Or shall we say, on the other hand, that the pain, that is, the pain itself, continued both before, during, and after their sleep, but that they were not consciously aware of the pain while they were asleep? My intuitions find the second just as natural, indeed probably more natural, than the first. However, the important thing is to see that there is no substantive issue involved. We are simply adopting an alternative vocabulary for describing the same sets of facts. But now consider the second vocabulary: On this vocabulary, we say that the pain was for a while conscious, then it was unconscious, then it was conscious again. Same pain, different states of consciousness. We might increase our urge to speak this way if we found that the person, though completely unconscious, made bodily movements during sleep that served to protect the painful portion of his body.

Now what exactly is the ontology of the pain when it is completely unconscious? The answer seems quite obvious to me. What inclines us to say that the pain continued to exist even though unconscious is that there was an underlying neurophysiological process that was capable of generating a conscious state and capable of generating behavior appropriate to someone who had that conscious state. And in the example as described, that is exactly what happened.

But now if I am right about this, then it is hard to see how there could be any factual substance to the old disputes between Freudians and their adversaries about whether unconscious mental states really exist. If you grant my argument so far, then I am unable to see how it could be other than a purely terminological matter, different only in complexity from the issue about the existence of unconscious pains as I just described it. One side insisted that there really are *unconscious mental* states; the other insisted that if they were really *mental*, why then, they must be *conscious*. But what facts in the world are supposed to correspond to these two different claims?

The evidence that the Freudians adduced involved causal histories, behavior, and conscious admissions by the agent—all of which seemed only interpretable on the assumption of an unconscious mental state, which was just like a conscious state except for being unconscious. Consider a typical sort of case. A man under hypnosis is given a posthypnotic suggestion to the effect that he must crawl around on the floor after coming out of the hypnotic trance. Later, when conscious, he gives some completely extraneous, but apparently rational justification for his behavior. He says, for example, "I think I may have lost my watch on this floor somewhere," whereupon he proceeds to crawl around on the floor. Now we suppose, with good reason I believe, that he is unconsciously obeying the order, that he unconsciously intends to crawl around on the floor because he was told to by the hypnotist, and that the reason he gives for his behavior is not the real reason at all.

But assuming that he is totally unconscious of his real motives, what is the ontology of the unconscious, right then and there, supposed to be? To repeat our earlier question, what *fact* corresponds to the attribution of the unconscious mental state at the time the agent is acting for a reason of which he is totally unconscious? If the state really is totally unconscious, then the only facts are the existence of neuro-physiological states capable of giving rise to conscious thoughts and to the sort of behavior appropriate for someone having those thoughts.

Sometimes there may be several inferential steps between the latent unconscious mental state and the manifest conscious intentionality. Thus, we are told, the adolescent boy who revolts against the authority of the school is unconsciously motivated by hatred of his father. The school symbolizes the father. But again, as in the hypnosis case we have to ask, what is the ontology of the unconscious supposed to be when unconscious? And in this case, as in the hypnosis case, the attribution of a specific aspectual shape to the unconscious must imply that there is in the neurophysiology a capacity to produce a conscious thought with that very aspectual shape.

Once you see that the description of a mental state as "unconscious" is the description of a neurophysiological ontology in terms of its causal capacity to produce conscious thoughts and behavior, then it seems there could not be any factual substance to the ontological question: Do unconscious mental states really exist? All that question can mean is: Are there *nonconscious* neurophysiological states of the brain capable of giving rise to conscious thoughts and to the sorts of behavior appropriate for someone having those thoughts? Of course neither side thought of the issue this way, but perhaps part of the intensity of the dispute derived from the fact that what looked like a straight ontological issue—do unconscious states exist?—was really not an ontological issue at all.

If I am right about this, then the old Freudian arguments—involving all the evidence from hypnotism, neuroses, etc.—are not so much conclusive or inconclusive as they are factually empty. The issue is not less important for being conceptual or terminological, but we should understand that it is not a factual issue about the existence of mental entities that are neither physiological nor conscious.

## V. Freud on the Unconscious

I want to conclude this chapter by comparing my conception of the unconscious and its relation to consciousness with Freud's. On my view, inside our skulls there is a mass of neurons embedded in glial cells, and sometimes this vast and intricate system is conscious. Consciousness is caused by the behavior of lower-level elements, presumably at neuronal, synaptic, and columnar levels, and as such it is a higher-level feature of the entire system. I do not mean to imply that there is anything simple about consciousness or about neurophysiology. Both seem to me immensely complex, and consciousness, in particular, comes as we have seen in a variety of modalities: perception, emotion, thought, pains, etc. But on my view, that is all that is going on inside the brain: neurophysiological processes and consciousness. On my account, talk of the unconscious mind is simply talk of the causal capacities of neurophysiology to cause conscious states and conscious behavior.

So much for my view. What about Freud? Where I see true ascriptions of unconscious mental life as corresponding to an objective neurophysiological ontology, but described in terms of its capacity to cause conscious subjective mental phenomena, Freud[5] sees these ascriptions as corresponding to mental states existing as mental states then and there. That is, Freud thinks that our unconscious mental states exist both as unconscious and as occurrent intrinsic intentional states even when unconscious. Their ontology is that of the mental, even when they are unconscious. Can he make such a picture coherent? Here is what he says: All mental states are "unconscious in themselves." And bringing them to consciousness is simply like perceiving an object (1915, reprinted in 1959, vol. 4, esp. p. 104ff.). So the distinction between conscious and unconscious mental states is not a distinction between two kinds of mental states, or even a distinction between two different modes of existence of mental states, but rather all mental states are really unconscious in themselves (*an sich*) and what we call "consciousness" is just a mode of perception of states that are unconscious in their mode of existence. It is as if the unconscious mental states really were like furniture in the attic of the mind, and to bring them to consciousness we go up in the attic and shine the flashlight of our perception on them. Just as the furniture "in itself" is unseen, so mental states "in themselves" are unconscious.

It is possible that I am misunderstanding Freud, but I cannot find or invent a coherent interpretation of this theory. Even if we leave out conscious states of perception and confine ourselves to propositional intentional states like beliefs and desires, it seems to me the theory is incoherent in at least two respects. First, I can't make his account of the ontology of the unconscious consistent with what we know about the brain, and second, I can't formulate a coherent version of the analogy between perception and consciousness.

Here is the first difficulty: Suppose I have a series of unconscious mental states. When I am completely unconscious, the only things going on in my brain are neurophysiological processes occurring in specific neuronal architectures. So what fact about these neurophysiological processes and architectures is supposed to *constitute* their being unconscious mental states? Notice the features that unconscious mental states have to have *qua* mental states. First, they have to have aspectual shape; and second, in some sense they have to be "subjective," because they are *my* mental states. It is easy to see how these conditions are satisfied for conscious states—such states are experienced as having aspectual shape. It is harder but still possible to see how they are satisfied for unconscious states if we think of the ontology of the unconscious in the way I have suggested—as an occurrent neurophysiology capable of causing conscious states and events. But how can the nonconscious neurophysiology have aspectual shape and subjectivity right then and there? The neurophysiology does indeed admit of different levels of description, but none of these objective neurophysiological levels of description—ranging all the way from the micro-anatomy of the synaptic cleft to large molar organs such as the hippocampus—is a level of aspectual shape or subjectivity.

Freud apparently thinks that, in addition to whatever neurophysiological features my brain has, there is also some level of description at which my unconscious mental states, though completely unconscious, have each and every one of the features of my conscious mental states, including intentionality and subjectivity. The unconscious has everything the conscious has, *only minus consciousness*. But he has not made intelligible what events could be going on in the brain in addition to the neurophysiological events to constitute unconscious subjectivity and intentionality.

The *evidence* that Freud gives us for the existence of the unconscious is invariably that the patient engages in behavior that is *as if* he had a certain mental state, but because we know independently that the patient does not have any such conscious mental state, Freud postulates an unconscious mental state as the cause of the behavior. A verificationist would have to say that the only meaning there is to the postulation is that the patient behaves in such and such ways and that such behavior would normally be caused by a conscious state. But Freud is not a verificationist. He thinks that there is something there causing the behavior that is not just neurophysiological, but is not conscious either. I cannot make this consistent with what we know about the brain, and it is hard to interpret it except as implying dualism, as Freud is postulating a class of non-neurophysiological mental phenomena; and thus it seems to constitute an abandonment of Freud's earlier project for a scientific psychology (1895).

What about the analogy between consciousness and perception? Once one adopts the view that mental states are both *in themselves* mental and *in themselves* unconscious, then it is not going to be easy to explain how consciousness fits into the picture. It looks as if the view that mental states are unconscious in themselves has the consequence that consciousness is totally extrinsic, not an essential part of any conscious state or event. It seems to me that Freud accepts this consequence, and the analogy between consciousness and perception is a way of trying to fit consciousness into the picture, given the consequence that consciousness is an extrinsic, nonessential feature of any conscious state. Once the theory of the unconscious is spelled out, the analogy with perception looks inevitable. To account for the fact of consciousness together with the theory of the unconscious, we are forced to postulate that consciousness is a kind of perception of states and events that in their intrinsic nature are unconscious.

But this solution takes us out of the frying pan and into the fire. As we saw in our discussion of introspection, the model of perception works on the assumption that there is a distinction between the object perceived and the act of perception. Freud needs this assumption to account for the consequence that consciousness is extrinsic, that for example, this very token conscious thought could have existed minus the consciousness. Let us try to take the analogy seriously. Suppose I see a bicycle. In such a perceptual situation there is a distinction between the object perceived and the act of perception. If I take away the perception, I am left with a bike; if I take away the bike, I am left with a perception that has no object, for example, a hallucination. But it is precisely these distinctions that we cannot make for the conscious thought. If I try to take away the conscious thinking of this token thought, say, that Bush is president, I have nothing left. If I try to take away the token occurrence of the thought from the conscious thinking of it, I don't succeed in taking anything away. The distinction between the act of perceiving and the object perceived does not apply to conscious thoughts.

Furthermore, we seem to get a vicious regress if we hold that the phenomenon of bringing unconscious states to consciousness consists in perceiving previously unconscious mental phenomena that, in themselves, are unconscious. For the question then arises: What about the act of perceiving—is this a mental phenomenon? If so, it must be "in itself" unconscious, and it would appear that for me to become conscious of that act, I would need some higher-level act of perceiving of my act of perceiving. I am not sure about this, but it looks like an infinite regress argument threatens.

A final difficulty with this perceptual analogy is the following: Perception works on the assumption that the object perceived exerts a causal impact on my nervous system, which causes my experience of it, so when I touch something or feel something, the object of the perception causes a certain experience. But how could this possibly work in the case in which the object perceived is itself an unconscious experience?

To summarize, it seems to me there are two objections to the Freudian account: One, we do not have a clear notion of how the ontology of the unconscious is supposed to match the ontology of the neurophysiology. Two, we do not have a clear notion of how to apply the perceptual analogy to the relation between consciousness and unconsciousness; and we would seem to get absurdity and an infinite regress if we try to take it seriously.

## VI. Remnants of the Unconscious

What is left of the unconscious? I said earlier that our naive pretheoretical notion of the unconscious was like the notions of fish in the sea or furniture in the dark attic of the mind. They keep their shapes even when unconscious. But now we can see that these pictures are inadequate in principle because they are based on the idea of a constant mental reality that appears and then disappears. But the submerged belief, unlike the submerged fish, can't keep its conscious shape when unconscious; for the only occurrent reality of that shape is the shape of conscious thoughts. The naive picture of unconscious states confuses the causal capacity to cause a conscious intentional state with a conscious state itself, that is, it confuses the latency with its manifestation. It is as if we thought the bottle of poison on the shelf had to be poisoning something all the time in order really to be poison. To repeat, *the ontology of the unconscious is strictly the ontology of a neurophysiology capable of generating the conscious.*

The final conclusion I want to draw from this discussion is that we have no unified notion of the unconscious. There are at least four different notions.

First, there are *as-if* metaphorical attributions of intentionality to the brain, which are not to be taken literally. For example, we might say that the medulla wants to keep us alive, so it keeps us breathing even while we are asleep.

Second, there are Freudian cases of shallow unconscious desires, beliefs, etc. It is best to think of these as cases of repressed consciousness, because they are always bubbling to the surface, though often in a disguised form. In its logical behavior the Freudian notion of the unconscious is quite unlike the cognitive science notion in the crucial respect that Freudian unconscious mental states are potentially conscious.

Third, there are the (relatively) unproblematic cases of shallow unconscious mental phenomena that just do not happen to form the content of my consciousness at any given point in time. Thus, most of my beliefs, desires, worries, and memories are not present to my consciousness at any given moment, such as the present one. Nonetheless, they are all *potentially* conscious in the sense I have explained (if I understand him correctly, these are what Freud meant by the "preconscious" as opposed to the "unconscious" (Freud 1949)).

Fourth, there is supposed to be a class of deep unconscious mental intentional phenomena that are not only unconscious but that are in principle inaccessible to consciousness. These, I have argued, do not exist. Not only is there no evidence for their existence, but the postulation of their existence violates a logical constraint on the notion of intentionality.

# Chapter 8
## Consciousness, Intentionality, and the Background

---

*I. Introduction to the Background*

The aim of this chapter is to explain the relationship between consciousness and intentionality on the one hand, and the capacities, abilities, and general know-how that enable our mental states to function on the other. I call these capacities, etc., collectively, "the Background," with a capital "B" to make it clear that I use the word as a technical term. Since my views of the Background have developed in some important respects since I wrote *Intentionality* (1983), I will also explain the changes and the motivation for them.

In the early 1970s I began investigating the phenomena that I later came to call "the Background" and to develop a thesis that I call "the hypothesis of the Background." The thesis was originally a claim about literal meaning (Searle 1978), but I believe what applies to literal meaning applies also to speaker's intended meaning, and indeed, to all forms of intentionality, whether linguistic or nonlinguistic. The thesis of the Background is simply this: Intentional phenomena such as meanings, understandings, interpretations, beliefs, desires, and experiences only function within a set of Background capacities that are not themselves intentional. Another way to state this thesis is to say that all representation, whether in language, thought, or experience, only succeeds in representing given a set of nonrepresentational capacities. In my technical jargon, intentional phenomena only determine *conditions of satisfaction* relative to a set of capacities that are not themselves intentional. Thus, the same intentional state can determine different conditions of satisfaction, given different Background capacities, and an intentional state will determine no conditions of satisfaction unless it is applied relative to an appropriate Background.

To further develop this thesis, I need to repeat a distinction I made earlier, between the Background and the Network. It is in general impossible for intentional states to determine conditions of satisfaction in isolation. To have one belief or desire, I have to have a whole Network of other beliefs and desires. Thus, for example, if I now want to eat a good meal at a local restaurant, I have to have a large number of other beliefs and desires, such as the beliefs that there are restaurants in the vicinity, restaurants are the sort of establishment where meals are served, meals are the sort of thing that can be bought and eaten inside restaurants at certain times of day for certain amounts of money, and so—more or less indefinitely—on. However, the problem is this: Even if I had the patience to list all of the other beliefs and desires that go to make up the Network that gives sense to my desire to eat a good meal in a restaurant, I would still be left with the problem that my initial desire posed for me, namely that the content of the intentionality is not, so to speak, self-interpreting. It is still subject to an indefinite range of different applications. As far as the actual intentional content of my desire is concerned, it is possible to have that very content and still apply it in an indefinite number of different and inconsistent ways. What exactly constitutes eating, what constitutes a meal, what constitutes a restaurant? All of these notions are subject to different interpretations, and these interpretations are not fixed by the content of the intentional state by itself. In addition to the Network, we need to postulate a Background of capacities that are not themselves part of that Network. Or rather, the whole Network stands in need of a Background, because the elements of the Network are not self-interpreting or self-applying.

The thesis of the Background (in which I am now including the claim about the Network) constitutes a very strong claim. It involves at least the following:

1. Intentional states do not function autonomously. They do not determine conditions of satisfaction in isolation.

2. Each intentional state requires for its functioning a Network of other intentional states. Conditions of satisfaction are determined only relative to the Network.

3. Even the Network is not enough. The Network only functions relative to a set of Background capacities.

4. These capacities are not and cannot be treated as more intentional states or as part of the content of any particular intentional state.

5. The same intentional content can determine different conditions of satisfaction (such as truth conditions) relative to different Backgrounds, and relative to some Backgrounds it determines none at all.

To think of the Background naively, think of Wittgenstein's example of the picture of the man walking uphill. It could be interpreted as a man sliding backward downhill. Nothing internal to the picture, even construed as a pictorial representation of a man in that position, forces the interpretation we find natural. The idea of the Background is that what goes for the picture goes for intentionality in general.

In the past century or so, the sort of phenomena I call "Background" has been recognized by a number of different philosophers with quite different commitments. Nietzsche is certainly not the first to have recognized the phenomenon, but he is one of those most aware of its contingency: The Background does not have to be the way it is. There are no proofs to the effect that the Background we have is one we must have of necessity. The work of the later Wittgenstein is in large part about the Background.[1] Among contemporary writers, it seems to me that Bourdieu's notion of *habitus* (1990) is closely related to my notion of the Background.

In this chapter I will first sketch an argument for the thesis of the Background, and thus attempt to justify the postulation of Background phenomena as a separate category for investigation. Second, I will restate the thesis of the Background, in light of the discussion of the relations between consciousness, the unconscious, and intentionality presented in chapter 7. Third, I will discuss various implications of the thesis of the Background; and in particular, I will try to avoid the various misunderstandings and misconceptions that it seems to me an awareness of the Background has generated. Fourth, I will begin a general account of the Background.

## II. Some Arguments for the Hypothesis of the Background

In earlier works (Searle 1978, 1980c, 1983, 1990) I have presented arguments for all five theses, and I won't repeat them all here. However to give a feel for the theses I am presenting, I will sketch a couple of the considerations that most impress me. The simplest way to see that representation presupposes a nonrepresentational Background of capacities is to examine the understanding of sentences. The beauty of starting with sentences is that they are well-defined syntactical objects, and the lessons to be learned from them can be applied generally to intentional phenomena. Point number 5 gives us the entering wedge of the argument: The same literal meaning will determine different conditions of satisfaction, for example, different truth conditions, relative to different Background presuppositions, and some literal meanings will determine no truth conditions because of the absence of appropriate Background presuppositions. Furthermore (point 4), those Background presuppositions are not and could not be included in literal meaning. So, for example, if you consider occurrences of the word "cut" in sentences such as "Sam cut the grass," "Sally cut the cake," "Bill cut the cloth," "I just cut my skin," you will see that the word "cut" means the same in each. This is shown, for example, by the fact that conjunction reduction works for the occurrences of this verb with these direct objects. For example, one can say "General Electric has invented a new device that will cut grass, cut cakes, cut cloth, and cut skin." One can simply then eliminate the last three occurrences of "cut" and put "General Electric has invented a new device that will cut grass, cake, cloth, and skin." Notice that the word "cut" differs in these occurrences from its genuinely metaphorical occurrences. If I say "Sally cut two classes last week," "The president cut the salaries of the professors," or "The Raiders cut the roster to forty-five," in each case, the word "cut" has a nonliteral use. Once again, conjunction reduction shows this. If I say "General Electric has invented a device that will cut grass, cake, cloth, and skin," and then add "and salaries, classes, and rosters," the whole becomes a bad joke. So the utterances contain the literal occurrence of the verb "cut," but that word, on a normal interpretation, is interpreted differently in each sentence. You can also see this if you imagine the corresponding imperative version of these utterances. If I say "Cut the grass," and you rush out and stab it with a knife, or if I say "Cut the cake," and you run over it with a lawn mower, there is a perfectly ordinary sense in which you did not do exactly what I asked you to do.

The lesson to be learned from these examples is this: The same literal expression can make the same contribution to the literal utterance of a variety of sentences, and yet although those sentences will be understood literally—there is no question of metaphor, ambiguity, indirect speech acts, etc.—the expression will be interpreted differently in the different sentences. Why? Because each sentence is interpreted against a Background of human capacities (abilities to engage in certain practices, know-how, ways of doing things, etc.), and those capacities will fix different interpretations, even though the literal meaning of the expression remains constant.

Now why is this an important result? Well, on our standard accounts of language, the meaning of a sentence is a compositional function of the meanings of its component parts and their syntactical arrangement in the sentence. Thus, we understand the sentence "John loves Mary" differently from the way we understand the sentence "Mary loves John" precisely because of the application of compositionality. Furthermore, we are able to understand sentences at all because they are composed of meaningful elements, elements whose meanings are matters of linguistic convention. Thus, the principle of compositionality and the notion of literal meaning are absolutely essential to any coherent account of language. However, though necessary for an account of language, it turns out that they are not sufficient. In addition, we need to postulate a nonrepresentational Background.

It is tempting to think that this argument rests on ambiguity, marginal cases, etc. But that is a mistake. Once full explicitness has been achieved, once all structural and lexical ambiguities have been removed, the problem of the Background still arises. You can see this if you see that progressive efforts at precision are not sufficient to remove the need for the Background. Suppose I go into the restaurant and order a meal. Suppose I say, speaking literally, "Bring me a steak with fried potatoes." Even though the utterance is meant and understood literally, the number of possible misinterpretations is strictly limitless. I take it for granted that they will not deliver the meal to my house, or to my place of work. I take it for granted that the steak will not be encased in concrete, or petrified. It will not be stuffed into my pockets or spread over my head. But none of these assumptions was made explicit in the literal utterance. The temptation is to think that I could make them fully explicit by simply adding them as further restrictions, making my original order more precise. But that is also a mistake. First, it is a mistake because there is no limit to the number of additions I would have to make to the original order to block possible misinterpretations, and second, each of the additions is itself subject to different interpretations.

Another argument for the Background is this: There are perfectly ordinary sentences of English and other natural languages that are uninterpretable. We understand all the meanings of the words, but we do not understand the sentence. So, for example, if you hear a sentence "Sally cut the mountain," "Bill cut the sun," " Joe cut the lake," or "Sam cut the building," you will be puzzled as to what these sentences could mean. If somebody gave you an order, "Go cut that mountain," you really would not know what to do. It would be easy to invent a Background practice that would fix a literal interpretation of each of these sentences, but without such a practice, we do not know how to apply the literal meaning of the sentence.

There is some recognition of Background problems in recent linguistics (see the articles in Davis 1991, by Robyn Carston and François Récanati, for example), but the discussions that I have seen only touch the surface of the problem. For example, a current discussion concerns the relationships between the literal meaning of the sentence uttered, the content of what the speaker says, and what the speaker implies by making the utterance. Thus, for example, in the sentence, "I have had breakfast," the literal meaning of the sentence makes no reference to the day of the utterance, but we would normally interpret that utterance as conveying the content that the speaker has had breakfast *today*, that is, the day of the utterance. Thus, "I have had breakfast" contrasts with "I have been to Tibet," an utterance which does not communicate that I have been to Tibet today. Or consider another much-discussed sentence, "Sally gave John the key, and he opened the door." An utterance of this sentence would normally convey that *first* Sally gave John the key, and *later* he opened the door, and that he opened the door *with* the key. There is much discussion about the mechanisms by which this additional content is conveyed, given that it is not encoded in the literal meaning of the sentence. The suggestion, surely correct, is that sentence meaning, to at least some extent, underdetermines what the speaker says when he utters the sentence. Now, the claim I am making is: Sentence meaning *radically* underdetermines the content of what is said. Consider the examples I just mentioned. No one would construe "I have had breakfast" on analogy with "I have had twins." That is, given our present Background, no one would interpret the utterance to mean, "I have just given birth to breakfast," but notice there is nothing whatever in the semantic content of the sentence that blocks that interpretation, or even compels the interpretation that I have *eaten* breakfast. It is very easy, though obscene, to imagine a culture where the two interpretations of "I have had. . ." are reversed. Similar problems arise for any sentence. Consider, "Sally gave John the key, and he opened the door." There is nothing whatever in the literal semantic content of that sentence to block the interpretation, "John opened the door with the key by battering the door down; the key was twenty feet long, made of cast iron, and weighed two hundred pounds." Nothing to block the interpretation, "John opened the door with the key by swallowing both door and key, and moving the key into the lock by way of the peristaltic contraction of his gut." Of course, such interpretations would be crazy, but there is nothing in the semantic content of the sentence, construed by itself, that blocks these crazy interpretations.

Is there some way we could account for the all these intuitions without a claim as extreme as the thesis of the Background? Well, let us try it. One idea, due to François Récanati,[2] is this. Any actual situation admits of an infinite number of true descriptions, so any linguistic representation will always be incomplete. If someone "cuts" the cake by running a lawn mower over it, it is true to say, "He cut the cake." But we would be surprised to have this event reported by this sentence. Our surprise, however, has nothing to do with semantics, understanding, etc. We simply have an inductively based set of expectations, and the report, though true, was incomplete in leaving out an account of how the cutting differed from the way we would normally expect.

Récanati tells me he does not agree with this view, but I find it important and challenging so I want to consider it further. The suggestion is: Literal meaning fixes truth conditions in isolation, but it is accompanied by a system of expectations, and this system works alongside literal meaning. The real problem suggested by the examples is that once all genuine ambiguities have been removed from a sentence, we are still left with vagueness and incompleteness. Words are inherently vague and descriptions are always incomplete. But further precision and completeness are added to understanding by the fact that meanings are *supplemented* with a a set of habitual expectations. So we should not say:

> Literal meaning only determines truth conditions relative to a Background.

Rather we should say:

> (Leaving indexicality and other context-dependent features aside) literal meaning determines truth conditions absolutely and in isolation. But literal meanings are vague, and literal descriptions are always incomplete. Greater precision and completeness are added by supplementing literal meaning with collateral assumptions and expectations. So for example, cutting is cutting however you do it, but we expect grass to be cut one way, and cake another. So if someone says "Go cut that mountain," the correct response is not "I do not understand." Of course you understand the English sentence! Rather the correct response is "How do you want me to cut it?"

I think this is a powerful and appealing argument. The answers I would give to it are two. First, if the question were one of incompleteness, then we ought in principle to approach completeness by adding further sentences. But we cannot. As I pointed out earlier, each sentence we add is subject to further misunderstandings unless fixed by the Background. Second, if you assume a radical break between literal meaning and collateral "assumptions," then you ought to be able to apply literal meaning no matter what the assumptions. But you cannot. So for example the application of the word "cut" proceeds against a presupposition that some objects in the world are solid and admit of penetration by the physical pressure of instruments. Without that assumption I cannot interpret most occurrences of "cut." But that assumption is not part of literal meaning. If it were, then the introduction of laser cutting devices would have involved a change in the meaning of the word, and it did not. Furthermore, I can imagine literal uses of "cut" in a universe where that assumption is false. One can imagine a set of Background capacities where "Cut the lake" is perfectly clear.

I believe that if one were to develop this argument fully, one could show that if you postulate a total break between literal meaning and Background, you would get a Kripke-Wittgenstein (Kripke 1982) style skepticism, because you would then be able to say anything and mean anything.[3] If you make a radical break between meaning and Background, then where meaning is concerned, anything goes; but that implies that normal understanding occurs only relative to a Background. I am not, however, trying to demonstrate any general theses about semantic skepticism.

My answers to this objection are, first, that incompleteness is not the problem, because efforts to complete the description don't help. In a sense they don't get started, because each additional sentence only adds further forms of incompleteness. And second, if you postulate a situation totally devoid of Background presuppositions, you cannot fix any definite interpretation.

A second question, also posed by Récanati is this: What is the argument for generalizing from literal meaning to all forms of intentionality? The only "argument" I would offer is that it is useful to have a taxonomy that captures our intuition that there is a match between thought and meaning. For example, I want to capture our ordinary intuition that the man who has the belief that Sally cut the cake has a belief with exactly the same propositional content as the literal assertion "Sally cut the cake." Because we are applying the technical terms "Background" and "intentionality," ordinary usage will not settle the issue. But if you use the notion of intentional content in such a way that literal meaning is an expression of intentional content, then it follows that Background constraints apply equally to both. I can imagine other taxonomies, but this one seems to work best.

A good way to observe the Background is in cases of breakdown: An example will illustrate this. A visiting philosopher came to Berkeley and attended some seminars on the Background. He was unconvinced by the arguments. One day a small earthquake occurred. This convinced him because, as he later told me, he had not, prior to that moment, had a belief or a conviction or a hypothesis that the earth does not move; he had simply taken it for granted. The point is "taking something for granted" need not name an intentional state on all fours with believing and hypothesizing.

A crucial step in understanding the Background is to see that one can be committed to the truth of a proposition without having any intentional state whatever with that proposition as content.[4] I can, for example, be committed to the proposition that objects are solid, without in any way, implicitly or explicitly, having any belief or conviction to that effect. Well then, what is the sense of commitment involved? At least this: I cannot, consistently with my behavior, deny that proposition. I cannot, while sitting in this chair, leaning on this desk, and resting my feet on this floor, consistently deny that objects are solid, because my behavior presupposes the solidity of these objects. It is in that sense that my intentional behavior, a manifestation of my Background capacities, commits me to the proposition that objects are solid, even though I need have formed no belief regarding the solidity of objects.

Furthermore, it is important to see that the Background concerns not merely such relatively sophisticated problems as the interpretation of sentences but such fundamental features as those that constitute the formal basis of all language. For example, we take for granted the fact that our present use of language identifies phonetic and graphemic tokens of the same syntactical type, in virtue of phonetic and graphemic shapes, but it is important to see that this is a contingent practice based on contingent Background capacities. Instead of a language in which the sequence, "France," "France," "France" involves three different occurrences of the same syntactical unit, we could easily imagine a language in which meanings attach not to a type identified phonetically or graphematically but to the numerical sequence of token occurrences of the type. So, for example, the first time in a discourse, the inscription "France" might be used to refer to France, but the second time, it refers to England, the third time to Germany, etc. The syntactical unit here is not a word in the traditional sense, but a sequence of token inscriptions. Similarly with the systems of opposition that the structuralists were so fond of: The apparatus of hot as opposed to cold, North to South, male to female, life to death, East to West, up to down, etc., are all Background based. There is nothing inevitable about accepting these oppositions. One could easily imagine beings for whom East was naturally opposed to South, for whom it was unintelligible to oppose East to West.

### III. The Network Is Part of the Background

I will now try to state exactly how my present view of the relationship between consciousness, unconsciousness, and intentionality, as stated in the previous chapter, produces a modification—and I hope an improvement—in my previous conception of the Background. On my earlier view, I thought of the mind as containing an inventory of mental states. At any given moment, some of these are conscious and some unconscious. For example, I might consciously think that Bush is president, or I might unconsciously have that belief, a token occurrence of that very belief, even when I am sound asleep. But consciousness was not essential to mental phenomena, not even to perceptual experiences, as the Weiskrantz experiments seem to show.

On this view, some phenomena that could be stated as beliefs seem unnaturally described if so stated. I do indeed have an unconscious belief that George Bush is president, when I am not thinking about it, but it seems I do not in that way have an unconscious belief that, for example, objects are solid. I simply behave in such a way that I take the solidity of objects for granted. The solidity of objects is part of my Background presuppositions; it is not an intentional phenomenon at all, unless it becomes such as part of some theoretical inquiry, for example.

But this way of thinking of matters poses some difficulties for me. What is the basis of the distinction between the Background and the Network? Well, begging the question, I can say the Background consists of phenomena that are not intentional states, and the Network is a network of intentionality; but how exactly is that distinction supposed to be delineated, if we are told, for example, that my unconscious belief that Bush is president is part of the Network and my presupposition that objects are solid is part of the Background? How about the belief that George Bush wears underwear or that he has two ears? Are those also part of my unconscious Network? We are making a mistake in posing the question in this way. And it ought to be obvious to us. On the view of the mind as containing an inventory of mental states, there must be a category mistake in trying to draw a line between Network and Background, because Background consists of a set of capacities, and Network is not a matter of capacities at all, but of intentional states.

I now think the real mistake was to suppose that there is an inventory of mental states, some conscious, some unconscious. Both language and culture tend to force this picture on us. We think of memory as a storehouse of propositions and images, as a kind of big library or filing cabinet of representations. But we should think of memory rather as a *mechanism* for generating current performance, including conscious thoughts and actions, based on past experience. The thesis of the Background has to be rewritten to get rid of the presupposition of the mind as a collection, an inventory, of mental phenomena, because the only occurrent reality of the mental as mental is consciousness.

The belief in an occurrent reality that consists of unconscious mental states, and that is distinct from Background capacities, is an illusion based largely on the grammar of our language. Even when Jones is asleep, we say that he believes Bush is president and that he knows the rules of French grammar. So we think lying in there in his brain, sleeping too, are his belief that Bush is president and his knowledge of French. But in fact all his brain contains is a set of neuronal structures, whose workings at present are largely unknown, that enable him to think and act, when he gets around to it. Among many other things, they enable him to think that Bush is president and to speak French.

The best way to think of these matters is this: In my brain there is an enormous and complex mass of neurons embedded in glial cells. Sometimes the behavior of the elements of this complex mass causes conscious states, including those conscious states that are parts of human actions. The conscious states have all of the color and variety that constitute our waking lives. But at the level of the mental, those are all the facts. What goes on in the brain, other than consciousness, has an occurrent reality that is neurophysiological rather than psychological. When we speak of unconscious states, we are speaking of the capacities of the brain to generate consciousness. Furthermore, some capacities of the brain do not generate consciousness, but rather function to fix the application of the conscious states. They enable me to walk, run, write, speak, etc.

Given this picture, how do we account for all those intuitions that led us to the original thesis of the Background and to the distinction between Background and Network? According to the account I gave in the last chapter, when we describe a man as having an unconscious belief, we are describing an occurrent neurophysiology in terms of its dispositional capacity to cause conscious thoughts and behavior. But if that is right, then it seems to follow that the Network of unconscious intentionality is part of the Background. The occurrent ontology of those parts of the Network that are unconscious is that of a neurophysiological capacity, but the Background consists entirely in such capacities.

So far so good. The question of how to distinguish between Network and Background disappears, because the Network is that part of the Background that we describe in terms of its capacity to cause conscious intentionality. But we are still not out of the morass, because we are left with the question, What is to become of the claim that intentionality functions against a set of nonintentional capacities? Why is the capacity to generate the belief that Bush is president to be treated any differently from the capacity to generate the belief that objects are solid, for example? And are we to make the distinction between the functioning of unconscious intentionality and nonintentional capacities? It seems we have traded the problem of distinguishing between Network and Background for the problem of distinguishing the intentional from the nonintentional within the Background capacities.

So we need to make some more distinctions:

1. We need to distinguish between what is at the center of our conscious attention from the periphery, boundary conditions, and situatedness of our conscious experiences, as described in chapter 6. In some sense this is a foreground-background distinction, but it is not the one concerning us now.

2. We need to distinguish within mental phenomena the representational from the nonrepresentational. Because intentionality is defined in terms of representation, what is the role, if any, of the nonrepresentational in the functioning of intentionality?

3. We need to distinguish capacities from their manifestations. One of our questions is: Which of the brain's capacities should be thought of as Background capacities?

4. We need to distinguish what we are actually concerned with from what we are taking for granted.

These distinctions cut across each other. In the light of these distinctions, and on the assumption that we have abandoned the inventory conception of the mind, it seems to me that we should restate the hypothesis of the Background as follows:

All conscious intentionality—all thought, perception, understanding, etc.—determines conditions of satisfaction only relative to a set of capacities that are not and could not be part of that very conscious state. The actual content by itself is insufficient to determine the conditions of satisfaction.

Of the original insight that intentional states require a nonintentional Background, this much remains: Even if you spell out all contents of the mind as a set of conscious rules, thoughts, beliefs, etc., you still require a set of Background capacities for their interpretation. This much is lost: There is no occurrent reality to an unconscious Network of intentionality, a Network that holistically supports its members, but that requires further support from a Background. Instead of saying "To have a belief, one has to have a lot of other beliefs," one should say "To have a conscious thought, one has to have the capacity to generate a lot of other conscious thoughts. And these conscious thoughts all require further capacities for their application."

Now within that set of capacities there will be some that one has acquired in the form of consciously learned rules, facts, etc. For example, I was taught the rules of baseball, the rule that in the U.S. we drive on the right side of the road, and the fact that George Washington was the first president. I was not taught any rules for walking, nor was I taught that objects are solid. The original intuition that there is a distinction between Network and Background derives from this fact. Some of one's capacities enable one to formulate and apply rules, principles, beliefs, etc., in one's conscious performances. But these are still in need of Background capacities for their application.

If one starts to think about the solidity of objects, then one may form a conscious belief that objects are solid. A belief in the solidity of objects then becomes a belief like any other, only much more general.

Of our original 5 theses, we now have the following revised list:

1. Intentional states do not function autonomously. They do not determine their conditions of satisfaction independently.
2. Each intentional state requires for its functioning a set of Background capacities. Conditions of satisfaction are determined only relative to these capacities.
3. Among these capacities will be some that are capable of generating other conscious states. To these others, conditions 1 and 2 apply.
4. The same *type* of intentional content can determine different conditions of satisfaction when it is manifest in

different conscious tokens, relative to different Background capacities, and relative to some Backgrounds it determines none at all.

## IV. Common Misunderstandings of the Background

There are several ways of misunderstanding the significance of the hypothesis of the Background, and I want to eliminate these now. First, many philosophers who become aware of the Background are extremely disconcerted by it. It suddenly seems to them that meaning, intentionality, rationality, etc., are somehow threatened if their application depends on contingently existing biological and cultural facts about human beings. There is a sense of panic that comes over a certain type of philosophical sensibility when it recognizes that the project of grounding intentionality and rationality on some pure foundation, on some set of necessary and indubitable truths, is mistaken in principle. It even seems to some people that it is impossible to have a theory of the Background, because the Background is the precondition of all theory, and in some extreme cases it even seems as if any theory is impossible, because the theory depends on what appear to be the shifting sands of unjustifiable presuppositions.

Against this view, I want to say that the discovery of the Background shows only that a certain philosophical conception was mistaken. It threatens no aspect of our daily life, including our theoretical daily life. That is, it does not show that meaning and intentionality are unstable or indeterminate, that we can never make ourselves understood, that communication is impossible or threatened; it merely shows that all of these function against a contingently existing set of Background capacities and practices. Furthermore, the thesis of the Background does not show that theorizing is impossible, on the contrary, the Background itself seems to me an excellent territory for theorizing, as I hope this chapter illustrates.

It is also important to point out that the Background has no metaphysical implications, since it is a feature of our *represen-*

*tations* of reality, and not a feature of the *reality* represented. Some find it tempting to think that on the hypothesis of the Background, somehow or other reality itself becomes relative to the Background, and that consequently some sort of relativism or idealism must follow. But that is a mistake. The real world does not care a damn about how we represent it, and though our system of representation requires a nonrepresentational set of capacities in order to function, the reality which that system is used to represent is not itself dependent on those capacities, or indeed on anything else. In short, the Background does not threaten our conviction of external realism, or the correspondence conception of truth, or the possibility of clear communication, or the possibility of logic. However, it does cast all of these phenomena in a different light, because they cannot provide transcendental justifications of our discourse. Rather, our acceptance of them is a Background presupposition of discourse.

One misunderstanding of the Background, particularly important in theories of textual interpretation, is the mistaken supposition that all understanding must involve some act of interpretation. From the fact that whenever one understands something, one understands it in a certain way and not in other ways, and from the fact that alternative interpretations are always possible, it simply does not follow that in all discourse one is engaged in constant "acts of interpretation." One's immediate, normal, instantaneous understanding of utterances is always possible only relative to a Background, but it does not follow from that that there is some separate logical step, some separate *act* of interpretation involved in normal understanding. A similar mistake is made in those theories of cognition that claim that we must have made an inference if, when we look at one side of a tree, we know that the tree has a back side. On the contrary, what we do is simply see a tree as a real tree. One could of course, given a different Background, interpret one's perception differently (e.g., see it as a two-dimensional stage prop tree), but from the fact that alternative interpretations are open to one, it does not follow either that ordinary perceptions always involve an act of interpreting or that some inferential step is made, as an actual temporal mental process, whereby one infers unperceived data from perceived data.

The Background is emphatically not a system of rules. This, it seems to me, was the weakness of Foucault's (1972) notion of a discursive formation and of Bourdieu's earlier discussion of practice in *Outline of a Theory of Practice* (1977). Both thought that rules were essential to the sorts of phenomena I am discussing. But it is important to see that rules only have application relative to the Background capacities. The rules are not self-interpreting, and in consequence they require a Background to function; they are not themselves explanatory or constitutive of the Background.

In light of these considerations, it sometimes seems as if the Background cannot be represented or made fully explicit. But that formulation already contains a mistake. When we say that, we already have a certain model of representation and explicitness. The difficulty is that the model is simply inapplicable to the Background. *Of course* the Background can be represented. Here goes: "the Background." That expression represents the Background, and of course the Background can be made "fully explicit" by using the same expression—or by writing a book about the Background.

The point is that we have a model of explicitness for the representation of mental states, which consists in providing sentences that have the same intentional content as the states represented. I can make the belief that water is wet fully explicit by saying it is the belief that water is wet, for example. But because the Background does not in that way have any intentional content, we cannot represent it as if it consisted of a set of intentional contents. This does not mean that we cannot describe the Background, or that its functioning is unanalyzable, or anything of the sort. It is precisely the beginnings of an analysis of the Background that I am attempting to provide.

*V. Further Features of the Background*

Can we do a geography of the Background? Can we do a taxonomy of its components? Well, any taxonomy requires principles of taxonomizing. Until we have a clear notion of how the Background functions, we will not be able to construct an adequate taxonomy. However, intuitively we can make a start. In *Intentionality* (Searle 1983) I argued that we need at least the following distinctions: A distinction between those features of the Background that are common to all human beings and those features that have to do with local, cultural practices. I oppose these two as "deep Background" versus "local practices." Differences in local Backgrounds make translation from one language to another difficult; the commonality of deep Background makes it possible at all. If you read the description of a dinner party at the home of the Geurmantes' in Proust, you are likely to find some features of the description puzzling. That has to do with differences in local cultural practices. But there are certain things you can take for granted. For example, the participants did not eat by stuffing the food in their ears. That is a matter of deep Background. I also made a distinction between knowing how to do things and knowing how things are. Roughly speaking, this was intended to capture our traditional distinction between the practical and the theoretical. Of course, both practical and theoretical reason are dependent on the Background, hence the Background itself is neither practical nor theoretical. But we still need to make this distinction. An example of how to do things is how to walk. An example of how things are would have to do with the permanence and stability of the objects we find around us. It is obvious, however, that these two are closely related, because one cannot know how to do things without taking for granted how things are. I cannot, for example, "know how" to chop wood without taking for granted that axes made of butter will not work and axes made of water are not axes at all.

There are certain laws of operation of the Background. Some of these are:

1. In general, *there is no action without perception, no perception without action.*

2. *Intentionality occurs in a coordinated flow of action and perception, and the Background is the condition of possibility of the forms taken by the flow.* Think of any normal slice of your waking life: You are eating a meal, taking a walk in the park, writing a letter, making love, or driving to work. In each case the condition of possibility of the performance is an underlying Background competence. The Background not only shapes the application of the intentional content—what counts as "driving to work," for example; but the existence of the intentional content in the first place requires the Background abilities—without a terrific apparatus you can't even have the intentionality involved in "driving to work," for example.

3. *Intentionality tends to rise to the level of the Background ability.* Thus, for example, the beginning skier may require an intention to put the weight on the downhill ski, an intermediate skier has the skill that enables him to have the intention "turn left," a really expert skier may simply have the intention "ski this slope." In a ski race, for example, the coaches will try to create a level of intentionality that is essential to winning the race, but that presupposes a huge underpinning of Background abilities. Thus, the coach may instruct the skier, "Stay close to the gates in the flush, take the red gate before the steep on the inside," and so on. Similarly, when I am speaking English, I do not have the intention to match singular nouns with singular verbs or plural nouns with plural verbs—I just talk.

4. Though intentionality rises to the level of the Background ability, *it reaches all the way down to the bottom of the ability.* This is another way of saying that all voluntary subsidiary actions performed within the scope of a higher-level intentional action are nonetheless intentional. Thus, for example, though I do not require a separate intention to move my arms and legs

when I ski or to move my mouth when I talk, nonetheless all of these movements are done intentionally.

Similarly with perception. I do not normally see at the level of colored patches; I see a Chevrolet station wagon with a rusting front fender, or I see a painting by Vermeer with a woman standing next to a window, reading a letter, while light streams in from the window onto her clothing, the letter, and the table. But notice that in these cases, though the intentionality of my perception rises to the level of my Background ability (my ability to recognize Chevrolet station wagons, Vermeers, etc.), nonetheless the lower-level components are also part of the intentional content; I do indeed see the blue of the station wagon and the brown of the table.

5. *The Background is only manifest when there is intentional content.* Though the Background is not itself intentional, any manifestation of the Background, whether in action, perception, etc., must itself come into play whenever there is some intentionality, conscious or unconscious. "The Background" does not name a sequence of events that can simply occur; rather the Background consists of mental capacities, dispositions, stances, ways of behaving, know-how, savoir faire, etc., all of which can only be manifest when there are some intentional phenomena, such as an intentional action, a perception, a thought, etc.

# Chapter 9
# The Critique of Cognitive Reason

*I. Introduction: The Shaky Foundations of Cognitive Science*

For over a decade, really since the beginnings of the discipline, I have been a practicing "cognitive scientist." In this period I have seen much valuable work and progress in the field. However, as a discipline, cognitive science suffers from the fact that several of its most cherished foundational assumptions are mistaken. It is possible to do good work on the basis of false assumptions, but it is more difficult than need be; and in this chapter I want to expose and refute some of those false assumptions. They derive from the pattern of mistakes that I described in chapters 1 and 2.

Not everybody in cognitive science agrees on the foundational principles, but there are certain general features of the mainstream that deserve a separate statement. If I were a mainstream cognitive scientist, here is what I would say:

Neither the study of the brain as such nor the study of consciousness as such is of much interest and importance to cognitive science. The cognitive mechanisms we study are indeed implemented in the brain, and some of them find a surface expression in consciousness, but our interest is in the intermediate level where the actual cognitive processes are inaccessible to consciousness. Though in fact implemented in the brain, they could have been implemented in an indefinite number of hardware systems. Brains are there, but inessential. The processes which explain cognition are unconscious not only in fact, but in principle. For example, Chomsky's rules of universal grammar (1986), or Marr's rules of vision (1982), or Fodor's language of thought (1975) are not the sort of phenomena that could become conscious. Furthermore, these processes are all computational. The basic assumption behind cognitive science is that the brain is a computer and mental processes are computational. For that reason many of us think that artificial intelligence (AI) is the heart of cognitive science. There is some dispute among us as to whether or not the brain is a digital computer of the old-fashioned von Neumann variety or whether it is a connectionist machine. Some of us, in fact, manage to have our cake and eat it too on this question, because we think the serial processes in the brain are implemented by a parallel connectionist system (e.g., Hobbs 1990). But nearly all of us agree on the following: Cognitive mental processes are unconscious; they are, for the most part, unconscious in principle; and they are computational.

I disagree with just about every substantive claim made in the previous paragraph, and I have already criticized some of them in earlier chapters, most notably the claim that there are mental states that are deep unconscious. The main aim of this chapter is to criticize certain aspects of the computational claim.

I think it will help explain what makes the research program seem so implausible to me if we nail the question down to a concrete example right away: In AI great claims have been made for programs run on SOAR.[1] Strictly speaking, SOAR is a type of computer architecture and not a program, but programs implemented on SOAR are regarded as promising examples of AI. One of these is embodied in a robot that can move blocks on command. So, for example, the robot will respond appropriately to the command "Pick up a cube-shaped block and move it three spaces to the left." To do this, it has both optical sensors and robot arms, and the system works because it implements a set of formal symbol manipulations that are connected to transducers that receive inputs from the optical sensors and send outputs to the motor mechanisms. But my problem is: What has all that got to do with actual human behavior? We know for example many of the details about how a human being does it in real life. First, she must be *conscious*. Furthermore she must *hear and understand* the order. She must *consciously see* the blocks, she must *decide* to carry out the command, and then she must perform the *conscious voluntary intentional action* of moving the blocks. Notice that these claims all support counterfactuals: for example, no consciousness, no movement of blocks. Also we know that all this mental stuff is caused by and realized in the neurophysiology. So before we ever get started on computer modeling, we know that there are two sets of levels: mental levels, many of them conscious, and neurophysiological levels.

Now where are the formal symbol manipulations supposed to fit into this picture? This is a fundamental foundational question in cognitive science, but you would be amazed at how little attention is paid to it. The absolutely crucial question for any computer model is, "How *exactly* does the model relate to the reality being modeled?" But unless you read skeptical critics like the present author, you will find very little discussion of this issue. The general answer, which is supposed to evade the demand for more detailed specific answers, is that between the level of intentionality in the human (what Newell [1982] calls "the knowledge level") and the various neurophysiological levels, there is an intermediate level of formal symbol manipulation. Now our question is, empirically speaking, what could that possibly mean?

If you read books about the brain (say, Shepherd 1983; or Bloom and Lazerson 1988), you get a certain picture of what is going on in the brain. If you then turn to books about computation (say, Boolos and Jeffrey 1989), you get a picture of the logical structure of the theory of computation. If you then turn to books about cognitive science (say, Pylyshyn 1984), they tell you that what the brain books describe is really the same as what the computation books were describing. Philosophically speaking, this does not smell right to me and I have learned, at least at the beginning of an investigation, to follow my sense of smell.

*II. Strong AI, Weak AI, and Cognitivism*

The basic idea of the computer model of the mind is that the mind is the program and the brain the hardware of a computational system. A slogan one often sees is: "The mind is to the brain as the program is to the hardware."[2]

Let us begin our investigation of this claim by distinguishing three questions:

1. Is the brain a digital computer?
2. Is the mind a computer program?
3. Can the operations of the brain be simulated on a digital computer?

In this chapter, I will be addressing 1, and not 2 or 3. In earlier writings (Searle 1980a, 1980b, and 1984b), I have given a negative answer to 2. Because programs are defined purely formally or syntactically, and because minds have an intrinsic mental content, it follows immediately that the program by itself cannot constitute the mind. The formal syntax of the program does not by itself guarantee the presence of mental contents. I showed this a decade ago in the Chinese room argument (Searle 1980a). A computer, me for example, could run the steps in the program for some mental capacity, such as understanding Chinese, without understanding a word of Chinese. The argument rests on the simple logical truth that syntax is not the same as, nor is it by itself sufficient for, semantics. So the answer to the second question is demonstrably "No."

The answer to 3 seems to me equally demonstrably "Yes," at least on a natural interpretation. That is, naturally interpreted, the question means: Is there some description of the brain such that under that description you could do a computational simulation of the operations of the brain. But given Church's thesis that anything that can be given a precise enough characterization as a set of steps can be simulated on a digital computer, it follows trivially that the question has an affirmative answer. The operations of the brain can be simulated on a digital computer in the same sense in which weather systems, the behavior of the New York stock market, or the pattern of airline flights over Latin America can. So our question is not, "Is the mind a program?" The answer to that is, "No." Nor is it, "Can the brain be simulated?" The answer to that is, "Yes." The question is, "Is the brain a digital computer?" And for purposes of this discussion, I am taking that question as equivalent to "Are brain processes computational?"

One might think that this question would lose much of its interest if question 2 receives a negative answer. That is, one might suppose that unless the mind is a program, there is no interest to the question of whether the brain is a computer. But that is not really the case. Even for those who agree that programs by themselves are not constitutive of mental phenomena, there is still an important question: Granted that there is more to the mind than the syntactical operations of the digital computer; nonetheless, it might be the case that mental states are *at least* computational states, and mental processes are computational processes operating over the formal structure of these mental states. This, in fact, seems to me the position taken by a fairly large number of people.

I am not saying that the view is fully clear, but the idea is something like this: At some level of description, brain processes are syntactical; there are so to speak, "sentences in the head." These need not be sentences in English or Chinese, but perhaps in the "language of thought" (Fodor 1975). Now, like any sentences, they have a syntactical structure and a semantics or meaning, and the problem of syntax can be separated from the problem of semantics. The problem of semantics is: How do these sentences in the head get their meanings? But that question can be discussed independently of the question: How does the brain work in processing these sentences? A typical answer to that latter question is: The brain works as a digital computer performing computational operations over the syntactical structure of sentences in the head.

Just to keep the terminology straight, I call the view that all there is to having a mind is having a program, Strong AI, the view that brain processes (and mental processes) can be simu-

lated computationally, Weak AI, and the view that the brain is
a digital computer, cognitivism. This chapter is about cognitivism.

### III. The Primal Story

Earlier I gave a preliminary statement of the assumptions of
mainstream cognitive science, and now I want to continue by
trying to state as strongly as I can why cognitivism has seemed
intuitively appealing. There is a story about the relation of
human intelligence to computation that goes back at least to
Turing's classic paper (1950), and I believe it is the foundation
of the cognitivist view. I will call it the primal story:

> We begin with two results in mathematical logic, the
> Church-Turing thesis and Turing's theorem. For our pur-
> poses, the Church-Turing thesis states that for any algo-
> rithm there is some Turing machine that can implement
> that algorithm. Turing's thesis says that there is a universal
> Turing machine that can simulate any Turing machine.
> Now if we put these two together, we have the result that a
> universal Turing machine can implement any algorithm
> whatever.

But now, why was this result so exciting? Well, what made it
send shivers up and down the spines of a whole generation of
young workers in artificial intelligence was the following
thought: Suppose the brain is a universal Turing machine.
    Well, are there any good reasons for supposing the brain
might be a universal Turing machine? Let us continue with the
primal story:

> It is clear that at least some human mental abilities are
> algorithmic. For example, I can consciously do long divi-
> sion by going through the steps of an algorithm for solving
> long-division problems. It is furthermore a consequence of
> the Church-Turing thesis and Turing's theorem that any-
> thing a human can do algorithmically can be done on a
> universal Turing machine. I can implement, for example,

the very same algorithm that I use for long division on a digital computer. In such a case, as described by Turing (1950), both I, the human computer, and the mechanical computer are implementing the same algorithm. I am doing it consciously, the mechanical computer nonconsciously. Now it seems reasonable to suppose that there might be a whole lot of other mental processes going on in my brain nonconsciously that are also computational. And if so, we could find out how the brain works by simulating these very processes on a digital computer. Just as we got a computer simulation of the processes for doing long division, so we could get a computer simulation of the processes for understanding language, visual perception, categorization, etc.

"But what about the semantics? After all, programs are purely syntactical." Here another set of logico-mathematical results comes into play in the primal story:

> The development of proof theory showed that within certain well-known limits the semantic relations between propositions can be entirely mirrored by the syntactic relations between the sentences that express those propositions. Now suppose that mental contents in the head are expressed syntactically in the head, then all we would need to account for mental processes would be computational processes between the syntactical elements in the head. If we get the proof theory right, the semantics will take care of itself; and that is what computers do: they implement the proof theory.[3]

We thus have a well-defined research program. We try to discover the programs being implemented in the brain by programming computers to implement the same programs. We do this in turn by getting the mechanical computer to match the performance of the human computer (i.e., to pass the Turing test) and then getting the psychologists to look for evidence that the internal processes are the same in the two types of computer.

In what follows I would like the reader to keep this primal story in mind. Notice especially Turing's contrast between the conscious implementation of the program by the human computer and the nonconscious implementation of the program, whether by the brain or by the mechanical computer. Notice also the idea that we might *discover* programs running in nature, the very same programs that we put into our mechanical computers.

If one looks at the books and articles supporting cognitivism, one finds certain common assumptions, often unstated, but nonetheless pervasive.

*First,* it is often assumed that the only alternative to the view that the brain is a digital computer is some form of dualism. I have discussed the reasons for this urge in chapter 2. Rhetorically speaking, the idea is to bully the reader into thinking that unless he accepts the idea that the brain is some kind of computer, he is committed to some weird antiscientific views.

*Second,* it is also assumed that the question of whether brain processes are computational is just a plain empirical question. It is to be settled by factual investigation in the same way that such questions as whether the heart is a pump or whether green leaves do photosynthesis were settled as matters of fact. There is no room for logic chopping or conceptual analysis, because we are talking about matters of hard scientific fact. Indeed, I think many people who work in this field would doubt that the question I am addressing is an appropriate philosophic question at all. "Is the brain really a digital computer?" is no more a philosophical question than "Is the neurotransmitter at neuromuscular junctions really acetylcholene?"

Even people who are unsympathetic to cognitivism, such as Penrose (1989) and Dreyfus (1972), seem to treat it as a straightforward factual issue. They do not seem to be worried about the question of what sort of claim it might be that they are doubting. But I am puzzled by the question: What sort of fact about the brain could constitute its being a computer?

*Third,* another stylistic feature of this literature is the haste and sometimes even carelessness with which the foundational questions are glossed over. What exactly are the anatomical and physiological features of brains that are being discussed? What exactly is a digital computer? And how are the answers to these two questions supposed to connect? The usual procedure in these books and articles is to make a few remarks about 0's and 1's, give a popular summary of the Church-Turing thesis, and then get on with the more exciting things such as computer achievements and failures. To my surprise, in reading this literature I have found that there seems to be a peculiar philosophical hiatus. On the one hand, we have a very elegant set of mathematical results ranging from Turing's theorem to Church's thesis to recursive function theory. On the other hand, we have an impressive set of electronic devices that we use every day. Since we have such advanced mathematics and such good electronics, we assume that somehow somebody must have done the basic philosophical work of connecting the mathematics to the electronics. But as far as I can tell, that is not the case. On the contrary, we are in a peculiar situation where there is little theoretical agreement among the practitioners on such absolutely fundamental questions as, What exactly is a digital computer? What exactly is a symbol? What exactly is an algorithm? What exactly is a computational process? Under what physical conditions exactly are two systems implementing the same program?

## IV. The Definition of Computation

As there is no universal agreement on the fundamental questions, I believe it is best to go back to the sources, back to the original definitions given by Alan Turing.

According to Turing, a Turing machine can carry out certain elementary operations: It can rewrite a 0 on its tape as a 1, it can rewrite a 1 on its tape as a 0, it can shift the tape 1 square to the left, or it can shift the tape 1 square to the right. It is controlled by a program of instructions and each instruction specifies a condition and an action to be carried out if the condition is satisfied.

That is the standard definition of computation, but, taken literally, it is at least a bit misleading. If you open up your home computer, you are most unlikely to find any 0's and 1's or even a tape. But this does not really matter for the definition. To find out if an object is really a digital computer, it turns out that we do not actually have to look for 0's and 1's, etc.; rather we just have to look for something that we could *treat as* or *count as* or that *could be used to* function as a 0's and 1's. Furthermore, to make the matter more puzzling, it turns out that this machine could be made out of just about anything. As Johnson-Laird says, "It could be made out of cogs and levers like an old fashioned mechanical calculator; it could be made out of a hydraulic system through which water flows; it could be made out of transistors etched into a silicon chip through which electric current flows; it could even be carried out by the brain. Each of these machines uses a different medium to represent binary symbols. The positions of cogs, the presence or absence of water, the level of the voltage and perhaps nerve impulses" (Johnson-Laird 1988, p. 39).

Similar remarks are made by most of the people who write on this topic. For example, Ned Block (1990) shows how we can have electrical gates where the 1's and 0's are assigned to voltage levels of 4 volts and 7 volts respectively. So we might think that we should go and look for voltage levels. But Block tells us that 1 is only "conventionally" assigned to a certain voltage level. The situation grows more puzzling when he informs us further that we need not use electricity at all, but we can use an elaborate system of cats and mice and cheese and make our gates in such as way that the cat will strain at the leash and pull open a gate that we can also treat as if it were a 0 or a 1. The point, as Block is anxious to insist, is "the irrelevance of hardware realization to computational description. These gates work in different ways but they are nonetheless computationally equivalent" (p. 260). In the same vein, Pylyshyn says that a computational sequence could be realized by "a group of pigeons trained to peck as a Turing machine!" (1984, p. 57)

But now if we are trying to take seriously the idea that the brain is a digital computer, we get the uncomfortable result that we could make a system that does just what the brain does out of pretty much anything. Computationally speaking, on this view, you can make a "brain" that functions just like yours and mine out of cats and mice and cheese or levers or water pipes or pigeons or anything else provided the two systems are, in Block's sense, "computationally equivalent." You would just need an awful lot of cats, or pigeons or water pipes, or whatever it might be. The proponents of cognitivism report this result with sheer and unconcealed delight. But I think they ought to be worried about it, and I am going to try to show that it is just the tip of a whole iceberg of problems.

## V. First Difficulty: Syntax Is Not Intrinsic to Physics

Why are the defenders of computationalism not worried by the implications of multiple realizability? The answer is that they think it is typical of functional accounts that the same function admits of multiple realizations. In this respect, computers are just like carburetors and thermostats. Just as carburetors can be made of brass or steel, so computers can be made of an indefinite range of hardware materials.

But there is a difference: The classes of carburetors and thermostats are defined in terms of the production of certain *physical* effects. That is why, for example, nobody says you can make carburetors out of pigeons. But the class of computers is defined syntactically in terms of the *assignment* of 0's and 1's. The multiple realizability is a consequence not of the fact that the same physical effect can be achieved in different physical substances, but that the relevant properties are purely syntactical. The physics is irrelevant except in so far as it admits of the assignments of 0's and 1's and of state transitions between them.

But this has two consequences that might be disastrous:

1. The same principle that implies multiple realizability would seem to imply universal realizability. If computa-

tion is defined in terms of the assignment of syntax, then everything would be a digital computer, because any object whatever could have syntactical ascriptions made to it. You could describe anything in terms of 0's and 1's.

2. Worse yet, syntax is not intrinsic to physics. The ascription of syntactical properties is always relative to an agent or observer who treats certain physical phenomena as syntactical.

Now why exactly would these consequences be disastrous?

Well, we wanted to know how the brain works, specifically how it produces mental phenomena. And it would not answer that question to be told that the brain is a digital computer in the sense that stomach, liver, heart, solar system, and the state of Kansas are all digital computers. The model we had was that we might discover some fact about the operation of the brain that would show that it is a computer. We wanted to know if there was not some sense in which brains were *intrinsically* digital computers in a way that green leaves intrinsically perform photosynthesis or hearts intrinsically pump blood. It is not a matter of us arbitrarily or "conventionally" assigning the word "pump" to hearts or "photosynthesis" to leaves. There is an actual fact of the matter. And what we were asking is, "Is there in that way a fact of the matter about brains that would make them digital computers?" It does not answer that question to be told, yes, brains are digital computers because everything is a digital computer.

On the standard textbook definition of computation, it is hard to see how to avoid the following results:

1. For any object there is some description of that object such that under that description the object is a digital computer.

2. For any program and for any sufficiently complex object, there is some description of the object under which it is implementing the program. Thus for example the wall behind my back is right now implementing the Wordstar program, because there is some pattern of molecule move-

ments that is isomorphic with the formal structure of Wordstar. But if the wall is implementing Wordstar, then if it is a big enough wall it is implementing any program, including any program implemented in the brain.

I think the main reason that the proponents do not see that multiple or universal realizability is a problem is that they do not see it as a consequence of a much deeper point, namely that "syntax" is not the name of a physical feature, like mass or gravity. On the contrary they talk of "syntactical engines" and even "semantic engines" as if such talk were like that of gasoline engines or diesel engines, as if it could be just a plain matter of fact that the brain or anything else is a syntactical engine.

I do not think that the problem of universal realizability is a serious one. I think it is possible to block the result of universal realizability by tightening up our definition of computation. Certainly we ought to respect the fact that programmers and engineers regard it as a quirk of Turing's original definitions and not as a real feature of computation. Unpublished works by Brian Smith, Vinod Goel, and John Batali all suggest that a more realistic definition of computation will emphasize such features as the causal relations among program states, programmability and controllability of the mechanism, and situatedness in the real world. All these will produce the result that the pattern is not enough. There must be a causal structure sufficient to warrant counterfactuals. But these further restrictions on the definition of computation are no help in the present discussion *because the really deep problem is that syntax is essentially an observer-relative notion. The multiple realizability of computationally equivalent processes in different physical media is not just a sign that the processes are abstract, but that they are not intrinsic to the system at all. They depend on an interpretation from outside.* We were looking for some facts of the matter that would make brain processes computational; but given the way we have defined computation, there never could be any such facts of the matter. We can't, on the one hand, say that anything is a digital computer if we can assign a syntax to it, and then suppose there is a factual question intrinsic to its physical operation whether or not a natural system such as the brain is a digital computer.

And if the word "syntax" seems puzzling, the same point can be stated without it. That is, someone might claim that the notions of "syntax" and "symbols" are just a manner of speaking and that what we are really interested in is the existence of systems with discrete physical phenomena and state transitions between them. On this view, we don't really need 0's and 1's; they are just a convenient shorthand. But, I believe, this move is no help. A physical state of a system is a computational state only relative to the assignment to that state of some computational role, function, or interpretation. The same problem arises without 0's and 1's because *notions such as computation, algorithm, and program do not name intrinsic physical features of systems.* Computational states are not *discovered within* the physics, they are *assigned to* the physics.

This is a different argument from the Chinese room argument, and I should have seen it ten years ago, but I did not. The Chinese room argument showed that semantics is not intrinsic to syntax. I am now making the separate and different point that syntax is not intrinsic to physics. For the purposes of the original argument, I was simply assuming that the syntactical characterization of the computer was unproblematic. But that is a mistake. There is no way you could discover that something is intrinsically a digital computer because the characterization of it as a digital computer is always relative to an observer who assigns a syntactical interpretation to the purely physical features of the system. As applied to the language of thought hypothesis, this has the consequence that the thesis is incoherent. There is no way you could discover that there are, intrinsically, unknown sentences in your head because something is a sentence only relative to some agent or user who uses it as a sentence. As applied to the computational model generally, the characterization of a process as computational is a characterization of a physical system from outside; and the identification of the process as computational does not identify an intrinsic feature of the physics; it is essentially an observer-relative characterization.

This point has to be understood precisely. I am not saying there are a priori limits on the patterns we could discover in nature. We could no doubt discover a pattern of events in my brain that was isomorphic to the implementation of the vi-editor program on my computer. But to say that something is *functioning as* a computational process is to say something more than that a pattern of physical events is occurring. It requires the assignment of a computational interpretation by some agent. Analogously, we might discover in nature objects that had the same sort of shape as chairs and that could therefore be used as chairs; but we could not discover objects in nature that were functioning as chairs, except relative to some agents who regarded them or used them as chairs.

To understand this argument fully, it is essential to understand the distinction between features of the world that are *intrinsic* and features that are *observer relative*. The expressions "mass," "gravitational attraction," and "molecule" name features of the world that are intrinsic. If all observers and users cease to exist, the world still contains mass, gravitational attraction, and molecules. But expressions such as "nice day for a picnic," "bathtub," and "chair" do not name intrinsic features of reality. Rather, they name objects by specifying some feature that has been assigned to them, some feature that is relative to observers and users. If there had never been any users or observers, there would still be mountains, molecules, masses, and gravitational attraction. But if there had never been any users or observers, there would be no such features as being a nice day for a picnic, or being a chair or a bathtub. The assignment of observer-relative features to intrinsic features of the world is not arbitrary. Some intrinsic features of the world facilitate their use as chairs and bathtubs, for example. But the feature of being a chair or a bathtub or a nice day for a picnic is a feature that only exists relative to users and observers. The point I am making here, and the essence of this argument, is that on the standard definitions of computation, computational features are observer relative. They are not intrinsic. The argument so far, then, can be summarized as follows:

*The aim of natural science is to discover and characterize features that are intrinsic to the natural world. By its own definitions of computation and cognition, there is no way that computational cognitive science could ever be a natural science, because computation is not an intrinsic feature of the world. It is assigned relative to observers.*[4]

## VI. Second Difficulty: The Homunculus Fallacy is Endemic to Cognitivism

So far, we seem to have arrived at a problem. Syntax is not part of physics. This has the consequence that if computation is defined syntactically, then nothing is intrinsically a digital computer solely in virtue of its physical properties. Is there any way out of this difficulty? Yes, there is, and it is a way standardly taken in cognitive science, but it is out of the frying pan and into the fire. Most of the works I have seen in the computational theory of the mind commit some variation on the homunculus fallacy. The idea always is to treat the brain as if there were some agent inside it using it to compute with. A typical case is David Marr (1982), who describes the task of vision as proceeding from a two-dimensional visual array on the retina to a three-dimensional description of the external world as output of the visual system. The difficulty is: Who is reading the description? Indeed, it looks throughout Marr's book, and in other standard works on the subject, as if we have to invoke a homunculus inside the system to treat its operations as genuinely computational.

Many writers feel that the homunculus fallacy is not really a problem because, with Dennett (1978), they feel that the homunculus can be "discharged." The idea is this: Because the computational operations of the computer can be analyzed into progressively simpler units, until eventually we reach simple flip-flop, "yes-no," "1–0" patterns, it seems that the higher-level homunculi can be discharged with progressively stupider homunculi, until finally we reach the bottom level of a simple flip-flop that involves no real homunculus at all. The idea, in short, is that recursive decomposition will eliminate the homunculi.

It took me a long time to figure out what these people were driving at, so in case someone else is similarly puzzled, I will explain an example in detail: Suppose that we have a computer that multiplies six times eight to get forty-eight. Now we ask "How does it do it?" Well, the answer might be that it adds six to itself seven times.[5] But if you ask "How does it add six to itself seven times?" the answer might be that, first, it converts all of the numerals into binary notation, and second, it applies a simple algorithm for operating on binary notation until finally we reach the bottom level at which the only instructions are of the form, "Print a zero, erase a one." So, for example, at the top level our intelligent homunculus says, "I know how to multiply six times eight to get forty-eight." But at the next lower level he is replaced by a stupider homunculus who says, "I do not actually know how to do multiplication, but I can do addition." Below him are some stupider ones who say "We do not actually know how to do addition or multiplication, but we know how to convert decimal to binary." Below these are stupider ones who say "We do not know anything about any of this stuff, but we know how to operate on binary symbols." At the bottom level are a whole bunch of a homunculi who just say "Zero one, zero one." All of the higher levels reduce to this bottom level. Only the bottom level really exists; the top levels are all just *as-if*.

Various authors (e.g., Haugeland 1981; Block 1990) describe this feature when they say that the system is a syntactical engine driving a semantic engine. But we still must face the question we had before: What facts intrinsic to the system make it syntactical? What facts about the bottom level or any other level make these operations into 0's and 1's? *Without a homunculus that stands outside the recursive decomposition, we do not even have a syntax to operate with.* The attempt to eliminate the homunculus fallacy through recursive decomposition fails, because the only way to get the syntax intrinsic to the physics is to put a homunculus in the physics.

There is a fascinating feature to all of this. Cognitivists cheerfully concede that the higher levels of computation, for example, "multiply 6 times 8," are observer relative; there is nothing really there that corresponds directly to multiplication; it is all in the eye of the homunculus/beholder. But they want to stop this concession at the lower levels. The electronic circuit, they admit, does not really multiply 6 x 8 as such, but it really does manipulate 0's and 1's and these manipulations, so to speak, add up to multiplication. But to concede that the higher levels of computation are not intrinsic to the physics is already to concede that the lower levels are not intrinsic either. So the homunculus fallacy is still with us.

For real computers of the kind you buy in the store, there is no homunculus problem, because each user is the homunculus in question. But if we are to suppose that the brain is a digital computer, we are still faced with the question "And who is the user?" Typical homunculus questions in cognitive science are such as the following: "How does the visual system compute shape from shading; how does it compute object distance from size of retinal image?" A parallel question would be, "How do nails compute the distance they are to travel in the board from the impact of the hammer and the density of the wood?" And the answer is the same in both sorts of case: If we are talking about how the system works intrinsically, neither nails nor visual systems compute anything. We as outside homunculi might describe them computationally, and it is often useful to do so. But you do not understand hammering by supposing that nails are somehow intrinsically implementing hammering algorithms, and you do not understand vision by supposing the system is implementing, for example, the shape from shading alogorithm.

## VII. Third Difficulty: Syntax Has No Causal Powers

Certain sorts of explanations in the natural sciences specify mechanisms that function causally in the production of the phenomena to be explained. This is especially common in the biological sciences. Think of the germ theory of disease, the account of photosynthesis, the DNA theory of inherited traits, and even the Darwinian theory of natural selection. In each case a causal mechanism is specified, and in each case the specification gives an explanation of the output of the mechanism. If you go back and look at the primal story it seems clear that this is the sort of explanation promised by cognitivism. The mechanisms by which brain processes produce cognition are supposed to be computational, and by specifying the programs we will have specified the causes of cognition. One beauty of this research program, often remarked, is that we do not need to know the details of brain functioning to explain cognition. Brain processes provide only the hardware implementation of the cognitive programs, but the program level is where the real cognitive explanations are given. On the standard account, as stated by Newell (1982), for example, there are three levels of explanation—hardware, program, and intentionality (Newell calls this last level the knowledge level)—and the special contribution of cognitive science is made at the program level.

But if what I have said so far is correct, then there is something fishy about this whole project. I used to believe that as a causal account, the cognitivist's theory was at least false, but I now am having difficulty formulating a version of it that is coherent even to the point where it could be an empirical thesis at all. The thesis is that there are a whole lot of symbols being manipulated in the brain, 0's and 1's flashing through the brain at lightning speed and invisible not only to the naked eye but even to the most powerful electron microscope, and it is these that cause cognition. But the difficulty is that the 0's and 1's as such have no causal powers because they do not even exist except in the eyes of the beholder. The implemented program has no causal powers other than those of the implementing medium because the program has no real existence, no ontology, beyond that of the implementing medium. Physically speaking, there is no such thing as a separate "program level."

You can see this if you go back to the primal story and remind yourself of the difference between the mechanical computer and Turing's human computer. In Turing's human
computer there really is a program level intrinsic to the system, and it is functioning causally at that level to convert input
to output. This is because the human is consciously following
the rules for doing a certain computation, and this causally
explains his performance. But when we program the mechanical computer to perform the same computation, the assignment of a computational interpretation is now relative to us,
the outside homunculi. There is no intentional causation
intrinsic to the system. The human computer is consciously
following rules, and this fact explains his behavior, but the
mechanical computer is not literally following any rules. It is
designed to behave exactly as if it were following rules; so for
practical, commercial purposes it does not matter that it is not
actually following any rules. It could not be following rules
because it has no intentional content intrinsic to the system
that is functioning causally to produce the behavior. Now cognitivism tells us that the brain functions like the commercial
computer and that this causes cognition. But without a
homunculus, both commercial computer and brain have only
patterns, and the patterns have no causal powers in addition to
those of the implementing media. So it seems there is no way
cognitivism *could* give a causal account of cognition.

There is a puzzle, however, for my view. Anyone who works
with computers even casually knows that we often do in fact
give causal explanations that appeal to the program. For
example, we can say that when I hit this key I got such-and-
such results because the machine is implementing the vi program and not the emacs program; and this looks like an
ordinary causal explanation. So the puzzle is, how do we
reconcile the fact that syntax, as such, has no causal powers
with the fact that we do give causal explanations that appeal to
programs? And more pressingly, would these sorts of explanations provide an appropriate model for cognitivism, will
they rescue cognitivism? Could we for example rescue the
analogy with thermostats by pointing out that just as the

notion "thermostat" figures in causal explanations independently of any reference to the physics of its implementation, so
the notion "program" might be explanatory while equally
independent of the physics?

To explore this puzzle, let us try to make the case for cognitivism by extending the primal story to show how the cognitivist investigative procedures work in actual research practice.
The idea, typically, is to program a commercial computer so
that it simulates some cognitive capacity, such as vision or
language. Then, if we get a good simulation, one that gives us
at least Turing equivalence, we hypothesize that the brain
computer is running the same program as the commercial
computer, and to test the hypothesis we look for indirect
psychological evidence, such as reaction times. So it seems
that we can causally explain the behavior of the brain computer by citing the program in exactly the same sense in which
we can explain the behavior of the commercial computer.
What is wrong with that? Doesn't it sound like a perfectly legitimate scientific research program? We know that the commercial computer's conversion of input to output is explained
by a program, and in the brain we discover the same program,
hence we have a causal explanation.

Two things ought to worry us immediately about this project. First, we would never accept this mode of explanation for
any function of the brain where we actually understood how it
worked at the neurobiological level. Second, we would not
accept it for other sorts of system that we can simulate computationally. To illustrate the first point, consider for example the
famous account of "What the Frog's Eye Tells the Frog's Brain"
(Lettvin, et al. 1959 in McCulloch 1965). The account is given
entirely in terms of the anatomy and physiology of the frog's
nervous system. A typical passage, chosen at random, goes
like this:

### Sustained Contrast Detectors

An unmyelinated axon of this group does not respond
when the general illumination is turned on or off. If the

sharp edge of an object either lighter or darker than the background moves into its field and stops, it discharges promptly and continues discharging, no matter what the shape of the edge or whether the object is smaller or larger than the receptive field. (p. 239)

I have never heard anyone say that all this is just the hardware implementation, and that they should have figured out which program the frog was implementing. I do not doubt that you could do a computer simulation of the frog's "bug detectors." Perhaps someone has done it. But we all know that once you understand how the frog's visual system *actually works*, the "computational level" is just irrelevant.

To illustrate the second worry, consider simulations of other sorts of systems. I am for example typing these words on a machine that simulates the behavior of an old-fashioned mechanical typewriter.[6] As simulations go, the word processing program simulates a typewriter better than any AI program I know of simulates the brain. But no sane person thinks: "At long last we understand how typewriters work, they are implementations of word processing programs." It is simply not the case in general that computational simulations provide causal explanations of the phenomena simulated.

So what is going on? We do not in general suppose that computational simulations of brain processes give us any explanations in place of or in addition to neurobiological accounts of how the brain actually works. And we do not in general take "X is a computational simulation of Y" to name a symmetrical relation. That is, we do not suppose that because the computer simulates a typewriter, therefore the typewriter simulates a computer. We do not suppose that because a weather program simulates a hurricane, that the causal explanation of the behavior of the hurricane is provided by the program. So why should we make an exception to these principles where unknown brain processes are concerned? Are there any good grounds for making the exception? And what kind of a causal explanation is an explanation that cites a formal program?

Here, I believe, is the solution to our puzzle. Once you remove the homunculus from the system, you are left only with a pattern of events to which someone from outside could attach a computational interpretation. The only sense in which the specification of the pattern by itself provides a causal explanation is that if you know that a certain pattern exists in a system, you know that some cause or other is responsible for the pattern. So you can, for example, predict later stages from earlier stages. Furthermore, if you already know that the system has been programmed by an outside homunculus, you can give explanations that make reference to the intentionality of the homunculus. You can say, for example, that this machine behaves the way it does because it is running vi. That is like explaining that this book begins with a bit about happy families and does not contain any long passages about a bunch of brothers, because it is Tolstoy's *Anna Karenina* and not Dostoevsky's *The Brothers Karamazov*. But you cannot explain a physical system such as a typewriter or a brain by identifying a pattern that it shares with its computational simulation, because the existence of the pattern does not explain how the system actually works *as a physical system*. In the case of cognition, the pattern is at much too high a level of abstraction to explain such concrete mental (and therefore physical) events as the occurrence of a visual perception or the understanding of a sentence.

I think it is obvious that we cannot explain how typewriters and hurricanes work by pointing to formal patterns they share with their computational simulations. Why is it not obvious in the case of the brain?

Here we come to the second part of our solution to the puzzle. In making the case for cognitivism, we were tacitly supposing that the brain might be implementing algorithms for cognition, in the same sense that Turing's human computer and his mechanical computer implement algorithms. But it is precisely that assumption that we have seen to be mistaken. To see this, ask yourself what happens when a system implements an algorithm. The human computer consciously goes through the steps of the algorithm, so the process is both causal and logical: logical because the algorithm provides a set of rules for deriving the output symbols from the input symbols, and causal because the agent is making a conscious effort to go through the steps. In the case of the mechanical computer, the whole working system includes an outside homunculus, and with the homunculus the system is both causal and logical: logical because the homunculus gives an interpretation to the processes of the machine, and causal because the hardware of the machine causes it to go through the processes. But these conditions cannot be met by the brute, blind, nonconscious neurophysiological operations of the brain. In the brain computer there is no conscious intentional implementation of the algorithm as there is in the human computer, but there can't be any nonconscious implementation as there is in the mechanical computer either, because that requires an outside homunculus to attach a computational interpretation to the physical events. The most we could find in the brain is a pattern of events that is formally similar to the implemented program in the mechanical computer, but that pattern, as such, has no causal powers to call its own and hence explains nothing.

In sum, the fact that the attribution of syntax identifies no further causal powers is fatal to the claim that programs provide causal explanations of cognition. To explore the consequences of this, let us remind ourselves of what cognitivist explanations actually look like. Explanations such as Chomsky's account of the syntax of natural languages or Marr's account of vision proceed by stating a set of rules according to which a symbolic input is converted into a symbolic output. In Chomsky's case, for example, a single input symbol, $S$, is converted into any one of a potentially infinite number of sentences by the repeated application of a set of syntactical rules. In Marr's case, representations of a two-dimensional visual array are converted into three-dimensional "descriptions" of the world in accordance with certain algorithms. Marr's tripartite distinction between the computational task, the algorithmic solution of the task, and the hardware implementation of the algorithm, has (like Newell's distinctions) become famous as a statement of the general pattern of the explanation.

If you take these explanations naively, as I do, it is best to think of them as saying that it is just as if a man alone in a room were going through a set of steps of following rules to generate English sentences or 3-D descriptions, as the case might be. But now, let us ask what facts in the real world are supposed to correspond to these explanations as applied to the brain. In Chomsky's case, for example, we are not supposed to think that the agent consciously goes through a set of repeated applications of rules; nor are we supposed to think that he is unconsciously thinking his way through the set of rules. Rather, the rules are "computational" and the brain is carrying out the computations. But what does that mean? Well, we are supposed to think that it is just like a commercial computer. The sort of thing that corresponds to the ascription of the same set of rules to a commercial computer is supposed to correspond to the ascription of those rules to the brain. But we have seen that in the commercial computer the ascription is always observer relative, the ascription is made relative to a homunculus who assigns computational interpretations to the hardware states. Without the homunculus, there is no computation, just an electronic circuit. So how do we get computation into the brain without a homunculus? As far as I know, neither Chomsky nor Marr ever addressed the question or even thought there was such a question. But without a homunculus, there is no explanatory power to the postulation of the program states. There is just a physical mechanism, the brain, with its various real physical and physical/mental causal levels of description.

*Summary of the Argument of this Section*
The discussion in this section has been more long-winded than I like, but I think it can be swiftly summarized as follows:

*Objection*: It is just a plain fact that computational explanations are causal. For example, computers fly airplanes, and the explanation of how they do it is given in terms of the program. What could be more causal than that?

*Answer*:  The sense in which the program gives a causal explanation is the following. There is an equivalence class of physical systems such that the patterns in the systems permit the encoding of information by us into intrinsic physical features of the system, such as voltage levels. And these patterns, together with transducers at the input and output ends of the system, enable us to use any member of this equivalence class to fly the airplane. The commonality of the patterns facilitates the assignments of computational interpretations (not surprisingly since the patterns were commercially designed for that purpose), but the interpretations are still not intrinsic to the systems. To the extent that the explanation makes reference to a program, it requires a homunculus.

*Objection*:  Yes, but suppose we could discover such patterns in the brain? All that computational cognitive science needs is the occurrence of such intrinsic patterns.

*Answer*:  Of course you can discover such patterns. The brain has more patterns than anybody needs. But even if we constrained the patterns by requiring the appropriate causal connections and consequent counterfactuals, the discovery of the pattern still would not explain what we are trying to explain. We are not trying to find out how an outside homunculus could assign a computational interpretation to brain processes. Rather, we are trying to explain the occurrence of such concrete biological phenomena as the conscious understanding of a sentence, or the conscious visual experience of a scene. That explanation requires an understanding of the brute physical processes that produce the phenomena.

*VIII. Fourth Difficulty: The Brain Does Not Do Information Processing*

In this section I turn finally to what I think is, in some ways, the central issue in all of this, the issue of information processing. Many people in the "cognitive science" scientific paradigm will feel that much of my discussion is simply irrelevant, and they will argue against it as follows:

There is a difference between the brain and all of the other systems you have been describing, and this difference explains why a computational simulation in the case of the other systems is a mere simulation, whereas in the case of the brain a computational simulation is actually duplicating and not merely modeling the functional properties of the brain. The reason is that the brain, unlike these other systems, is an *information processing* system. And this fact about the brain is, in your words, "intrinsic." It is just a fact about biology that the brain functions to process information, and as we can also process the same information computationally, computational models of brain processes have a different role altogether from computational models of, for example, the weather.

So there is a well-defined research question: Are the computational procedures by which the brain processes information the same as the procedures by which computers process the same information?

What I just imagined an opponent saying embodies one of the worst mistakes in cognitive science. The mistake is to suppose that in the sense in which computers are used to process information, brains also process information. To see that that is a mistake contrast what goes on in the computer with what goes on in the brain. In the case of the computer, an outside agent encodes some information in a form that can be processed by the circuitry of the computer. That is, he or she provides a syntactical realization of the information that the computer can implement in, for example, different voltage levels. The computer then goes through a series of electrical stages that the outside agent can interpret both syntactically and semantically even though, of course, the hardware has no intrinsic syntax or semantics: It is all in the eye of the beholder. And the physics does not matter, provided only that you can get it to implement the algorithm. Finally, an output is produced in the form of physical phenomena, for example, a printout, which an observer can interpret as symbols with a syntax and a semantics.

But now contrast that with the brain. In the case of the brain, none of the relevant neurobiological processes are observer relative (though of course, like anything they can be described from an observer-relative point of view), and the specificity of the neurophysiology matters desperately. To make this difference clear, let us go through an example. Suppose I see a car coming toward me. A standard computational model of vision will take in information about the visual array on my retina and eventually print out the sentence, "There is a car coming toward me." But that is not what happens in the actual biology. In the biology a concrete and specific series of electrochemical reactions are set up by the assault of the photons on the photo receptor cells of my retina, and this entire process eventually results in a concrete visual experience. The biological reality is not that of a bunch of words or symbols being produced by the visual system; rather it is a matter of a concrete specific conscious visual event—this very visual experience. That concrete visual event is as specific and as concrete as a hurricane or the digestion of a meal. We can, with the computer, make an information processing model of that event or of its production, as we can make an information processing model of the weather, digestion, or any other phenomenon, but the phenomena themselves are not thereby information processing systems.

In short, the sense of information processing that is used in cognitive science is at much too high a level of abstraction to capture the concrete biological reality of intrinsic intentionality. The "information" in the brain is always specific to some modality or other. It is specific to thought, or vision, or hearing, or touch, for example. The level of information processing described in the cognitive science computational models of cognition, on the other hand, is simply a matter of getting a set of symbols as output in response to a set of symbols as input.

We are blinded to this difference by the fact that the sentence, "I see a car coming toward me," can be used to record both the visual intentionality and the output of the computational model of vision. But this should not obscure the fact that the visual experience is a concrete conscious event and is produced in the brain by specific electrochemical biological processes. To confuse these events and processes with formal symbol manipulation is to confuse the reality with the model. The upshot of this part of the discussion is that in the sense of "information" used in cognitive science, it is simply false to say that the brain is an information processing device.

### IX. Summary of the Argument

1. On the standard textbook definition, computation is defined syntactically in terms of symbol manipulation.

2. But syntax and symbols are not defined in terms of physics. Though symbol tokens are always physical tokens, "symbol" and "same symbol" are not defined in terms of physical features. Syntax, in short, is not intrinsic to physics.

3. This has the consequence that computation is not discovered in the physics, it is assigned to it. Certain physical phenomena are used or programmed or interpreted syntactically. Syntax and symbols are observer relative.

4. It follows that you could not *discover* that the brain or anything else was intrinsically a digital computer, although you could assign a computational interpretation to it as you could to anything else. The point is not that the claim "The brain is a digital computer" is simply false. Rather, it does not get up to the level of falsehood. It does not have a clear sense. The question "Is the brain a digital computer?" is ill defined. If it asks, "Can we assign a computational interpretation to the brain?" the answer is trivially yes, because we can assign a computational interpretation to anything. If it asks, "Are brain processes intrinsically computational?" the answer is trivially no, because nothing is intrinsically computational, except of course conscious agents intentionally going through computations.

5. Some physical systems facilitate the computational use much better than others. That is why we build, program, and

use them. In such cases we are the homunculus in the system interpreting the physics in both syntactical and semantic terms.

6. But the causal explanations we then give do not cite causal properties different from the physics of the implementation and from the intentionality of the homunculus.

7. The standard, though tacit, way out of this is to commit the homunculus fallacy. The homunculus fallacy is endemic to computational models of cognition and cannot be removed by the standard recursive decomposition arguments. They are addressed to a different question.

8. We cannot avoid the foregoing results by supposing that the brain is doing "information processing." The brain, as far as its intrinsic operations are concerned, does no information processing. It is a specific biological organ and its specific neurobiological processes cause specific forms of intentionality. In the brain, intrinsically, there are neurobiological processes and sometimes they cause consciousness. But that is the end of the story. All other mental attributions are either dispositional, as when we ascribe unconscious states to the agent, or they are observer relative, as when we assign a computational interpretation to his brain processes.

# Chapter 10

# The Proper Study

In any book on the philosophy of mind, the author, explicitly or implicitly, has an overall vision of the mind and its relation to the rest of the natural world. The reader who has followed my argument so far will have no difficulty in recognizing my vision. I see the human brain as an organ like any other, as a biological system. Its special feature, as far as the mind is concerned, the feature in which it differs remarkably from other biological organs, is its capacity to produce and sustain all of the enormous variety of our consciousness life.[1] By consciousness I do not mean the passive subjectivity of the Cartesian tradition, but all of the forms of our conscious life—from the famous "four f's" of fighting, fleeing, feeding, and fornicating to driving cars, writing books, and scratching our itches. All of the processes that we think of as especially mental—whether perception, learning, inference, decision making, problem solving, the emotions, etc.—are in one way or another crucially related to consciousness. Furthermore, all of those great features that philosophers have thought of as special to the mind are similarly dependent on consciousness: subjectivity, intentionality, rationality, free will (if there is such a thing), and mental causation. More than anything else, it is the neglect of consciousness that accounts for so much barrenness and sterility in psychology, the philosophy of mind, and cognitive science.

The study of the mind is the study of consciousness, in much the same sense that biology is the study of life. Of course, biologists do not need to be constantly thinking about life, and indeed, most writings on biology need not even make use of the concept of life. However, no one in his right mind denies that the phenomena studied in biology are forms of life. Now similarly, the study of the mind is the study of consciousness, even though one may not explicitly make any mention of consciousness when one is doing a study of inference, perception, decision making, problem solving, memory, speech acts, etc.

No one can or should try to predict or legislate the future of research whether in philosophy, science, or other disciplines. New knowledge will surprise us, and one of the surprises we should expect is that advances in knowledge will give us not only new explanations, but new *forms* of explanation. In the past, for example, the Darwinian revolution produced a new type of explanation, and I believe we have not fully understood its importance for our present situation.

In this final chapter I want to explore some of the consequences of the general philosophical position that I have been advocating for the study of the mind. I begin with a discussion of the connection principle and its implications.

## II. The Inversion of Explanation

I believe that the connection principle has some quite striking consequences. I will argue that many of our explanations in cognitive science lack the explanatory force that we thought they had. To rescue what can be salvaged from them, we will have to perform an inversion on their logical structure analogous to the inversion that Darwinian models of biological explanation forced on the old teleological biology that preceded Darwin.

In our skulls there is just the brain with all of its intricacy, and consciousness with all its color and variety. The brain produces the conscious states that are occurring in you and me right now, and it has the capacity to produce many others which are not now occurring. But that is it. Where the mind is concerned, that is the end of the story. There are brute, blind neurophysiological processes and there is consciousness, but there is nothing else. If we are looking for phenomena that are intrinsically intentional but inaccessible in principle to consciousness, there is nothing there: no rule following, no mental information processing, no unconscious inferences, no mental models, no primal sketches, no 2 1/2-D images, no three-dimensional descriptions, no language of thought, and no universal grammar. In what follows I will argue that the entire cognitivist story that postulates all these inaccessible mental phenomena is based on a pre-Darwinian conception of the function of the brain.

Consider the case of plants and the consequences of the Darwinian revolution on the explanatory apparatus that we use to account for plant behavior. Prior to Darwin, it was common to anthropomorphize plant behavior and say such things as that the plant turns its leaves toward the sun to aid in its survival. The plant "wants" to survive and flourish, and "to do so," it follows the sun. On this pre-Darwinian conception there was supposed to be a level of intentionality in the behavior of the plant. This level of supposed intentionality has now been replaced by two other levels of explanation, a "hardware" level and a "functional" level. At the hardware level we have discovered that the actual movements of the plant's leaves in following the sun are caused by the secretion of a specific hormone, auxin. Variable secretions of auxin account for the plant's behavior, without any extra hypothesis of purpose, teleology, or intentionality. Notice furthermore that this behavior plays a crucial role in the plant's survival, so at the functional level we can say such things as that the light-seeking behavior of the plant functions to help the plant survive and reproduce.

The original intentionalistic explanation of the plant's behavior turned out to be false, but it was not just false. If we get rid of the intentionality and invert the order of the explanation, the intentionalistic claim emerges as trying to say something true. In order that what happened should be absolutely clear, I want to show how in replacing the original intentionalistic explanation by a combination of the mechanical hardware explanation and a functional explanation, we are inverting the explanatory structure of the original intentionalistic explanation.

a.  The original intentionalistic explanation:
*Because it wants to survive,* the plant turns its leaves
toward the sun.
or
*In order to survive,* the plant turns its leaves toward the
sun.
b.  The mechanical hardware explanation:
Variable secretions of auxin cause plants to turn their
leaves toward the sun.
c.  The functional explanation:
Plants that turn their leaves toward the sun *are more
likely to survive than plants that do not.*

In (a) the form of the explanation is teleological. The
*representation* of the goal, that is, survival, functions as the *cause*
of the behavior, namely turning toward the sun. But in (c) the
teleology is eliminated and the behavior that now, by (b), has a
mechanical explanation, causes the brute fact of survival,
which is now no longer a goal, but just an effect that simply
happens.

The moral I will later draw from this entire discussion can
now be stated, at least in a preliminary form: *Where nonconscious processes are concerned, we are still anthropomorphizing the
brain in the same way in which we were anthropomorphizing plants
before the Darwinian revolution.* It is easy to see why we make
the mistake of anthropomorphizing the brain—after all, the
brain is the home of anthropos. Nevertheless, to ascribe a vast
array of intentional phenomena to a system in which the conditions on that ascription are being violated is a mistake. Just
as the plant has no intentional states because it does not meet
the conditions for having intentional states, so those brain
processes that are in principle inaccessible to consciousness
have no intentionality, because they do not meet the conditions
for having intentionality. When we ascribe intentionality to
processes in the brain that are in principle inaccessible to consciousness, what we say is either metaphorical—as in metaphorical ascriptions of mental states to plants—or false.
Ascriptions of intentionality to plants would be false if we took

them literally. But notice that they are not *just* false; they are trying to say something true, and to get at what is true in them, we have to invert many of the explanations in cognitive science as we did in plant biology.

To work out this thesis in detail, we will have to consider some specific cases. I will start with theories of perception and then proceed to theories of language to show what a cognitive science that respects the facts of the brain and the facts of consciousness might look like.

Irvin Rock concludes his excellent book on perception (Rock 1984) with the following observations: "Although perception is autonomous with respect to such higher mental faculties as are exhibited in conscious thought and in the use of conscious knowledge, I would still argue that it is intelligent. By calling perception 'intelligent' I mean to say that it is based on such thoughtlike mental processes as description, inference, and problem solving, although these processes are rapid-fire, unconscious, and nonverbal. . . . 'Inference' implies that certain perceptual properties are computed from given sensory information using unconsciously known rules. For example, perceived size is inferred from the object's visual angle, its perceived distance, and the law of geometrical optics relating the visual angle to object distance" (p. 234).

But now let us apply this thesis to the explanation of the Ponzo illusion as an example.

**Figure 10.1**
Ponzo illusion

Though the two parallel lines are equal in length, the top line looks longer. Why? According to the standard explanation, the agent is unconsciously following two rules and making two unconscious inferences. The first rule is that converging lines from lower to higher in the visual field imply greater distance in the direction of the convergence, and the second is that objects that occupy equal portions of the retinal image vary in perceived size depending on perceived distance from the observer (Emmert's law). On this account the agent unconsciously infers that the top parallel line is farther away because of its position in relation to the converging lines, and second, he infers that the top line is larger because it is farther away. Thus there are two rules and two unconscious inferences, none of whose operations are accessible to consciousness even in principle. It should be pointed out that this explanation is controversial and there are lots of objections to it (see Rock 1984, p. 156ff.). But the point here is that the *form* of the explanation is not challenged, and that is what I am challenging now. I am interested in this type of explanation, not just in the details of this example.

There is no way that this type of explanation can be made consistent with the connection principle. You can see this if you ask yourself, "What facts in the brain are supposed to correspond to the ascription of all these unconscious mental processes?" We know that there are conscious visual experiences, and we know that these are caused by brain processes, but where is the additional mental level supposed to be in this case? Indeed, this example is very hard to interpret literally at all without a homunculus: We are postulating logical operations performed over retinal images, but who is supposed to be performing these operations? Close inspection reveals that this explanation in its very form is anthropomorphizing the nonconscious processes in the brain in the same way that the pre-Darwinian explanations of plant behavior anthropomorphized the nonconscious operations of the plant.

The problem is not, as is sometimes claimed, that we lack sufficient empirical evidence for the postulation of mental processes that are in principle inaccessible to consciousness, rather it is not at all clear what the postulation is supposed to mean. We cannot make it coherent with what we know about the nature of mental states and what we know about the operation of the brain. We think, in our pathetic ignorance of brain functioning, that some day an advanced brain science will locate all of these unconscious intelligent processes for us. But you only have to imagine the details of a perfect science of the brain to see that even if we had such a science, there could be no place in it for the postulation of such processes. A perfect science of the brain would be stated in neurophysiological (i.e., "hardware") vocabulary. There would be several hardware levels of description, and as with the plant there would also be functional levels of description. These functional levels would identify those features of the hardware that we find interesting in the same way that our functional descriptions of the plant identify those hardware operations in which we take an interest. But just as the plant knows nothing of survival, so the nonconscious operations of the brain know nothing of inference, rule following, nor size and distance judgments. We attribute these functions to the hardware relative to our interests, but there are no additional mental facts involved in the functional attributions.

The crucial difference between the brain on the one hand and the plant on the other is this: The brain has an intrinsically mental level of description because at any given point it is causing actual conscious events and it is capable of causing further conscious events. Because the brain has both conscious and unconscious mental states, we are also inclined to suppose that in the brain there are mental states that are intrinsically inaccessible to consciousness. But this thesis is inconsistent with the connection principle, and we need to make the same inversion of the explanation here as we did in the explanations of the plant's behavior. Instead of saying, "We see the top line as larger because we are unconsciously following two rules and making two inferences," we should say, "We consciously see the top line as farther away and larger." Period. End of the intentionalistic story.

As with the plant, there is a functional story and a (largely unknown) mechanical hardware story. The brain functions in such a way that lines converging above appear to be going away from us in the direction of the convergence, and objects that produce the same size of retinal image will appear to vary in size if they are perceived to be at different distances away from us. *But there is no mental content whatever at this functional level.* In such cases the system functions to cause certain sorts of conscious intentionality, but the causing is not itself intentional. And the point, to repeat, is not that the ascription of deep unconscious intentionality is insufficiently supported by empirical evidence, but that it cannot be made to cohere with what we already know to be the case.

"Well," you might say, "the distinction does not really make much difference to cognitive science. We continue to say what we have always said and do what we have always done, we simply substitute the word "functional" for the word "mental" in these cases. This is a substitution many of us have been doing unconsciously anyway, as many of us tend to use these words interchangeably."

I think that the claim I am making does have important implications for cognitive science research, because by inverting the order of explanation we get a different account of cause-and-effect relations, and in so doing we radically alter the structure of psychological explanation. In what follows, I have two aims: I want to develop the original claim that cognitive science requires an inversion of the explanation comparable to the inversion achieved by evolutionary biology, and I want to show some of the consequences that this inversion would have for the conduct of our research.

I believe the mistake persists largely because in the case of the brain, we lack hardware explanations of the auxin type. I want to explain the inversion in a case in which we do have something like a hardware explanation. Anyone who has seen home movies taken from a moving car is struck by how much more the world jumps around in the movie than it does in real life. Why? Imagine that you are driving on a bumpy road. You consciously keep yours eyes fixed on the road and on the other traffic even though the car and its contents, including your body, are bouncing around. In addition to your conscious efforts to keep your eye on the road, something else is happening unconsciously: Your eyeballs are constantly moving inside their sockets in such a way as to help you to continue to focus on the road. You can try the experiment right now by simply focusing on the page in front of you and shaking your head from side to side and up and down.

In the car case it is tempting to think that we are following an unconscious rule. A first approximation of this rule would be: Move the eyeballs in the eye sockets relative to the rest of the head in such a way as to keep vision focused on the intended object. Notice that the predictions of this rule are nontrivial. Another way to do it would have been to keep the eyes fixed in their sockets and move the head, and in fact some birds keep retinal stability in this way. (If an owl could drive, this is how he would have to do it, since his eyeballs are fixed.) So we have two levels of intentionality:

A conscious intention: Keep your visual attention on the road.
A deep unconscious rule: Make eyeball movements in relation to the eye sockets that are equal and opposite to head movements to keep the retinal image stable.

In this case the result is conscious, though the means for achieving it are unconscious. But the unconscious aspect has all the earmarks of intelligent behavior. It is complex, flexible, goal directed, and it involves information processing and has a potentially infinite generative capacity. That is, the system takes in information about body movements and prints out instructions for eyeball movements, with no limit on the number of possible combinations of eyeball movements that the system can generate. Furthermore, the system can learn because the rule can be systematically modified by putting magnifying or miniaturizing spectacles on the agent. And without much difficulty one could tell any standard cognitive science story about the unconscious behavior: a story about information processing, the language of thought, and computer programs, just to mention obvious examples. I leave it to the reader as a five-finger exercise to work out the story according to his or her favorite cognitive science paradigm.

The problem is, however, that all these stories are false. What actually happens is that fluid movements in the semicircular canals of the inner ear trigger a sequence of neuron firings that enter the brain over the eighth cranial nerve. These signals follow two parallel pathways, one of which can "learn" and one of which cannot. The pathways are in the brain stem and cerebellum and they transform the initial input signals to provide motor output "commands," via motorneurons that connect to the eye muscles and cause eyeball movements. The whole system contains feedback mechanisms for error correction. It is called the vestibular ocular reflex (VOR).[2] The actual hardware mechanism of the VOR has no more intentionality or intelligence than the movement of the plant's leaves due to the secretion of auxin. The appearance that there is an unconscious rule being followed, unconscious information processing, etc., is an optical illusion. All the intentional ascriptions are *as-if*. So here is how the inversion of the explanation goes. Instead of saying:

> Intentional: To keep my retinal image stable and thus improve my vision while my head is moving, I follow the deep unconscious rule of eyeball movement.

We should say:

> Hardware: When I look at an object while my head is moving, the hardware mechanism of the VOR moves my eyeballs.
> Functional: The VOR movement keeps the retinal image stable and this improves my vision.

Why is this shift so important? In scientific explanations, we
are characteristically trying to say exactly what causes what.
In the traditional cognitive science paradigms, there is supposed to be a deep unconscious mental cause that is supposed
to produce a desired effect, such as perceptual judgments, or
grammatical sentences. But the inversion eliminates this mental cause altogether. There is nothing there except a brute
physical mechanism that produces a brute physical effect.
These mechanisms and effects are describable at different levels, none of which so far is mental. The apparatus of the VOR
functions to improve visual efficiency, but the only intentionality is the conscious perception of the object. All the rest of the
work is done by the brute physical mechanism of the VOR. So
the inversion radically alters the ontology of cognitive science
explanation by *eliminating a whole level of deep unconscious
psychological causes*. The normative element that was supposed
to be *inside the system* in virtue of its psychological content now
comes back in when *a conscious agent outside the mechanism
makes judgments about its functioning*. To clarify this last point I
have to say more about functional explanations.

## III. The Logic of Functional Explanations

It might appear that I am proposing that there are, unprob-
lematically, three different levels of explanation—hardware,
functional, and intentional—and that where deep unconscious
processes are concerned, we should simply substitute
hardware and functional for intentional explanations. But, in
fact, the situation is a bit more complicated than that. Where
functional explanations are concerned, the metaphor of levels
is somewhat misleading, because it suggests that there is a
separate functional level different from the causal levels. That
is not true. The so called "functional level" is not a separate
level at all, but simply one of the causal levels *described in terms
of our interests*. Where artifacts and biological individuals are
concerned, our interests are so obvious that they may seem
inevitable, and the functional level may seem intrinsic to the

system. After all, who could deny, for example, that the heart *functions* to pump blood? But remember when we say that the heart functions to pump blood, the only facts in question are that the heart does, in fact, pump blood; that fact is important to us, and is causally related to a whole lot of other facts that also are important to us, such as the fact that the pumping of blood is necessary to staying alive. If the only thing that interested us about the heart was that it made a thumping noise or that it exerted gravitational attraction on the moon, we would have a completely different conception of its "functioning" and correspondingly of, for example, heart disease. To put the point bluntly, in addition to its various causal relations, the heart does not have any functions. When we speak of its functions, we are talking about those of its causal relations to which we attach some *normative* importance. So the elimination of the deep unconscious level marks two major changes: It gets rid of a whole level of psychological causation and it shifts the normative component out of the mechanism to the eye of the beholder of the mechanism. Notice for example the normative vocabulary that Lisberger uses to characterize the function of the VOR. "The function of the VOR is to stabilize retinal images by generating smooth eye movements that are equal and opposite to each head movement." Furthermore, "An accurate VOR is important because we require stable retinal images for good vision" (Lisberger 1988, pp. 728–729).

The intentional level, on the other hand, differs from nonintentional functional levels. Though both are causal, the causal features of intrinsic intentionality combine the causal with the normative. Intentional phenomena such as rule following and acting on desires and beliefs are genuinely causal phenomena; but as intentional phenomena they are essentially related to such normative phenomena as truth and falsity, success and failure, consistency and inconsistency, rationality, illusion, and conditions of satisfaction generally.[3] In short, the actual facts of intentionality contain normative elements, but where functional explanations are concerned, the only *facts* are brute, blind physical facts and the only norms are in us and exist only from our point of view.

The abandonment of the belief in a large class of mental phenomena that are in principle inaccessible to consciousness would, therefore, result in treating the brain as an organ like any other. Like any other organ, the brain has a functional level—indeed many functional levels—of description, and like any other organ it *can be described as if* it were doing "information processing" and implementing any number of computer programs. But the truly special feature of the brain, the feature that makes it the organ of the mental, is its capacity to cause and sustain conscious thoughts, experiences, actions, memories, etc.

The notion of an unconscious mental *process* and the correlated notion of the principles of unconscious mental processes are also sources of confusion. If we think of a conscious process that is "purely" mental, we might think of something like humming a tune soundlessly to oneself in one's head. Here there is clearly a process and it has a mental content. But there is also a sense of "mental process" where it does not mean, "process with mental content," but rather "process by which mental phenomena are related." Processes in this second sense may or may not have a mental content. For example, on the old associationist psychology there was supposed to be a process by way of which the perception of A reminds me of B, and that process works on the principle of resemblance. If I see A, and A resembles B, then I will have a tendency to form an image of B. In this case the process by which I go from the perception of A to the image of B does not necessarily involve any additional mental content at all. There is supposed to be a principle on which the process works, namely resemblance, but the existence of the process according to the principle does not imply that there has to be any further mental content other than the perception of A and the thought of B or the thought of B as resembling A. In particular it does not imply that when one sees A and is reminded of B, one follows a rule whose content requires that if I see *A* and *A* resembles *B*, then I should think of *B*. In short, *a process by which mental contents are related need not have any mental content at all in addition to that of the relata*; even though, of course, our theoretical talk and thoughts of that principle will have a content referring to the principle. This distinction is going to prove important, because many of the discussions in cognitive science move from the claim that there are processes that are "mental" in the sense of causing conscious phenomena (the processes in the brain that produce visual experiences, for example) to the claim that those processes are mental processes in the sense of having mental content, information, inference, etc. The nonconscious processes in the brain that cause visual experiences are certainly mental in one sense, but they have no mental content at all and thus in that sense are not mental processes.

To make this distinction clear, let us distinguish between those processes, such as rule following, that have a mental content that functions causally in the production of behavior, and those processes that do not have a mental content but that associate mental contents with input stimuli, output behavior, and other mental contents. The latter class I will call "association patterns." If, for example, whenever I eat too much pizza I get a stomachache, there is definitely an association pattern, but no rule following. I do not follow a rule: When you eat too much pizza, get a stomachache; it just happens that way.

*IV. Some Consequences: Universal Grammar, Association Patterns, and Connectionism*

It is characteristic of intentionalistic explanations of human and animal behavior that *patterns* in the behavior are explained by the fact that the agent has a representation of that very pattern or a representation logically related to that very pattern in its intentional apparatus, and that representation functions causally in the production of the pattern of behavior. Thus, we say that people in Britain drive on the left because they follow the rule: Drive on the left; and that they do not drive on the right because they follow that same rule. The intentional content functions causally in producing the behavior it represents. There are two qualifications immediately. First, the intentional content of the rule does not produce the behavior all by itself. Nobody, for example, goes for a drive just to be following the rule, and nobody talks just for the sake of following the rules of English. And second, the rules, principles, etc., may be unconscious and, for all practical purposes, they are often unavailable to consciousness, even though, as we have seen, if there really are such rules, they must be, at least in principle, accessible to consciousness.

A typical strategy in cognitive science has been to try to discover complex patterns such as those found in perception or language and then to postulate combinations of mental representations that will explain the pattern in the appropriate way. Where there is no conscious or shallow unconscious representation, we postulate a deep unconscious mental representation. Epistemically, the existence of the patterns is taken as evidence for the existence of the representations. Causally, the existence of the representations is supposed to explain the existence of the patterns. But both the epistemic and the causal claims presuppose that the ontology of deep unconscious rules is perfectly in order as it stands. I have tried to challenge the ontology of deep unconscious rules, and if that challenge is successful, the epistemic and the causal claims collapse together. Epistemically, both the plant and the VOR exhibit systematic patterns, but that provides no evidence at all for the existence of deep unconscious rules—an obvious point in the case of the plant, less obvious but still true in the case of vision. Causally, the pattern of behavior plays a functional role in the overall behavior of the system, but the representation of the pattern in our theory does not identify a deep unconscious representation that plays a causal role in the production of the pattern of behavior, because there is no such deep unconscious representation. Again, this is an obvious point in the case of the plant, less obvious but still true in the case of vision.

Now, with this apparatus in hand, let us turn to a discussion of the status of the alleged rules of universal grammar. I concentrate my attention on universal grammar, because grammars of particular languages, like French or English, whatever else they contain, obviously contain a large number of rules that are accessible to consciousness. The traditional argument for the existence of universal grammar can be stated quite simply: The fact that all normal children can readily acquire the language of the community in which they grow up without special instruction and on the basis of very imperfect and degenerate stimuli, and further that children can learn certain sorts of languages, such as are exemplified by natural human languages, but cannot learn all sorts of other logically possible language systems, provides overwhelming evidence that each normal child contains in some unknown way in his or her brain a special language acquisition device (LAD), and *this language acquisition device consists at least in part of a set of deep unconscious rules.*

With the exception of the last italicized clause, I agree entirely with the foregoing argument for a "language acquisition device." The only problem is with the postulation of deep unconscious rules. That postulation is inconsistent with the connection principle. It is not surprising that there has been a great deal of discussion about the sorts of evidence that one might have for the existence of these rules. These discussions are always inconclusive, because the hypothesis is empty.

Years ago, I raised epistemic doubts about Chomsky's confidence in the attribution of deep unconscious rules and suggested that any such attribution would require evidence that the specific content, the specific aspectual shape, of the rule was playing a causal role in the production of the behavior in question (Searle 1976). I claimed that simply predicting the right patterns would not be enough to justify the claim that we are following deep unconscious rules; in addition we would need evidence that the rule was "causally efficacious" in the production of the pattern. With certain qualifications, Chomsky accepts the requirements. Since we are agreed on these requirements, it might be worth spelling them out:

1. The use of the word "rule" is not important. The phenomenon in question could be a principle, or a parameter, or a constraint, and so on. The point, however, is that it is at a level of intrinsic intentionality. For both Chomsky and me, it is not merely a matter of the system behaving *as if* it were following a rule. There must be a difference between the role of rules in the language faculty and, for example, the role of "rules" in the behavior of plants and planets.

2. "Behavior" is not at issue, either. Understanding sentences, intuitions of grammaticality, and manifestations of linguistic competence in general are what we are referring to by the use of the short-hand term "behavior." There is no behaviorism implicit in the use of this term and no confusion between competence and performance.

3. Neither of us supposes that all of the behavior (in the relevant sense) is caused by the rules (in the relevant sense). The point, however, is that in the best causal explanation of the phenomena, the rules "enter into" (Chomsky's phrase) the theory that gives the explanation.

Now, with these constraints in mind, what exactly was Chomsky's answer to the objection?

> Suppose that our most successful mode of explanation and description attributes to Jones an initial and attained state including certain rules (principles with parameters fixed or rules of other sorts) and explains Jones's behavior in these terms; that is, the rules form a central part of the best account of his use and understanding of language and are directly and crucially invoked in explaining it in the best theory we can devise . . . . I cannot see that anything is involved in attributing causal efficacy to rules beyond the claim that these rules are constituent elements of the states postulated in an explanatory theory of behavior and enter into our best account of this behavior. (Chomsky 1986, pp. 252–253)

In the same connection, Chomsky also quotes Demopoulos and Matthews (1983).

> As Demopoulos and Matthews (1983) observe, "the apparent theoretical indispensability of appeals to grammatically characterized internal states in the explanation of linguistic behavior is surely the best sort of reason for attributing to these states [and, we may add, to their relevant constituent elements] a causal role in the production of behavior." (Chomsky 1986, p. 257)

So the idea is this: The claim that the rules are causally efficacious is justified by the fact that the rules are constituent elements of the states postulated by the best causal theory of the behavior. The objection that I want to make to this account should by now be obvious: In stating that the "best theory" requires the postulation of deep unconscious rules of universal grammar, all three authors are presupposing that the postulation of such rules is perfectly legitimate to begin with. But once we cast doubt on the legitimacy of that assumption, then it looks like the "best theory" might just as well treat the evidence as association patterns that are not produced by mental representations that in some way reflect those patterns, but are produced by neurophysiological structures that need have no resemblance to the patterns at all. The hardware produces patterns of association, in the sense defined above, but the patterns of association play no causal role in the production of the patterns of behavior—they just are those patterns of behavior.

Specifically, the evidence for universal grammar is much more simply accounted for by the following hypothesis: There is, indeed, a language acquisition device innate in human brains, and LAD constrains the form of languages that human beings can learn. There is, thus, a hardware level of explanation in terms of the structure of the device, and there is a functional level of explanation, describing which sorts of languages can be acquired by the human infant in the application of this mechanism. No further predictive or explanatory power is added by saying that there is in addition a level of deep unconscious rules of universal grammar, and indeed, I have tried to suggest that that postulation is incoherent anyway. For example, suppose that children can only learn languages that contain some specific formal property $F$. Now that is evidence that the LAD makes it possible to learn $F$ languages and not possible to learn Non-$F$ languages. But that is it. There is no further evidence that the child has a deep unconscious rule, "Learn $F$ languages and don't learn Non-$F$ languages." And no sense has been given to that supposition anyway.

The situation is exactly analogous to the following: Humans are able to perceive colors only within a certain range of the spectrum. Without formal training, they can see blue and red, for example, but they cannot see infrared or ultraviolet. This is overwhelming evidence that they have a "vision faculty" that constrains what sorts of colors they can see. But now, is this because they are following the deep unconscious rules "If it is infrared, don't see it," or "If it is blue, it is OK to see it"? To my knowledge, no argument has ever been presented to show that the rules of "universal linguistic grammar" have any different status from the rules of "universal visual grammar." Now ask yourself why exactly are you unwilling to say that there are such rules of universal visual grammar? After all, the evidence is just as good as, indeed it is identical in form with, the evidence for the rules of universal linguistic grammar. The answer, I believe, is that it is quite obvious to us from everything else we know that there is no such mental level. There is simply a hardware mechanism that functions in a certain way and not in others. I am suggesting here that there is no difference between the status of deep unconscious universal visual grammar and deep unconscious universal linguistic grammar: Both are non-existent.

Notice that to rescue the cognitive science paradigm, it is not enough to say that we can simply decide to treat the attribution of rules and principles as *as-if* intentionality, because *as-if* intentional states, not being real, have no causal powers whatever. They explain nothing. The problem with *as-if* intentionality is not merely that it is ubiquitous—which it is—but its identification does not give a causal explanation, it simply restates the problem that the attribution of real intentionality is supposed to solve. Let us see how this point applies in the present instance. We tried to explain the facts of language acquisition by postulating rules of universal grammar. If true, this would be a genuine causal explanation of language acquisition. But suppose we abandon this form of explanation and say simply that the child acts *as if* he were following rules, but of course he is not really doing so. If we say that, we no longer have an explanation. The cause is now left open. We have converted a psychological explanation into speculative neurophysiology.

If I am right, we have been making some stunning mistakes. Why? I believe it is in part because we have been supposing that if the input to the system is meaningful and the output is meaningful, then all the processes in between must be meaningful as well. And certainly there are many meaningful processes in cognition. But where we are unable to find meaningful conscious processes, we postulate meaningful unconscious processes, even deep unconscious processes. And when challenged we invoke that most powerful of philosophical arguments: "What else could it be?" "How else could it work?" Deep unconscious rules satisfy our urge for meaning, and besides, what other theory is there? Any theory is better than none at all. Once we make these mistakes our theories of the deep unconscious are off and running. But it is simply false to assume that the meaningfulness of the input and output implies a set of meaningful processes in between, and it is a violation of the connection principle to postulate in principle inaccessible unconscious processes.

One of the unexpected consequences of this whole investigation is that I have quite inadvertently arrived at a defense—if that is the right word—of connectionism. Among their other merits, at least some connectionist models show how a system might convert a meaningful input into a meaningful output without any rules, principles, inferences, or other sorts of meaningful phenomena in between. This is not to say that existing connectionist models are correct—perhaps they are all wrong. But it is to say that they are not all obviously false or incoherent in the way that the traditional cognitivist models that violate the connection principle are.

## V. Conclusion

In spite of our modern arrogance about how much we know, in spite of the assurance and universality of our science, where the mind is concerned we are characteristically confused and in disagreement. Like the proverbial blind men and the elephant, we grasp onto some alleged feature and pronounce it the essence of the mental. "There are invisible sentences in there!" (the language of thought). "There is a computer program in there!" (cognitivism). "There are only causal relations in there!" (functionalism). "There is nothing in there!" ( eliminativism). And so, depressingly, on.

Just as bad, we let our research methods dictate the subject matter, rather than the converse. Like the drunk who loses his car keys in the dark bushes but looks for them under the streetlight, "because the light is better here," we try to find out how humans might resemble our computational models rather than trying to figure out how the conscious human mind actually works. I am frequently asked, "But how could you study consciousness *scientifically*? How could there be a *theory*?"

I do not believe there is any simple or single path to the rediscovery of the mind. Some rough guidelines are:

First, we ought to stop saying things that are obviously false. The serious acceptance of this maxim might revolutionize the study of the mind.

Second, we ought to keep reminding ourselves of what we know for sure. For example, we know for sure that inside our skulls there is a brain, sometimes it is conscious, and brain processes cause consciousness in all its forms.

Third, we ought to keep asking ourselves what actual facts in the world are supposed to correspond to the claims we make about the mind. It does not matter whether "true" means corresponds to the facts, because "corresponds to the facts" does mean corresponds to the facts, and any discipline that aims to describe how the world is aims for this correspondence. If you keep asking yourself this question in the light of the knowledge that the brain is the only thing in there, and the brain causes consciousness, I believe you will come up with the results I have reached in this chapter, and indeed many of the results I have come up with in this book.

But that is only to take a first step on the road back to the mind. A fourth and final guideline is that we need to rediscover the social character of the mind.

# Notes

## Chapter 1

1. Or at least they are investigating the preliminaries of such questions. It is surprising how little of contemporary neuroscience is devoted to investigating, e.g., the neurophysiology of consciousness.

2. The best-known proponent of this view is Thomas Nagel (1986), but see also Colin McGinn (1991).

3. See, for example, P. S. Churchland 1987.

4. I will confine my discussion to analytic philosophers, but apparently the same sort of implausibility affects so-called Continental philosophy. According to Dreyfus (1991), Heidegger and his followers also doubt the importance of consciousness and intentionality.

5. The best-known exponent of this view is Daniel Dennett (1987).

6. But for an explicit statement, see Georges Rey (1983).

7. In different ways, I believe this is done by Armstrong (1968, 1980), and Dennett (1991).

8. Another form of incredibility, but from a different philosophical motivation, is the claim that each of us has at birth all of the concepts expressible in any words of any possible human language, so that, for example, Cro-Magnon people had the concepts expressed by the word "carburetor" or by the expression "cathode ray oscillograph." This view is held most famously by Fodor (1975).

9. Howard Gardner, in his comprehensive summary of cognitive science (1985), does not include a single chapter—indeed not a single index entry—on consciousness. Clearly the mind's new science can do without consciousness.

10. On my view, an inner process such as feeling a pain, for example, does not "stand in need" of anything. Why should it?

11. Oddly enough, my views have been confidently characterized by some commentators as "materialist," by some others, with equal confidence, as "dualist." Thus, for example, U. T. Place writes, Searle "presents the materialist position" (1988, p. 208), while Stephen P. Stich writes, "Searle is a property dualist" (1987, p. 133).

12. A closely related point is made by Noam Chomsky (1975).

*Chapter 2*

1. A good example is Richard Rorty (1979), who asks us to imagine a tribe that does not say "I am in pain," but rather "My C-fibers are being stimulated." Well, let us imagine such a case. Imagine a tribe that refuses to use our mentalistic vocabulary. What follows? Either they have pains as we do or they do not. If they do, then the fact that they refuse to call them pains is of no interest. The facts remain the same regardless of how we or they choose to describe them. If, on the other hand, they really do not have any pains, then they are quite different from us and their situation is of no relevance to the reality of our mental phenomena.

2. It is an interesting fact that in three recent books all of which contain the word "consciousness" in their titles—Paul Churchland's *Matter and Consciousness* (1984), Ray Jackendoff's *Consciousness and the Computational Mind* (1987), and William Lycan's *Consciousness* (1987)—there is little or no effort to give any account of or theory of consciousness. Consciousness is not a subject that is treated as a worthy topic in its own right, but rather simply as an annoying problem for the materialist philosophy of mind.

3. In his review of Marvin Minsky's book *Society of Mind*, Bernard Williams (1987) writes: "What is at issue in this [A.I.] research, in part, is precisely whether intelligent systems can be compounded of unintelligent matter."

4. I do not know the origin of this phrase, but it is probably derived from Ogden and Richards's characterization of Watson as "affecting general anaesthesia" (1926, p. 23 of 1949 edition).

5. I mention this talk of "C-fibers" with some embarrassment because the entire discussion is misinformed. Regardless of the merits or demerits of materialism, it is out of the question for purely neurophysiological reasons that C-fibers should be the locus of pain sensations. C-fibers are a type of axon that transmits certain sorts of pain signals from peripheral nerve endings to the central nervous system. Other pain signals are transmitted by A-Delta fibers. The C-fibers function as pathways for taking the stimuli to the brain, where the real action takes place. As far as we know, the neurophysiological events responsible for sensations of pain occur in the thalamus, the limbic system, the somato-sensory cortex, and possibly other regions as well. (See any standard textbook on this question.)

6. In this chapter I am not concerned to defend my solution to the mind-body problem, but it is worth pointing out that it is not subject to this objection. Kripke and his opponents both accept the dualistic vocabulary with its opposition between "mental " and "physical," which I reject. Once you reject that opposition, then, on my view, my present state of pain is a higher-level feature of my brain. It is therefore necessarily identical with a certain feature of my brain, namely itself. Equally necessary, it is not identical with any other features of my brain, though it is caused by certain lower-level events in my brain. It is possible that such features might be caused by other sorts of events and might be features of other sorts of systems. So there is no necessary con-

nection between pains and brains. Everything is what it is and not another thing.

7. For example, McGinn (1977). McGinn defends Davidson's argument for "anomalous monism," which both he and Davidson take to be a version of token identity theory.

8. After the British philosopher F. P. Ramsey, (1903–1930).

9. The terminology of "chauvinism" and "liberalism" was introduced by Ned Block (1978).

10. The argument is found in the work of several philosophers, for example, Steven Schiffer (1987) and Paul Churchland. Churchland gives a succinct statement of the premise: "If we do give up hope of a reduction, then elimination emerges as the only coherent alternative" (1988).

11. I will have more to say about these issues in chapter 7.

## Chapter 3

1. In the style of Thomas Nagel's article, "What Is It Like to Be a Bat?" (1974).

2. For example, "As one might expect, cells whose receptive fields are specifically color-coded have been noted in various animals, including the monkey, the ground squirrel, and some fishes. *These animals, in contradistinction to the cat, possess excellent color vision* and an intricate neural mechanism for processing color" (Kuffler and Nicholls 1976, p. 25, my italics).

3. For an example of this misunderstanding, see P. M. and P. S. Churchland 1983.

4. I am indebted to Dan Rudermann for calling my attention to this article.

5. See, for example, Dennett 1987.

## Chapter 4

1. There is one qualification to this point. The sense of body location does have intentionality, because it refers to a portion of the body. This aspect of pains is intentional, because it has conditions of satisfaction. In the case of a phantom limb, for example, one can be mistaken, and the possibility of a mistake is at least a good clue that the phenomenon is intentional.

2. The metaphor of "left-right" derives, of course, from the arbitrary convention of European languages of writing from left to right.

3. The term "functional" is somewhat misleading because the functional level is also causal, but it is common in biology to speak of the two types of causal explanation as "functional" and "causal." However we describe it, the distinction is important and I make further use of it in chapter 10.

4. Sometimes people resist my views because of a mistaken conception of the relations between causation and identity. U. T. Place (1988), for example, writes:"According to Searle mental states are both identical with and causally dependent on the corresponding states of the brain. I say you can't have your

cake and eat it. Either mental states are identical with brain states or one is causally dependent on the other. They can't be both" (p. 209).

Place is thinking of cases such as "These footprints can be causally dependent on the shoes of the burglar, but they can't also be identical with those shoes." But how about: "The liquid state of this water can be causally dependent on the behavior of the molecules, and can also be a feature of the system made up of the molecules"? It seems to me just obvious that my present state of consciousness is caused by neuronal behavior in my brain and that very state just is a higher level feature of the brain. If that amounts to having your cake and eating it too, let's eat.

5. This is not an argument for "privileged access" because there is no privilege and no access. I will have more to say about this topic later in this chapter.

6. "Logically, "consciousness" is a stuff term, as "matter" is; and I see nothing wrong, metaphysically, with recognizing that consciousness is a kind of stuff (p. 60)."

7. The alternative explanation is that we have other more general biological urges that are satisfied by these various activities. Compare Elliot Sober's distinction between what is *selected* and what is *selected for* (1984, ch. 4).

## Chapter 5

1. For further discussion of this point, see chapter 2.

## Chapter 6

1. Even such obvious points as that when one is bored, "time passes more slowly" seem to me to require explanation. Why should time pass more slowly when one is bored?

2. This expression is due to Edelman (1991).

3. Hume, by the way, thought that there couldn't be any such feeling, because if there were, it would have to do a lot of epistemic and metaphysical work that no mere feeling could do. I think in fact we all have a characteristic sense of our own personhood, but it is of little epistemic or metaphysical interest. It does not guarantee "personal identity," "the unity of the self," or any such thing. It is just how, for example, it feels like to me to be me.

4. E.g., by David Woodruff Smith (1986).

## Chapter 7

1. Lashley 1956. I don't think Lashley means this literally. I think he means that the processes by which the various features of conscious states are produced are never conscious. But even that is an overstatement, and the fact that he resorts to this sort of hyperbole is revealing of the theme I am trying to identify.

2. See also Searle 1980b, 1984b, and especially 1984a.

3. For these purposes I am contrasting "neurophysiological" and "mental," but of course on the view of mind-body relations that I have been expounding throughout this book, the mental is neurophysiological at a higher level. I contrast mental and neurophysiological as one might contrast humans and animals without thereby implying that the first class is not included in the second. There is no dualism implicit in my use of this contrast.

4. Specifically David Armstrong, Alison Gopnik, and Pat Hayes.

5. For this discussion I am ignoring Freud's distinction between preconscious and unconscious. For present purposes I call both "unconscious."

## Chapter 8

1. Especially *On Certainty* (1969), which I believe is one of the best books on the subject.

2. In discussion.

3. The correct answer to this style of skepticism, I believe, is to explain the role of the Background in meaning and understanding (Searle, unpublished).

4. This is a change from the view I held in Searle 1991. I was convinced of this point by William Hirstein.

## Chapter 9

1. SOAR is a system developed by Alan Newell and his colleagues at Carnegie Mellon University. The name is an acronym for "State, Operator, And Result." For an account see Waldrop 1988.

2. This view is announced and defended in a large number of books and articles many of which appear to have more or less the same title, e.g., *Computers and Thought* (Feigenbaum and Feldman, eds., 1963), *Computers and Thought* (Sharples et al. 1988), *The Computer and the Mind* (Johnson-Laird 1988), *Computation and Cognition* (Pylyshyn 1984), "The Computer Model of the Mind" (Block 1990), and of course, "Computing Machinery and Intelligence" (Turing 1950).

3. This whole research program has been neatly summarized by Gabriel Segal (1991) as follows: "Cognitive science views cognitive processes as computations in the brain. And computation consists in the manipulation of pieces of syntax. The content of the syntactic objects, if any, is irrelevant to the way they get processed. So, it seems, content can figure in cognitive explanations only insofar as differences in content are reflected in differences in the brain's syntax" (p. 463).

4. Pylyshyn comes very close to conceding precisely this point when he writes, "The answer to the question what computation is being performed requires discussion of semantically interpreted computational states" (1984, p. 58). Indeed. And who is doing the interpreting?

5. People sometimes say that it would have to add six to itself *eight* times. But that is bad arithmetic. Six added to itself eight times is fifty-four, because six added to itself zero times is still six. It is amazing how often this mistake is made.

6. The example was suggested by John Batali.

## Chapter 10

1. The brain has, of course, many other features as well that have nothing to do with consciousness. For example, the medulla regulates breathing even when the system is totally unconscious.

2. Lisberger 1988, Lisberger and Pavelko 1988.

3. See Searle 1983, especially chapter 5, for an extended discussion.

# Bibliography

Armstrong, D. M. (1968) *A Materialist Theory of Mind*. London: Routledge and Kegan Paul.

Armstrong, D. M. (1980) *The Nature of Mind*. Sydney: University of Queensland Press.

Block, N. (1978) "Troubles with Functionalism," in *Minnesota Studies in the Philosophy of Science* IX: 261–325. Minneapolis: University of Minnesota Press.

Block, N., ed. (1980) *Readings in Philosophy of Psychology*. Vol. 1. Cambridge, MA: Harvard University Press.

Block, N. (1990) "The Computer Model of the Mind," in D. Osherson and E. E. Smith (eds.), *An Invitation to Cognitive Science* 3: 247–289. Cambridge, MA: MIT Press.

Block, N. (unpublished), "Two Concepts of Consciousness."

Block, N., and Fodor, J. (1972) "What Psychological States are Not," *Philosophical Review* 81: 159–181.

Bloom, Floyd E., and Lazerson, Arlyne (1988) *Brain, Mind, and Behavior* 2nd ed. New York: W. H. Freeman.

Boolos, G. S., and Jeffrey, R. C. (1989) *Computationality and Logic*. Cambridge: Cambridge University Press.

Bourdieu, P. (1977) *Outline of a Theory of Practice*. R. Nice, tr. Cambridge: Cambridge University Press.

Bourdieu, P. (1990) *The Logic of Practice*. R. Nice, tr. Stanford, CA: Stanford University Press.

Changeux, J. P. (1985) *Neuronal Man: The Biology of Mind*. L. Garey, tr. New York: Pantheon Books.

Chisholm, R. M. (1957) *Perceiving: A Philosophical Study*. Ithaca: Cornell University Press.

Chomsky, N. (1975) *Reflections on Language*. New York: Pantheon Books.

Chomsky, N. (1986) *Knowledge of Language: Its Nature, Origin and Use*. New York and Philadelphia: Praeger Special Studies.

Churchland, P. M. (1981) "Eliminative Materialism and the Propositional Attitudes," *Journal of Philosophy* 78: 67–90.

Churchland, P. M. (1984) *Matter and Consciousness: A Contemporary Introduction to the Philosophy of Mind*. Cambridge, MA: MIT Press.

Churchland, P. M. (1988) "The Ontological Status of Intentional States: Nailing Folk Psychology to Its Perch," *Behavorial and Brain Sciences* 11, 3: 507–508.

Churchland, P. M., and Churchland, P. S. (1983) "Stalking the Wild Epistemic Engine," *Nous* 17: 5–18. Reprinted in W. G. Lycan (ed.), 1990.

Churchland, P. S. (1987) "Reply to McGinn," in *Times Literary Supplement*, Letters to the Editor, March 13.

Davis, S., ed. (1991) *Pragmatics: A Reader*. New York and Oxford: Oxford University Press.

Demopoulos, W., and Matthews, R. J. (1983) "On the Hypothesis that Grammars are Mentally Represented," *Behavioral and Brain Sciences* 6, 3: 405–406.

Dennett, D. C. (1978) *Brainstorms: Philosophical Essays on Mind and Psychology*. Cambridge, MA: MIT Press.

Dennett, D. C. (1987) *The Intentional Stance*. Cambridge, MA: MIT Press.

Dennett, D. C. (1991) *Consciousness Explained*. Boston: Little, Brown and Company.

Dreyfus, H. L. (1972) *What Computers Can't Do*. New York: Harper and Row.

Dreyfus, H. L. (1991) *Being-In-the-World: A Commentary On Heidegger's Being and Time, Division I*. Cambridge, MA: MIT Press.

Edelman, G. M. (1989) *The Remembered Present: A Biological Theory of Consciousness*. New York: Basic Books.

Feigenbaum, E. A., and Feldman, J., eds. (1963) *Computers and Thought*. New York: McGraw-Hill Company.

Feigl, H. (1958) "The 'Mental' and the 'Physical,'" in *Minnesota Studies in the Philosophy of Science: vol II: Concepts, Theories, and the Mind-Body Problem*. Minneapolis: University of Minnesota Press.

Feyerabend, P. (1963) "Mental Events and the Brain," *Journal of Philosophy* 60: 295–296.

Fodor, J. (1975) *The Language of Thought*. New York: Thomas Y. Crowell.

Fodor, J. (1986) "Banish DisContent," in Butterfield, J. (ed.), *Language, Mind, and Logic*. Cambridge: Cambridge University Press, 1986.

Fodor, J. (1987) *Psychosemantics: The Problem of Meaning in the Philosophy of Mind*. Cambridge, MA: MIT Press.

Foucault, M. (1972) *The Archaeology of Knowledge*, A. M. Sheridan Smith, tr. New York: Harper and Row.

Freud, S. (1895) "Project for Scientific Psychology," in *The Standard Edition of the Complete Psychological Works of Sigmund Freud*, vol. 1, pp. 295–343, James Strachey, tr. London: Hogarth Press, 1966.

Freud, S. (1915) "The Unconscious in Psychoanalysis," in *Collected Papers*, vol. 4. pp. 98–136. J. Riviere tr. New York: Basic Books, 1959.

Freud, S. (1949) *Outline of Psychoanalysis*. James Strachey, tr. London: Hogarth Press.

Gardner, H. (1985) *The Mind's New Science: A History of the Cognitive Revolution*. New York: Basic Books.

Gazzaniga, M. S.(1970) *The Bisected Brain*. New York: Appleton Century Crofts.

Geach, P. (1957) *Mental Acts*. London: Routledge and Kegan Paul.

Grice, P. (1975) "Method in Philosophical Psychology (From the Banal to the Bizarre)," *Proceedings and Addresses of the American Philosophical Association*, vol. 48, November 1975, pp. 23–53.

Griffin, D. R. (1981) *The Question of Animal Awareness: Evolutionary Continuity of Mental Experience*. New York: Rockefeller University Press.

Hampshire, S. (1950) "Critical Notice of Ryle, *The Concept of Mind*." *Mind* LIX, 234: 237–255.

Hare, R. M. (1952) *The Language of Morals*. Oxford: Oxford University Press.

Haugeland, J., ed. (1981) *Mind Design*. Cambridge, MA: MIT Press.

Haugeland, J. (1982) " Weak Supervenience," *American Philosophical Quarterly* 19, 1: 93–104.

Hempel, C. G. (1949) "The Logical Analysis of Psychology," in H. Feigl and W. Sellars (eds.), *Readings in Philosophical Analysis*. New York: Appleton Century Crofts.

Hobbs, J. R. (1990) "Matter, Levels, and Consciousness," *Behaviorial and Brain Sciences* 13, 4: 610–611.

Horgan, T., and Woodward, J. (1985) "Folk Psychology is Here to Stay," *Philosophical Review* XCIV, 2: 197–220.

Jackendoff, R. (1987) *Consciousness and the Computational Mind*. Cambridge, MA: MIT Press.

Jackson, F. (1982) "Epiphenomenal Qualia," *Philosophical Quarterly* 32: 127–136.

Johnson-Laird, P. N. (1983) *Mental Models: Towards a Cognitive Science of Language, Inference, and Consciousness*. Cambridge, MA: Harvard University Press.

Johnson-Laird, P. N. (1988) *The Computer and the Mind*. Cambridge, MA: Harvard University Press.

Kim, J. (1979) "Causality, Identity and Supervenience in the Mind-Body Problem," *Midwest Studies in Philosophy* 4: 31–49.

Kim, J. (1982) "Psychophysical Supervenience," *Philosophical Studies* 41, 1: 51–70.

Kripke, S. A. (1971) "Naming and Necessity," in D. Davidson and G. Harman (eds.), *Semantics of Natural Language*. Dordrecht: Reidel, pp. 253–355 and 763–769.

Kripke, S. A. (1982) *Wittgenstein on Rules and Private Language*. Oxford: Basil Blackwell.

Kuffler, S. W., and Nicholls, J. G. (1976) *From Neuron to Brain*. Sunderland, MA: Sinauer Associates.

Lashley, K. (1956) "Cerebral Organization and Behavior," in *The Brain and Human Behavior*, H. Solomon, S. Cobb, and W. Penfield (eds.) Baltimore: Williams and Wilkins Press.

Lepore, E., and van Gulick, R., eds. (1991) *John Searle and His Critics*. Oxford: Basil Blackwell.

Lettvin, J. Y., Maturana, H. R., McCulloch, W. S., and Pitts, W. H. (1959) "What the Frog's Eye Tells the Frog's Brain," *Proceedings of the Institute of Radio Engineers* 47, 1940–51. Reprinted in W. S. McCulloch (1965).

Lewis, D. (1966) "An Argument for the Identity Theory," *Journal of Philosophy* 63, 1:17–25. Reprinted in D. Rosenthal (ed.) (1971).

Lewis, D. (1972) "Psychological and Theoretical Identification," *Australasian Journal of Philosophy* 50: 249–258.

Lisberger, S. G. (1988) "The Neural Basis for Learning of Simple Motor Skills," *Science* 4, 242: 728–735.

Lisberger, S. G., and Pavelko, T. A. (1988) "Brain Stem Neurons in Modified Pathways for Motor Learning in the Primate Vestibulo-Ocular Reflex," *Science* 4, 242: 771–773.

Lycan, W. G. (1971) "Kripke and Materialism," *Journal of Philosophy* 71, 18: 677–689.

Lycan, W. G. (1987a) *Consciousness*. Cambridge, MA: MIT Press.

Lycan, W. G. (1987b) "What is the 'Subjectivity' of the Mental," *Philosophical Perspectives* 4: 109–130.

Lycan, W. G., ed. (1990) *Mind and Cognition: A Reader*. Cambridge, MA: Basil Blackwell.

Marr, D. (1982) *Vision*. San Francisco: W. H. Freeman and Company.

McCulloch, W. S. (1965) *The Embodiment of Mind*. Cambridge, MA: Harvard University Press.

McGinn, C. (1977) "Anomalous Monism and Kripke's Cartesian Intuitions," *Analysis* 37, 2: 78–80.

McGinn, C. (1987) "Review of P. S. Churchland, *Neurophilosophy*," *Times Literary Supplement*, Feb. 6, pp. 131–132.

McGinn, C. (1991) *The Problem of Consciousness*. Oxford: Basil Blackwell.

Millikan, R. (1984) *Language, Thought and Other Biological Categories: New Foundations for Realism*. Cambridge, MA: MIT Press.

Minsky, M. L. (1986) *Society of Mind*. New York: Simon and Schuster.

Moore, G. E. (1922) *Philosophical Studies*. London: Routledge and Kegan Paul.

Nagel, T. (1974) "What Is It Like to Be a Bat?" *Philosophical Review* 4 LXXXIII: 435–450.

Nagel, T. (1986) *The View from Nowhere*. Oxford: Oxford University Press.

Newell, A. (1982) "The Knowledge Level," *Artificial Intelligence* 18: 87–127.

Ogden, C. K., and Richards, I. A. (1926) *The Meaning of Meaning*. London: Harcourt, Brace & Company.

Penfield, W. (1975) *The Mystery of the Mind: A Critical Study of Consciousness and the Human Brain*. Princeton: Princeton University Press.

Penrose, R. (1989) *The Emperor's New Mind*. Oxford: Oxford University Press.

Place, U. T. (1956) "Is Consciousness a Brain Process?" *British Journal of Psychology* 47: 44–50.

Place, U. T. (1988) "Thirty Years On—Is Consciousness Still a Brain Process?" *Australasian Journal of Philosophy* 66, 2: 208–219.

Postman, L., Bruner, J., and Walk, R., (1951) "The Perception of Error," *British Journal of Psychology* 42: 1–10.

Putnam, H. (1960) "Minds and Machines," in S. Hook (ed.), *Dimensions of Mind*. New York: Collier Books.

Putnam, H. (1963) "Brains and Behavior," in R. Butler (ed.), *Analytical Philosophy*. Oxford: Basil Blackwell.

Putnam, H. (1967) "The Mental Life of Some Machines," in H. Castaneda (ed.), *Intentionality, Minds, and Perception*. Detroit, MI: Wayne State University Press.

Putnam, H. (1975a) "Philosophy and Our Mental Life," in *Mind, Language and Reality: Philosophical Papers, vol. 2*. Cambridge: Cambridge University Press.

Putnam, H. (1975b) "The Meaning of 'Meaning,'" in K. Gunderson (ed.), *Language, Mind and Knowledge: Minnesota Studies in the Philosophy of Science*, VII. Minneapolis: University of Minnesota Press.

Pylyshyn, Z. W. (1984) *Computation and Cognition: Toward a Foundation for Cognitive Science*. Cambridge, MA: MIT Press.

Quine, W. V. O. (1960) *Word and Object*. Cambridge, MA: MIT Press.

Rey, G. (1983) "A Reason for Doubting the Existence of Consciousness," in R. Davidson, G. Schwartz, D. Shapiro (eds.), *Consciousness and Self-Regulation*, 3, 1–39. New York: Plenum.

Rey, G. (1988) "A Question about Consciousness," in H. Otto, J. Tuedio (eds.), *Perspectives on Mind*. Dordrecht: Reidel.

Rock, I. (1984) *Perception*. New York: Scientific American Library, W.H. Freeman.

Rorty, R. (1965) "Mind-Body Identity, Privacy and Categories," *Review of Metaphysics* 29, 1: 24–54.

Rorty, R. (1970) "Incorrigibility as the Mark of the Mental," *Journal of Philosophy* LXVII, 12: 399–424.

Rorty, R. (1979) *Philosophy and the Mirror of Nature*. Princeton: Princeton University Press.

Rosenthal, D., ed. (1971) *Materialism and the Mind-Body Problem*. Englewood Cliffs, N.J.: Prentice Hall.

Rosenthal, D., ed. (1991) *The Nature of Mind*. New York: Oxford University Press.

Ryle, G. (1949) *The Concept of Mind*. New York: Barnes and Noble.

Sacks, O. (1985) *The Man Who Mistook His Wife For a Hat: And Other Clinical Tales*. New York: Simon and Schuster.

Sarna, S. K., and Otterson, M. F. (1988) "Gastrointestinal Motility: Some Basic Concepts," in *Pharmacology: Supplement* 36: 7–14.

Schiffer, S. R. (1987) *Remnants of Meaning*. Cambridge, MA: MIT Press.

Searle, J. R. (1976) "The Rules of the Language Game," review of Noam Chomsky, *Reflections on Language*. *The Times Literary Supplement*, 10 September.

Searle, J. R. (1978) "Literal Meaning," *Erkenntnis* 1: 207–224. Reprinted in Searle (1979).

Searle, J. R. (1979) *Expression and Meaning*. Cambridge: Cambridge University Press.

Searle, J. R. (1980a) "Minds, Brains, and Programs," *Behavorial and Brain Sciences* 3: 417–424.

Searle, J. R. (1980b) "Intrinsic Intentionality: Reply to Criticisms of Minds, Brains, and Programs," *Behavorial and Brain Sciences*, 3: 450–456.

Searle, J. R. (1980c) "The Background of Meaning," in J. R. Searle, F. Kiefer, and M. Bierwisch (eds.), *Speech Act Theory and Pragmatics*. Dordrecht, Holland: Reidel.

Searle, J. R. (1982) "The Chinese Room Revisited: Response to Further Commentaries on 'Minds, Brains, and Programs,'" *Behavioral and Brain Sciences* 5, 2: 345–348.

Searle, J. R. (1983) *Intentionality: An Essay in the Philosophy of Mind*. Cambridge: Cambridge University Press.

Searle, J. R. (1984a) "Intentionality and Its Place in Nature," *Synthese* 61: 3–16.

Searle, J. R. (1984b) *Minds, Brains, and Science: The 1984 Reith Lectures*. Cambridge, MA: Harvard University Press.

Searle, J. R. (1987) "Indeterminacy, Empiricism, and the First Person," *Journal of Philosophy* LXXXIV, 3: 123–146.

Searle, J. R. (1990) "Collective Intentionality and Action," in *Intentions in Communications*, P. Cohen, J. Morgan, and M. E. Pollack (eds.). Cambridge, MA: MIT Press.

Searle, J. R. (1991) "Response: The Background of Intentionality and Action," in E. Lepore and R. van Gulick (eds.) (1991), pp. 289–299.

Searle, J. R. (Unpublished) "Skepticism about Rules and Intentionality."

Segal, G. (1991) "Review of Garfield, J., *Belief in Psychology*," *Philosophical Review* C, 3: 463–466.

Shaffer, J. (1961) "Could Mental States be Brain Processes?" *Journal of Philosophy* 58, 26: 813–822.

Sharples, M., Hogg, D., Hutchinson, C., Torrence, S., and Young, D. (1988) *Computers and Thought: A Practical Introduction to Artificial Intelligence*. Cambridge, MA: MIT Press.

Shepherd, G. M. (1983) *Neurobiology*. Oxford and New York: Oxford University Press.

Sher, G. (1977) "Kripke, Cartesian Intuitions, and Materialism," *Canadian Journal of Philosophy* 7.

Smart, J. J. C. (1959) "Sensations and Brain Processes," *Philosophical Review* 68: 141–156.

Smith, D. W. (1986) "The Structure of (Self-)Consciousness," *Topoi* 5, 2: 149–156.

Sober, E. (1984) *The Nature of Selection: Evolutionary Theory in Philosophical Focus*. Cambridge, MA: MIT Press.

Stevenson, J. T. (1960) "Sensations and Brain Processes: A Reply to J. J. C. Smart," *Philosophical Review* 69: 505–510.

Stich, S. P. (1983) *From Folk Psychology to Cognitive Science: The Case Against Belief.* Cambridge, MA: MIT Press.

Stich, S. P. (1987) "Review of Searle, J., *Minds, Brains and Science.*" *Philosophical Review* XCVI, 1: 129–133.

Turing, A. (1950) "Computing Machinery and Intelligence," *Mind* 59: 433–460.

Waldrop, M. M. (1988) "Toward a Unified Theory of Cognition," and "SOAR: A Unified Theory of Cognition," *Science* 241 (July 1), 1988, pp 27–29 and (July 15), pp. 296–298.

Watson, J. B. (1925) *Behaviorism.* New York: Norton Press.

Weiskrantz, L., et al. (1974) "Visual Capacity in the Hemianopic Field Following a Restricted Occipital Ablation," *Brain* 97: 709–728.

Williams, B. (1987) "Leviathan's Program: Review of Marvin Minsky, *The Society of Mind*," *New York Review of Books,* 11 June.

Wittgenstein, L. (1953) *Philosophical Investigations.* Oxford: Basil Blackwell.

Wittgenstein, L. (1969) *On Certainty.* Oxford: Basil Blackwell.

# Subject Index

# Name Index